Property
Edward A. Free M.D.
33 Crest Rd
Piedmont, Cal

DESOLATION WILDERNESS

A complete guide to over 200 miles of
trail and 139 trout streams and lakes

by

Robert S. Wood

Photographs and maps by the author

Drawings by Helen S. Wood

 Wilderness Press   Berkeley

To keep this guide accurate and up-to-date, a new edition will be published every four or five years. The author therefore will appreciate receiving — via Wilderness Press — all corrections, additions and suggestions.

Revised second printing 1971

Acknowledgements

I am pleased to express my gratitude to Mike Carver, who hiked so many miles with me and helped in innumerable ways, to Jim Olson and Jim Chapin of the USFS for their patient assistance, to DFG fisheries biologist Dick Johnson for a wealth of angling information, to Haven (Jorgy) Jorgensen and Skip Wollenberg, the companions who guided my early travels, and to my wife Freda for her help and encouragement. I am also indebted to Jim Culver, Ralph H. Cross, Jr., Margaret Grosse, Annie Nilsson and Cece Walrond.

—ROBERT S. WOOD, Berkeley, January 1970.

About the author

Robert S. Wood was born in Berkeley, graduated from the University of California in Forestry, and served as San Francisco reporter for LIFE magazine and *Sports Illustrated*. For twenty-five years he has backpacked throughout the California Sierra, and he has spent ten summers exploring the Desolation Wilderness country from his cabin on Upper Echo Lake.

Table of Contents

Chapter 1

Desolation Wilderness

Desolation Wilderness Area must surely offer as much beauty per square mile as any alpine region in the world. But the attributes that keep it the most popular roadless area in the state are its compactness and its ease of access. No wild section of the Sierra crest is friendlier, more easily reached or easier to travel. This combination of wildness, popularity and beauty suggests why Congress, in October 1969, conferred upon it full Wilderness Area status while expanding its boundaries by nearly fifty percent.

The Wilderness Area in outline resembles an irregular oval with its long axis draped over the Sierra crest; it ranges six to eight miles in width, about fifteen miles in length, and comprises just better than one hundred square miles. Topographically, the area is most easily envisioned as two back-to-back glacially excavated valleys lying between two parallel ranges of mountains.

In the east rises the main crest of the Sierra Nevada: Rubicon Peak (9183), Phipps Peak (9234), Dicks Peak (9974), Jacks Peak (9856), Mt. Tallac (9735), Echo Peak (8895) and Ralston Peak (9235). Roughly paralleling it in the west lies the twelve-mile-long Crystal Range: Tells Peak (8872), McConnell Peak (9099), Silver Peak (8930), Red Peak (9307), Mt. Price (9975) and Pyramid Peak (9983).

Between these ranges in the north lies 10-mile-long Rockbound Valley, which runs northward down the Rubicon River from Mosquito Pass to Rockbound Lake. Between these ranges in the south lies 5-mile-long Desolation Valley, which runs south from Mosquito Pass down Pyramid Creek to Horsetail Falls. The Wilderness Area is completed in the west by a broad strip of land embracing a series of lake-filled valleys and canyons along the western slope of the Crystal Range, and in the east by a smaller and more irregular series of lake basins on the Tahoe slope of the main Sierra crest.

The region covered by this book includes, in addition to the Wilderness Area proper, all the surrounding buffer zone that lies between it and the roads that provide the twenty-one principal points of access. Generally speaking, this region is bounded by Highway 89 along Lake Tahoe in the east, Highway 50 in the south, the Wrights and Loon Lakes roads in the west, and the

Miller Lake Jeep Trail to Wentworth Springs in the north. Altitudes within the Wilderness Area range from 6400 on lower Pyramid Creek to the 9983' summit of Pyramid Peak (a mile away), with an average elevation of 8000 feet.

One of the area's greatest assets is its proximity to major centers of population, principally to the San Francisco Bay region and the city of Sacramento. As more and more of the connecting Highway 50 is converted to freeway, travel time to the mountains, despite increased traffic, steadily drops. Except during the heaviest traffic, motorists from the Bay Area should reach Echo Summit, principal gateway to the Wilderness, in 3-4 hours. From Sacramento the driving time should be 1½ hours less. There is Greyhound Bus service on Highway 50 and passengers can arrange to be let off at Twin Bridges and Pinecrest Camp, as well as at the Wrights and Echo Lakes roads.

Ease of travel within the Wilderness region will amaze habitues of the mighty southern Sierra, where a six-hour climb from the trailhead may be required simply to reach the first bleak pass. By comparison, a much easier three-hour hike in Desolation will generally take the traveler over a pass and far enough into the Wilderness to choose a campsite from any of several lakes and streams. And dayhikers can easily visit half a dozen lakes in several watersheds before returning to camp or car. It is even practical to make an east-west traverse of the region in a single day.

Although most of the use is crowded between the Fourth of July and Labor Day, hiking trips of some sort are often possible from late May to early November, and ski touring is excellent in the winter. In the mythical average year, trails at lower elevations on south-facing slopes are largely free of snow by mid-May, and the ice melts on the lowest lakes about a week later. The roads to Echo and Wrights lakes open about the first of June, lakes under 8000' thaw by the middle of the month, and Mosquito Pass and all but the highest lakes are open by the first of July.

Rockbound Pass opens about a week later and the Dicks Pass Trail becomes usable about the middle of the month; at about the same time the two lowest fords on the Rubicon become safely wadable. By August even the highest country is open, but the human population is at its greatest, the springs and meadows have begun to dry and the wildflowers are past their prime. The quality of the fishing declines as the predominant brook trout move down to colder water, but the nights are often balmy, the mosquitos are nearly gone and the water is at its warmest for swimming.

Shortly after Labor Day, with the opening of the schools, back country travel drops off. Nights are cooler and generally there is a snow storm before the end of the month. The human population picks up during the latter half of the month as deer hunters move in to send bullets ricocheting through the canyons. In October the days are measurably shorter and the nights are colder, but the cold brings an astonishing variety of autumn reds and browns and golds to country which at first seems entirely evergreen.

The weather in October is often warm and still and perhaps it is the least windy month of the year—although ice begins to form on the higher lakes. November, on the other hand, must be the least inviting month, with rain, occasional heavy snows and long cold nights. By Christmas, Echo Lakes are generally frozen and the ice skating is good as long as the wind keeps the ice free of snow. In January and February the snow is deep and well-packed (average snowfall in the area is thirty feet) and the ski touring and snow camping for experienced and well-equipped parties can be excellent.

By late April, south-facing slopes have begun to shed their snow and in fine weather it is often possible to climb Flagpole and even Echo Peak. During the winter the old Echo Summit (Johnson Pass) Road, from which the Echo Road branches, is kept more or less open and passable to cars with chains. Highway 50 is the only road in the area kept continuously open in winter. By the end of April there are patches of open water in the lower lakes, the skiing grows wet and mushy, and the lengthening days herald the coming of spring and summer.

Desolation Wilderness, because of its compactness, its small size and comparatively low elevation, is justly famous as the gentlest, friendliest, most inviting section of the Sierra Nevada crest. But visitors should not be lulled by any false sense of security. The land is wild and can be hazardous, even to the experienced and prepared. Foolhardy visitors during the summer have been swept down rivers, fallen off cliffs and otherwise been injured. And more than one poorly prepared winter traveler has perished.

The least menacing aspect of the environment is its wildlife. There are no rattlesnakes or scorpions (or poison oak) and the relatively docile black bear rarely ventures into such open, unsheltered country. The shy coyote, like the deer, makes himself scarce during the busy summer months but moves freely through the country during the winter, spring and fall. The greatest menace from wildlife is provided by mosquitos. Nothing ruins a trip so often as being unprepared for mosquitos.

During the first few weeks after the ice melts in the lakes, the air is mercifully free of insects. Then suddenly, mosquitos are everywhere. The worst is over in about two weeks, but there follows another month during which insects are more or less active. Very dry weather hastens their disappearance; extensive summer rains extend their breeding. The mosquito season depends on temperature, which is closely related to altitude; for example, the season at 7500' may begin several weeks earlier than at 8500'. In a few boggy meadows and damp forests sheltered from wind, mosquitos may be active to the end of August.

Protection begins with a long-sleeved shirt and long trousers. But mosquitos can bite through Levis and all but the thickest wool shirts and socks, so repellents are necessary on clothes as well as skin and hair. During the height of insect activity, I carry a fresh aerosol can of spray repellent for quick relief during a sudden attack; in addition I carry a lightweight plastic vial of Cutter Laboratories' preparation for use when there is ample time to prepare for battle. Many backpackers will not carry an aerosol can, considering it a luxury on the basis of weight, but when mosquitos are thick in early season I rank it high on my list of necessities.

Another menace worth mentioning are other people's firearms. Guns of all kinds are unwelcome within the area covered by this book, except during deer season. Much of the private land has already been posted against both hunting and shooting, and the USFS is considering the prohibition of firearms during the summer, when ricochet from rock or water presents a real hazard to the heavy population of visitors. Firearms are never necessary for protection from wild animals; target practice mars the country; and the hunting of small animals and birds ranges from reprehensible to illegal. Lastly, gunfire disturbs the peace and solitude of other visitors for miles around. Considerate travelers leave their guns at home.

Thoughtful visitors also take care to leave no sign of their passing on the landscape. Since old firepits exist in every suitable campsite, there is no need to blacken fresh rocks with new fireplaces. There was a time when burial was a satisfactory means of disposing of debris, but that time has passed. Edible garbage, not including egg shells and orange peels, may be scattered unobtrusively for animals and birds; paper and some plastics may be burned; but cans and glass (no longer carried by knowledgeable backpackers) and foil, plastic, metal and other nonburnable debris should be compacted and reduced in weight (if possible) and carried (in doubled plastic garbage bags brought for that purpose) out of the wilderness to a garbage can (preferably your own).

Lightly burdened day hikers are invited to join those of us who automatically pick up and carry out trailside trash on the

4

homeward journey. A refreshing back-country swim can provide an opportunity to remove debris thoughtlessly thrown in a lake. Cleanup parties, sponsored by the Sierra Club and other interested outdoorsmen, occasionally make more thorough cleanup trips through the Wilderness, sacking refuse for pack animals to carry out.

Enormously increased use of the Wilderness in the late 1960s has forced the USFS to adopt a drastic two-phase program to protect and restore the area's wilderness character and solitude. Phase one, beginning in the summer of 1971, requires all visitors to carry "Wilderness permits." These are issued without charge for individual trips to applicants aware of the problems regarding fire, litter and sanitation. Day hikers may be granted longer-term permits. All USFS offices, staffed campgrounds, and probably principal resorts will issue permits. They will also be available by mail. An increased force of Wilderness rangers will issue misdemeanor citations to regulation-violators and visitors without permits. Sometime between 1972 and 1975 phase two will limit group size and also limit the number of persons permitted to visit or camp in any one place at a given time. Length of stay will likewise be limited to give a maximum number of visitors a chance to camp in wilderness. Advance reservations will be required.

Water in the lakes and streams of the region is pure and safe to drink, except where contamination is obvious (usually due to grazing cattle or inconsiderate campers). Water from snowpools and ponds should be avoided. Firewood, though often scarce, is available in sufficient quantity for cooking. The two heaviest and least necessary items of equipment mistakenly carried by backpackers in the region are an ax or hatchet and a filled canteen. Travelers accustomed to brisk evening temperatures in the higher southern Sierra are apt to be driven out of their mummy bags on balmy midsummer nights; a light bag cover enables the camper to sleep on top of his bag while maintaining protection against insects. On the other hand, the wind often blows hard during summer months, and snow has been known to fall in every month of the year, including July and August. For most people, however, parkas and down jackets are unnecessary. There are summers, when, despite afternoon thunderheads, rain is virtually nonexistent. In other years sizable storms reach the area and there are daily thundershowers in the afternoons for a week or more thereafter. Clothing and gear must be chosen carefully to protect against most contingencies while keeping weight to a minimum. Beyond that there is nothing to do but hope for fair weather and sally forth.

Chapter 2

A Short History

The wild, open landscape of Desolation Wilderness owes much of its beauty and distinctive character to the violent movements within the earth which formed it and to the series of powerful glaciers which polished it.

The country as we know it today had its origin not more than two million years ago with the onset of the Pleistocene Epoch. Violent deformation within the earth thrust the Sierra approximately to its present height and the first of four glacial stages (or ice ages) began. At that time, polar climates extended over a far greater area than they do today, including high altitude country far from the poles.

As the climate grew colder less and less of the winter snow in the Sierra high country was melted. Gradually the snow and ice blanket grew deeper until, in areas of principal concentration like Desolation Valley, it formed ice caps hundreds of feet thick. The weight of these ice caps grew so great that the outward force along its margins produced moving fronts or tongues of ice called glaciers. Heavy snow and ice accumulations in the tops of high canyons beyond the ice caps and their glaciers formed small, independent moving ice masses known as cirque and valley glaciers.

Four times in the last million or two years, for unknown reasons, the land grew cold, an ice cap formed in Desolation Valley, and glaciers came forth to grind their way north, east, southeast and south. The first of these ice ages began around a million years ago, and the ice only began to retreat from the fourth about 25,000 years ago.

The narrow tongue of ice forming the Echo Lakes glacier flowed over the long north ridge of Ralston Peak from the Desolation ice cap, excavating Echo basin before it plunged in a giant ice cascade over the low ridge south of Flagpole Peak and down the cliffs to Lake Valley at the south end of Lake Tahoe. The upper Echo basin was hollowed by its passage; the lower lake owes its existence to a combination of glacial excavation and the creation of a lateral moraine that formed a dam across the south shore.

Rockbound Valley was deepened by a river of ice pushed northward over Mosquito Pass from the Desolation ice cap. The Rockbound Glacier extended northwest well beyond the northern boundary of the Wilderness Area. But the longest of the tongues from the Desolation ice cap cascaded south over Horsetail Falls into the south fork of the American River and turned to plough its way downstream an additional two miles. The Glen Alpine Glacier moved east down the canyon to the foot of Fallen Leaf Lake.

As a representative example, the topography of Glen Alpine Canyon suggests how greatly glaciation influenced the scenery of today. Heather, Susie, Half Moon, Alta Morris and Grass lakes owe their existence to glaciers which excavated the hollows they fill, and Gilmore is impounded behind a lateral moraine laid down by the passing ice. There are several prominent cirques (steep-walled, round-bottomed, glacially dug amphitheaters at the heads of canyons) notably the one cradling Half Moon and Alta Morris. The canyon walls exhibit evidence of powerful glacial erosion, the valley bottom is sprinkled with *roches moutonnées* (rounded knobs of hard rock which resisted the glaciers) and Fallen Leaf Lake itself is dammed by a succession of terminal moraines.

The canyons that lead east to Cascade Lake, Emerald Bay and Meeks Bay lay beyond range of the Desolation-centered ice mass, and they were excavated by independent valley glaciers. Many of the canyons and basins on the western slope of the Crystal Range were likewise shaped by cirque or valley glaciers. At the time of maximum ice thickness and main movement, all of the lower ridges and divides were covered, and glacial erosion is principally responsible for the lowness of the passes in most of the Desolation region of the Wilderness.

But even at its deepest, the snow and ice never covered either the narrow, ragged spine of the Crystal Range or the more rounded summits of the main Sierra crest (Rubicon, Phipps, Dicks, Jacks, Tallac, Ralston). These isolated summits rode just above the river of ice, and though they were subject to heavy weathering, avalanching and frostwedging, they differ markedly in appearance from the glaciated land. The high mark of the ice flows is nowhere more evident than on the eastern slope of Pyramid Peak and Mt. Price, around the 9000' level.

When the warming climate melted the ice cap and glaciers after the fourth ice age, about 10,000 years ago, the many hollows scraped from the granitoid bedrock were filled with water. The Pleistocene, or Glacial, Epoch had created in the Desolation country hundreds of ponds and lakes where previously there had been none. As the land warmed vegetation moved up the canyons and valleys. Brush, grass and trees began to grow, and wildlife, insects and birds came with them.

About 4000 years ago, the earth reached its climatic optimum (maximum warmth). Since then the climate has grown measurably colder and both lakes and glaciers have formed in the highest parts of the southern Sierra. But in the Desolation country the land has mellowed. Much of the glacier polish has eroded away, soil has formed, and forests have spread over much of the land. Many of the glacial tarns are filling with sediment and turning to meadow, and meadows are evolving into forest.

Today, a quarter of the Wilderness Area is classified as forest; the largest barren area, not surprisingly, is centered in upper Desolation Valley, site of the ice cap. Three quarters of the total area consists of quartz-bearing granitic rock. This igneous rock, solidified from molten masses beneath the earth's surface, is principally composed of light-colored quartz and feldspar. Dark-colored grains of iron and magnesium minerals complete its salt-and-pepper appearance.

The remainder of the area consists of metamorphic rock remnants. Enormous pressure over long periods deep within the earth alters the characteristic of rock, causing it to be classified as metamorphic. A segment of land bounded by Lake Schmidell, Middle Velma, Half Moon and Susie is basically metasedimentary rock. And an area bordered by Mt. Tallac, Dicks Pass and Lily and Susie Lakes is composed of metavolcanic rock. Several other kinds of rock, including volcanic basalt and marble, are represented in small areas, and much of the borderlands are covered with low hills and ridges of unconsolidated morainal deposits left behind by the glaciers.

Since the Wilderness Area lies between the gold- and silver-rich Comstock Lode to the east and the Mother Lode to the west, it is safe to say that the area was carefully prospected during Gold Rush days. But repeated glaciation had stripped the country to bedrock and rushing streams had carried away the remaining debris. It was not surprising then that nothing was found before the mid 1890s, when the first gold claims were registered. In the past hundred years only 22 claims (8 lode and 14 placer) have been located in the area; all are now abandoned and there is no record of mineral production from the area.

The only area of remaining interest lies half a mile directly south of Gilmore Lake on the west side of the creek between the T-Y and Mt. Tallac trails. Here, atop a north-running ridge, at 8000-8200 feet, significant amounts of gold have been found in erratically distributed surface outcrops. The "Josie" claims were filed in 1931, a number of pits and several trenches up to 1500 feet long were dug, and samples assaying as high as $50 a ton were taken. But the deposits proved to be too low in grade, too erratically distributed and too difficult of access to be commercially exploitable, and the claims were abandoned in 1938.

INDIANS

Archeological finds reveal that Indians lived in or near the central Sierra for hundreds, perhaps thousands, of years. But the hunting and fishing were so good in the more comfortable climates of the lower Sierra and the Tahoe basin that there was little to draw Indians into the high barren region that is now the Wilderness. The heavily forested Tahoe basin was rich with deer, and the lake was alive with native cutthroat trout, which spawned in the tributary creeks. By comparison, the high country was largely barren of fish and the thin forests sheltered little game.

The lower lands near the Wilderness boundary, however, were heavily used by Indians. Fallen Leaf, Cascade Lake, Emerald Bay and Meeks Bay all show heavy Indian use, mainly by Washoes who wintered in the Carson Valley and moved up to the lush mountains in the summer to hunt, fish and trade. Travelers shunned the high region blocked by the snow-covered Crystal Range, but ancient, well-used trails passed both north and south of it.

In the north, a trail from the middle of the western shore of Lake Tahoe crossed the Sierra's main crest at only 7100 feet, forded the Rubicon River, skirted the north end of Loon Lake, and descended the lower Rubicon through the foothills to the valley. Today the Miller Lake Jeep Trail, through Rubicon and Wentworth Springs, takes much the same route, and Indian artifacts may still be found along the way.

A still more popular route across the Sierra, used by Indians from the Carson Valley bound for both Tahoe and the central valley, led over Carson Pass and then northwest into the canyon of the South Fork of the American River. An alternate route led up the Kingsbury Grade route to Tahoe and then over Echo Summit to the South Fork. Echo Lakes lay close to the trail from Tahoe and were popular by virtue of their population of cutthroat trout, which had somehow climbed up from the Upper Truckee River. Relics found at the foot of the lower lake indicate this was a favorite camping ground for visiting Washoes, and to the end of the last century Indians came to seine and dry the native trout and to trap in the basin for muskrat, white fox, ermine and mink. As recently as the 1920s they came every fall to hunt marmot for both food and fur.

Although farther from the South Fork, Wrights Lake offered sheltered camping, good hunting and easy access from the central valley. Relics found in 1961 near the lake's outlet suggest that Washoe families moved up from the Carson Valley in the summer, and while the men hunted, the women shaped arrowheads and spearpoints from obsidian and chert native to what is now Nevada.

Materials native to the coast and valley suggest that the Wrights Indian campground (now a USFS public campground) was a trading post to which Digger Indians, as well as other tribes, came from considerable distances to exchange such necessities as food, obsidian and furs.

The Wrights campground was also a landmark on the various Indian trails that joined the South Fork with the Miller Lake Indian trail. Indians continued to make use of traditional trails and camping grounds on the Wilson Ranch south of Wrights well after the turn of the century.

THE GOLD RUSH ROUTES

Led by the lure of gold in the Mother Lode, white men took over the country with astonishing speed in the mid-19th century. The country was wild and unknown when, in the winter of 1844, the first white man to reach the area, John C. Fremont, led an exploration expedition guided by Kit Carson, across the Sierra on the same route used by the Washoe Indians. Fremont climbed west out of the Carson Valley, crossed Carson Pass in February, and followed a ridge (with a view north into Lake Tahoe) that led him to the South Fork of the American, from which he descended into the central valley.

When the news of the discovery of gold reached population centers of the east, the great migration began, and the route favored by many followed Fremont's tracks down the South Fork. By 1848 there was a road of sorts, really a marked route, that followed ancient Indian trails over Carson Pass and down the American River canyon. A number of entrepreneurs took over development of the route and opened a series of toll roads. By 1849 a growing stream of Conestoga wagons and pack trains arrived from the east across the plains to laboriously work their way over what by then was known as the Johnson Cutoff or Johnson Pass Toll Road.

The first recorded trip by a six-horse Concord stage was made in 1857, and after that the rush was on. On one August day in 1860 an observer counted 353 wagons crawling over the Johnson Pass Road. That same year along the road there were more than fifty inns, hostelries, toll houses and way stations between Placerville and Echo Summit, employing better than two thousand people.

The heyday of the region ended abruptly in 1868 when the

Central Pacific Railroad's crossing of the Sierra was completed over Donner Summit, to the north.

DAIRIES AND CATTLE

During boom times entrepreneurs of all kinds moved into the region to supply the immigrants' needs. Bert and Ed Wright, who operated dairies in the central valley, rightly determined that there would be a brisk demand for butter on the road, and they each filed on 640 acres of meadowland north of Wrights Lake in the early 1850s. The brothers were soon followed by a friend named Sawyer, who opened another dairy on Peavine Ridge at the base of Pyramid Peak. Sawyer later sold to cattleman John Forni, whose name was given to several lakes and whose family still holds the Peavine Ridge land.

The Lyons dairy lay roughly between the Sawyer and Wrights dairies, at what now is the junction of the Bloodsucker and Lyons Creek trails, and a trail (part of which is now Bloodsucker) joined the three. In those days virtually all the land along the creeks from Lyons Creek to Barrett Lake was lush meadow and offered excellent grazing. When the demand for dairy products dwindled, shortly after the turn of the century, the dairymen turned to raising beef cattle. As forest rapidly replaced meadow, the cattle business faded somewhat and much of the private land was logged.

Cattlemen in the early days of the century drove their herds cross-country over the Crystal Range to graze in Rockbound Valley on the grass beside the Rubicon. After a herd was nearly trapped by heavy snow early one fall around 1915, the USFS hired a Swiss stone mason named Joe Minghetti to build the first Rockbound Pass trail, which was to be used by cattle only in emergency.

From the 1850s to the 1930s cattle were grazed on the shores of Upper Echo and at Haypress Meadows to the northwest. A shepherd ran sheep during the summer on what is now sage slope under Echo Peak, and a cheesemaker kept a herd of goats in spring-fed Tamarack Pass on Ralston Peak's north ridge. The tall, thick grasses of Haypress Meadows were regularly harvested with scythes and compressed into bales by a horse-powered, screw-driven press at the foot of the meadows. Pack trains carried the bales down a trail along the south shore of the lakes (before a dam raised the water) to the hungry teams climbing through Johnson Pass. In 1872 the Lowery brothers built a log cabin on the northwesternmost island in Upper Echo Lake, from which they seined cutthroat trout and trapped muskrat and fox, selling their fish and furs to the immigrants.

In 1875 the first dam was built at the foot of what now is Lake Aloha, and the following year a four-foot-wide flume was completed to divert the normal eastward flow from Echo Lakes into the westward-running American River. The Echo Dam was raised, bringing the two lakes to their present level and filling the channel that joins them. Hamden "El Dorado" Cagwin, shaggy "Hermit of the Lake," built a cabin in 1897 in a cluster of trees on the north side of the outlet stream, from which he maintained the dam and flume and served as a fishing guide and boatman for occasional visitors.

EARLY TRAILS

The early trails in the region were mainly on the perimeter, outside the Wilderness Area proper. The earliest, of course, were the Indian trails: the Miller Lake trail, the Meeks Creek trail (now the Tahoe-Yosemite Trail), and myriad paths around Emerald Bay, Cascade, Fallen Leaf, Echo and Wrights Lakes. The first white men operated in essentially the same areas. Health-seekers crowded Rubicon Springs and Wentworth Springs reached by the Miller Lake trail (then known as the Bigler Indian trail—Bigler Lake was an early name for Lake Tahoe) during the 1880s.

In 1863 Nathan Gilmore, in the process of rounding up his cattle, discovered Lily Lake and Glen Alpine Springs, and the latter was extremely popular with the gentry toward the end of the century as a health spa. Cascade (known until 1885 as Silver Lake) became the home of Jimmie Walker, who in the 1880s built a stone cabin near the outlet from which to operate a fishing and trapping business. In later years Cascade was visited by John Muir and Mark Twain, and John Steinbeck was the lake's caretaker during the summer of 1926.

Another section of the Tahoe-Yosemite Trail that saw very early use lay between Echo Lakes and the grass-harvesting operation in Haypress Meadows. The most active region, thanks to extensive dairy and cattleraising operations, lay along the gentle west slope of the Crystal Range. The Forni, Lyons Creek, Bloodsucker and Island Lake trails all owe their origin to the early ranches. So do the Barrett Lake Jeep trail and the Red Peak trail. Latter-day cattle operations are largely responsible for the Tells Peak-Highland trail, Cattlemen's Stock Driveway and Rockbound Pass trail.

It is certain that Indians made their way some distance up the Rubicon River into what now is Rockbound Valley. After the primitive area was established in 1931, USFS trail crews constructed sections of trail in the heart of the wilderness to link together into a continuous trail system the paths established by Indians, cattlemen and pioneers.

PUBLIC USE POLICY

The Eldorado National Forest was created out of public lands in El Dorado County in 1910, and divided for purposes of administration into ranger districts. The Chief of the Forest Service (USFS), in April 1931, established 41,383 acre Desolation Valley Primitive Area, to protect the wild country along the Sierra crest from development and to manage it for public recreation and water production. Unfortunately, the Primitive Area fell within the boundaries of three separate ranger districts: Pacific in the west, Lake Valley in the east and Placerville in the south (see accompanying map for boundaries).

Since the districts are largely independent of one another, and since their budgets for recreation vary, management has tended to be only accidentally similar and largely uncoordinated. The result has been inconsistent and sometimes contradictory trail signing, uncoordinated trail maintenance; and many rangers are unable to provide needed information about areas beyond their immediate district.

For may years, most of the public use and nearly all the money for trails went to the Lake Valley District. In the meantime, Pacific District had little to spend and was virtually unable to maintain or sign its lightly used trails. Placerville District, even today, has virtually nothing to spend on the two trails for which it is responsible: the Ralston Peak trail from Pinecrest Camp and the alleged Horsetail Falls trail from Twin Bridges to Avalanche Lake. In the last several years, Pacific has been rapidly developing its trail system, while Lake Valley has grown concerned with the heavy use of its popular network.

Visitor use of the Wilderness more than doubled in the five years ending in 1967, when some 40,000 visitor days (a USFS unit of measure meaning a 12-hour stay within the boundaries) were recorded. In 1968, Lake Valley alone reported 43,200 visitor days. If we add Pacific and Placerville districts, in addition to the far more frequently visited area surrounding the Wilderness, it seems likely that as many as 100,000 visitor days might be expected in the early 1970s.

When visitor use was low the USFS, to encourage camping. built improved campsites, with concrete fireplaces, privies, and sometimes picnic tables and garbage cans, at five locations: Lake Schmidell, China Flat, Lake Aloha, Crag Lake and Velma Lakes. Now that the problem has turned from under-use to over-use, these improvements are being destroyed or removed, both to discourage camper concentration and because improvements are inconsistent with wilderness.

Some years ago the USFS maintained resident rangers in the back country, equipped with radios for communicating with headquarters. The present-day counterpart is the "Wilderness Ranger," whose job it is to help back-country travelers, clean up litter and put out fires. Under the Wilderness permit program an increased number of rangers are empowered to issue misdemeanor citations to regulation-violators and visitors without permits.

To better protect the buffer zone between the roads and the wilderness, the USFS developed a vehicle control plan for Eldorado Forest land surrounding the Wilderness Area. Inside the boundary vehicles are permitted only on specified roads and trails. The regulations, which went into effect in May 1969, state (in summary) that the various unmaintained vehicle routes have been designated for either two- or four-wheel drive vehicles, or both.

Within the area (shown on a new USFS Vehicle Control Map) vehicles must never leave approved roads and must be equipped with approved spark arresters; drivers must pack out all cans and debris, obtain permits from the owners of private land, and give right-of-way to hikers and horsemen. Motorists are not to smoke while driving, except in enclosed vehicles. Four-wheel vehicles will need four-wheel drive for the roads in question. Violators of these regulations are subject to prosecution.

Added to the requirements should be a provision requiring oversize mufflers. Trail bikes with undersized mufflers (or none at all) can be heard for several miles, effectively destroying wilderness experience for everyone in range of the sound.

Unfortunately and unnecessarily, the vehicle-control-area boundary coincides with the Wilderness boundary in the northwest between Loon Lake and Buck Island reservoirs, leaving no buffer zone at all, and allowing jeeps and motorcycles unwarranted access to the wilderness border. This situation hopefully will be reconsidered by the USFS Forest Supervisor and a vital buffer zone added to keep motorcycles from the new Loon Lake and Rockbound Valley trails, both of which seem destined for heavy use by hikers.

After considerable study the USFS, under provisions of the Wilderness Act, proposed to Congress in 1966 that the Desolation Valley Primitive Area be enlarged from 41,383 acres to 64,097 and be made part of the National Wilderness Preservation System (i.e. given full Wilderness Area status). Since there was neither mining nor lumbering in the area to be added, opposition was slight, and though progress was slow, eventual passage seemed assured.

But Pacific Gas & Electric and Sacramento Municipal Utility District, whose water and power rights were soon due for review, asked for non-wilderness-conforming right-of-ways to their dams, claiming that roads would be necessary to maintain the dams in the future. Certain purist legislators felt that if these right-of-ways were necessary, the areas through which they passed should be stricken from the proposed Wilderness. In the case of Buck Island and Rubicon reservoirs and Rockbound Lake (SMUD) this would have been disappointing, but in the case of Aloha dam, the right-of-way would have been a major disaster, ironically excluding Desolation Valley, from which the Wilderness takes its name.

Urgent appeals by the Sierra Club and other conservation organizations overrode the requests of the two utilities at the eleventh hour, common sense prevailed, and in October 1969 the bill enlarging and reclassifying the Desolation preserve passed both houses of Congress to become law, very largely intact. Utility access remained essentially unchanged.

In a time when use of the high country is increasing at an almost alarming rate, and development in the surrounding area grows larger and closer, the passage of this bill can only be viewed as a triumph of major proportions. The enlargement moved the western boundary from the spine of the Crystal Range almost two miles west to annex all the sculptured canyons and glacially excavated lake basins along the western slope. And a large block of land was added in the south and southeast.

Passage of the bill should insure the area better and more cohesive management. The USFS is taking this occasion for a reappraisal of its policy, and to this end a new Wilderness Resource Plan was scheduled for completion before the summer of 1970. Improved and better coordinated management between the administering ranger districts is one aim, and this may mean a new alignment of district boundaries, based on ease of access.

With the recent increase in use, and predictions of still heavier demand, there has been a shift in USFS policy toward "preventing overuse" and "maintaining wilderness quality." As one USFS recreation officer puts it, the emphasis will be ". . . away from the trend toward making the Wilderness Area a big amusement park, with something for everyone. Wilderness is supposed to be wild. That's the way we want it."

To implement this policy, designated campground improvements are being removed or destroyed. The trail system is being scrutinized, with the probable result that few if any big, high-standard trails will again be built. Trail maintenance may be modified to turn the boulevards into paths, and a growing number of trails will be reserved for hikers only. An indication of the direction management will take can be seen in the Wilderness Resource Plan's preliminary suggestions for signing.

Trail signs will be of a new design, simpler and smaller. Instead of being painted brown they will be stained a "weathered grey," and the carved-out text will no longer be painted white. Only two or three destinations will be offered on each sign, and mileages will be deliberately omitted to place the initiative on the traveler to obtain maps, plan his trips, and find his own way. To mark the new Wilderness boundaries there will be large wooden signs at all trail crossings. And small metal signs will be strung along the entire boundary perimeter, spaced three or four to the mile.

With California's population expected to double within the next 20 years, the USFS looks toward the day when, to maintain a wilderness environment, it may be necessary to limit the number of visitors at any one time. Looking still further into the future, the USFS is thinking about the possibility of such radical measures as banning stock, discontinuing trails altogether and prohibiting hunting. Firearms, presently unwelcome, will probably be prohibited, except during deer season, in the near future.

For maps, Wilderness permits, information and regulations, write to: U. S. Forest Service Recreation Officer, at either Lake Valley Ranger Station, P. O. Box 8465, South Lake Tahoe, Calif. 95705, or, Pacific Ranger Station, Pollock Pines, Calif. 95726.

Something should be said about the "improvements" within the boundaries of the new Wilderness preserve. In addition to 22 low and unobtrusive streamflow maintenance dams on naturally occurring lakes, there is the somewhat larger P G & E dam, first built in 1875, then raised in 1917 on Lake Aloha. The dam itself is unobtrusive but its effects are profound. The dam transformed a series of small lakes (Medley Lakes) in the shallow polished granite basin into the giant and ill-named Aloha. In the fall when the water is let out, the basin becomes a desolate scene of cracked mud and drowned snags. And in all seasons the flow through Pyramid Creek and through the Chain of Lakes along it is largely dependent upon release from Aloha Dam.

At the north end of Rockbound Valley, in response to growing demands for hydroelectric power, construction was begun in 1957, under power withdrawal rights predating the Primitive Area (1875), on a project to create 237,000 kilowatts of power for SMUD customers. A road was built from Loon Lake to Buck Island Lake and then into the primitive area past Rockbound Lake to Onion Flat on the then-wild Rubicon River.

A dam was built across the Rubicon to transform Onion Flat

into a 146-acre reservoir, and a tunnel was drilled through the granite to carry the flow to Rockbound Lake, from which it flows to Buck Island. Another dam at Buck Island raised the surface twenty feet, turning the lake into a reservoir, and a 1½ mile tunnel was drilled to empty the Rockbound Valley runoff into Loon Lake. The project was completed in 1963, all equipment removed, and the crushed granite road blocked off and converted (in name only) to USFS trail.

Chapter 3

Key to Trail Descriptions

The country described in this guide logically divides itself, largely on the basis of drainages, into eight separate regions (see accompanying map). Each of these constitutes a chapter within the text, beginning with Echo Basin and running clockwise in a circle. The trails and routes in each chapter are divided into sections; each section is a continuous stretch of trail. Trails are usually described from the trailhead inward; some are described in the direction of most frequent travel.

To find the description of a given stretch of trail, first determine which region it falls into from the map, then turn to the appropriate chapter and scan the list of sections that heads it. It should then be a simple matter to thumb through the chapter and locate the desired description.

The primary intent of this guide is to direct the visitor from the road to the country of his choice, and to provide some idea about what both trail and country are like. The more obscure the trailhead, the more confusing the junctions, the fainter the track—the more detailed the descriptions are liable to be. Many previously unmapped and rarely shown trails and routes are set forth and these, together with confusing and obscure sections of mapped trails, are shown in large-scale maps inserted among the trail descriptions.

At the beginning of each chapter a list of the trail sections to be described serves as a table of contents. There immediately follows a summary description of the region covered, its general characteristics and peculiarities, the nature of its trail system, directions for reaching the trailheads, and supplies and facilities (packers, restaurants, boat service, telephones, etc.) to be found at or near the end of the road.

Each section, in turn, begins with its own table of contents, followed by a brief specific account of trail conditions and the country traversed. The table of contents lists a series of readily recognized points along the trail (usually lakes or trail junctions), giving for each point the elevation, distance from the preceding point, and cumulative distance from the beginning of the section. The trail descriptions that follow are keyed to these same points, and elevation and distance from the preceding point are included in the text, e.g. **Triangle Lake Trail** (7640 — 2.1).

Each regional chapter is designed to stand separate and complete in itself for easy reference in the field, and to minimize cross-referencing. Consequently some duplication will be discovered along the regional boundaries. All the trails and routes described in this book were hiked by the author in either 1968 or 1969, and all the signs, official and otherwise, standing at that time, as well as USFS signs ordered for installation, are represented, at least in summary.

In the interests of accuracy it must be reported that approximately a quarter of the entries on USFS signs are to some extent wrong, misleading or contradictory of other signs. And virtually all USFS-signed distances are at variance with the far more accurate distances shown on the USFS trail map. Nevertheless, all signs are reproduced in this guide because they provide unmistakable reference points on the trail, and because they indicate the principal destinations of intersecting trails.

The USFS has assigned each trail a name and a number. These numbers are mentioned only when they appear in the text of a sign and are not used in trail descriptions. Trail names, on the other hand, are useful and have usually been included. Since any given trail can be hiked in two directions, the terms "left" and "right" have no meaning. As a consequence all directions are given in terms of points of the compass: north, northeast, east, and so forth.

To give travelers some idea of the availability of drinking water along their intended routes, an attempt has been made to indicate how long springs, rills and creeks are likely to flow in the mythical "average" year. My admittedly arbitrary seasonal breakdown runs as follows: "early season," mid-June to mid-July; "midseason," mid-July to mid-August; and "late season," mid-August through September. These seasonal references are also occasionally applied to the melting of ice and snow, the opening of passes, the blooming of wildflowers, etc.

To clarify commonly used terms: "Duck"—1, 2 or 3 rocks stacked one upon another to mark a route. "Cairn"—a larger pile of rocks or a monument serving the same purpose. "Blaze"—a shallow axe cut in a tree about head height, the size of a man's hand (sometimes 2 cuts, one above the other). "Paint blaze"—any of a variety of painted marks on rock to define a route. "Groove" —the shallow indentation made by hikers' feet through impressionable terrain.

Chapter 4

Maps and Their Use

For maximum benefits, this book is designed to be used with a compass and a good map. By far the finest available map is the U. S. Geological Survey (USGS) Topographic map in 7½ minute sheets, referred to in the text as the "topo map." The scale is a generous 2.6 inches to the mile, the contour interval is only 40 feet, and every feature of the land and most of the trails are shown with great accuracy and clarity.

The second-best map, carried by many travelers, is the USGS 15-minute topo map, offering about half the scale (1″ = 1 mile) and twice as large a contour interval. More widely known and more readily available than its 7½ minute big brother, its biggest advantage is that a single sheet (the Fallen Leaf Quadrangle) covers nearly all the Wilderness Area. The 7½ offers about twice as much information per square mile as the 15, and with practice it becomes possible almost to see the country in advance by studying the map.

Desolation visitors are fortunate in having a choice between topo maps. In no other section of the Sierra crest is the 7½ minute series available. The 7½'s only drawback is its size, but this can be overcome by a little off-season effort. After buying whatever sheets are needed (at about 50c apiece) cut off the margins and extraneous areas and lay the resulting pieces on an old bed sheet. Next, determine the largest rectangular size in which the folded map will fit comfortably in the largest outside pocket on your pack or shirt.

Then cut the pieced-together map into rectangles of the size determined — without regard for the original margins — and again lay them out on the sheet. After spacing the rectangles a quarter of an inch apart all around, glue them down with rubber cement. Once the excess sheet has been trimmed off, you have an easily folded map which, if kept flat and dry, should last for a number of seasons.

The third-best map is the USFS trail map of the Wilderness, a 1970 edition of which will show the new trails and the new Wilderness boundaries. The scale is about one mile to the inch and no topography or elevations are given, but all principal trails are shown clearly and the length of each trail segment is recorded to the nearest tenth of a mile. A few trails are vaguely drawn and others shown are virtually non-existent, but this is probably the best map on which to plot trips because the trails are so prominently set forth. The map is especially useful in the northwest where new trails, roads and reservoirs render the topo maps inaccurate.

The USFS publishes several other special-use maps which are useful. (All USFS maps are available at no charge from ranger stations and other USFS offices.) The Vehicle Control Area Map offers only a 1 inch = 2 miles scale but shows the new Wilderness boundary, the Vehicle Control boundary and the roads in between that are open for vehicular traffic. Rules and regulations are on the back. A map entitled "Lake Tahoe Area," though of equally small scale, shows the boundaries of all holdings of private land, and consequently is useful at the trip-planning stage.

To get any use from your map you need to know directions, which usually means you need a compass. There is a rather surprising tendency among amateur outdoorsmen to look upon the compass as a toy for Boy Scouts. But in strange country where landmarks are unknown to you and a sure knowledge of directions is vital for map use, a compass is indispensable. More than once during the research for this book I was able to avoid a wrong turn, and all the fruitless effort that inevitably follows, by referring to a small plastic compass that weighs a fraction of an ounce and costs less than a dollar.

My friends and I play a game on the trail — while taking a breather — which has proved as interesting as it is instructive. Each of us draws a line in the dirt with a stick toward what he believes is true north. Then the compass is brought out, the declination is marked off, and the winner is declared. It is surprising how quickly this game develops a sharp sense of direction.

The usefulness of any map depends largely on the effort invested by the traveler. Winter is a fine time to study maps, plan trips and become familiar with topography. The first principle of map use is orientation — lining up the map with the country. Since all the above-listed maps are laid out north-south, this means pointing the top of your map toward true north.

First, lay your map on the ground and place your compass upon it. After the compass needle stops moving, carefully rotate the compass until the needle points 17 degrees to the east of north (each topo sheet shows the 17 degree angle of declination). This corrects for the discrepancy between true and magnetic north. The "N" on your compass now points to true north. Gently lift the compass in order to rotate your map until the top (or vertical section lines) point to true north; your map is now oriented.

If you know approximately where you are on the trail, you can easily identify the peaks and landmarks visible around you by laying a straight edge (pencil, notebook or grass stem) from your location on the map toward the landmark you wish to identify. If the map is oriented the straight edge should point to the appropriate landmark on the map. Using this procedure in reverse, if you know the landmarks around you, you can find out where you are.

Reading the rise and fall of the land on a topo map is more a matter of practice than talent. On the 7½ minute map the contour interval is 40 feet, and every fifth line is darkened, so the elevation change between dark lines is 200 feet. To become adept at using contour maps, one must learn to visualize the actual shapes of landforms shown on the map. The best place to begin is with solitary peaks or hills where the contour lines form concentric rings that get smaller as they go higher toward the summit in the center.

It is also useful to note that contour lines generally form arrows which point upstream as they cross running water. Starting with peaks and streams one can, by projection and with practice, determine the slope of the land in any part of the map.

Surprisingly often, travelers fail to make use of the shading and color presented on the topo map. The color areas are quite accurate and tell a good deal about the country. Green represents forest; dotted green shows brush or sparse woodland; and white means either bare rock or meadow. White areas in flat or rolling forest tend to be meadow, while white on peaks, cliffs and ridges most often represents bare rock.

Chapter 5

Trip Planning Guide

and Index to Trailheads

There are 27 principal trails into the Wilderness Area from 21 major trailheads. Like the regional divisions, the trailheads are presented below in clockwise fashion, beginning at Echo Lake. Material is arranged in tabular form to simplify making comparisons between trails.

From this trip planning guide the hiker should be able to judge which of several trails to a given area best suits his aims. The guide should also be useful in planning circuit and shuttle trips. The "Region-Section" index will enable the reader to quickly find a more detailed account of each trail in the text.

Since most trails in the area are interconnected, they offer access to a large number of possible destinations. From these, for each trail, I have listed the three or four most popular. And one of these has been selected as the *principal* destination (indicated by an *). This makes possible specific comparisons between trailheads in terms of climb and distance.

The "Remarks" column for each trail is a qualitative judgment of scenic attributes, terrain, trail condition, popularity and limitations. Trails are judged solely from the viewpoint of a hiker. ("Trailhead No." refers to number on map in back pocket.)

Region Section	Trailhead location	Trail name	Popular destinations
		Trailhead No. 1	
1-1	Lower Echo L. at So. end of dam (7420)	Tahoe-Yosemite	Haypress Meadows, Tamarack, Aloha,* Lake of the Woods
1-3	Echo Corral (7460)	South Rim	Cup, Saucer lakes, Ralston Peak*
1-4	Lower Echo (7420)	North Rim	Flagpole, Echo peaks*
1-9	Lower Echo (7420)	South Shore	Saucer Lake Trail*, T-Y
		Trailhead No. 2	
1-2	Paved road opposite 45-mile Campground on US 50 (6550)	Ralston Peak	Ralston Peak,* Lake of the Woods, Haypress Meadows
		Trailhead No. 3	
2-2	Twin Bridges: on US 50 (6100)	Horsetail Falls	Desolation Valley Rim*, Lakes of lower basin, Lake of the Woods
		Trailhead No. 4	
3-1	Jctn.: Wrights Lake, Lyons Creek roads (6900)	Lyons Creek	Lyons, Sylvia,* Bloodsucker lakes, Pyramid Pk.
		Trailhead No. 5	
3-2	Foot of Wrights Lake at Horse Camp (6960)	Bloodsucker	Bloodsucker Lake,* Lyons Creek
		Trailhead No. 6	
3-3	Road's end N.E. of Wrights Lake (6940)	Island Lake	Grouse, Hemlock, Smith, Twin, Island*, Clyde lakes
3-4	Road's end N.E. of Wrights Lake (6940)	Willow Flat	Maud, Gertrude, Tyler lakes, Rockbound Pass* and Valley

*principal destination

| Distance, climb to | | Principal Destination |
(Miles)	(feet)	Remarks
6.7	920	Easiest, fastest, most popular Wilderness access on big, dusty, scenic boulevard. Echo boat service pleasant, saves 3 miles.
4.0	1775	Brushy, rugged; for energetic ridgewalkers from Ralston Peak. Becker Peak climb easy.
2.8	1475	Easy climbs; beautiful open country. For day-hikers; fine views.
1.8	30	Winding, level, wooded, vague cabin-owner path.
4.1	2685	Long, hot, steep, dry, rarely maintained trail; usually descended.
2.0	1400	Steep, poorly marked, unmaintained route located by usage not design; not for novices, the heavily laden or stock.
5.0	1160	Pleasant, shaded, easy grade beside stream; offers easiest Pyramid Peak ascent route.
2.2	460	Despite logging roads, stumps, a nice. easy walk to shallow, fishless Bloodsucker Lake.
3.1	1200	Smith Lake Trail is wooded, higher, and less traveled than open, barren Island Trail country.
5.0	1610	Tyler-Gertrude Trail delightful, little traveled; Rockbound Pass Trail long, dreary, steep.

Region Section	Trailhead location	Trail name	Popular destinations
		Trailhead No. 7	
3-5	East end Dark Lake (6900)	Barrett Lake Jeep Trail	Barrett*, Lawrence lakes
		Trailhead No. 8	
4-3	Van Vleck Ranch gate (6100)	Tells Peak-Highland	Forni Lake, Tells Peak*
4-4	Van Vleck Ranch gate (6100)	Red Peak	Lake No. 3,* and 5
		Trailhead No. 9	
4-2	South end Loon Lake (6420)	Loon Lake	Spider Lake, Buck Island Reservoir*, Rockbound Valley
		Trailhead No. 10	
4-1	Wentworth Springs (6013)	Wentworth Springs Jeep Trail	North Tells Peak Tr., Buck Island Reservoir*, Rockbound Valley
		Trailhead No. 11	
5-1	Jctn.: Miller, Richardson Lake Rds. (7150)	Miller Lake Jeep Trail	Rubicon Springs, Buck Island Reservoir*, Rockbound Valley
6-1	Jctn.: Miller, Richardson Lake Rds. (7150)	General Cr. Trail Lateral	Wilderness boundary*, Lost, Duck lakes, T-Y Trail Velma lakes
		Trailhead No. 12	
6-3	Sugar Pine Point Campground State 89 (6340)	Lower General Creek	Wilderness boundary*, Lost, Duck lakes, T-Y Trail, Velma Lakes
		Trailhead No. 13	
6-2	End Meeks Creek Rd. from State 89 (6250)	T-Y	Lake Genevieve,* Upper General Creek, Phipps Pass, Velma lakes

*principal destination

Distance, climb to Principal Destination		
(Miles)	**(feet)**	**Remarks**
5.0	720	4-wheel-drive jeep road through dull forest to Barrett; Lawrence handsome.
8.2	2772	Private land provides access quandary; ranch land dull; trail poorly marked.
7.9	2120	Same as above, but access, trail better.
6.5	400	Big new motorbike boulevard hooks to construction road for easiest Rockbound Valley access; dismal hiking.
6.7	735	Western half of trans-Sierra trail for 4-wheel-drive jeeps; roundabout, dusty, unlovely.
6.6	—650	Eastern half of trans-Sierra 4-wheel-drive jeep trail; a steep, dusty, dreary descent on old Indian trail.
1.5	190	Longest but easiest access to Velma Lakes Basin on little traveled, unexciting trail through rolling wooded country.
5.1	1000	Pleasant streamside walk, partly on logging road; General Creek lateral (above) offers better access.
3.1	1170	High-standard, heavily traveled T-Y climbs through wooded country past a variety of trout lakes.

Region Section	Trailhead location	Trail name	Popular destinations
	Trailhead No. 14		
7-1	Eagle Falls Campground, State 89 (6600)	Eagle Falls	Velma lakes*, Dicks Pass, Rockbound Valley, Upper General Creek
	Trailhead No. 15		
7-2	Bay View Campground. State 89 (6850)	Bay View	Velma lakes*, Dicks Pass, Rockbound Valley, Upper General Creek
	Trailhead No. 16		
7-5	End Cascade Rd. from Bay View Campground (6900)	Cascade Basin	Snow*, Azure lakes, Velma lakes, Dicks Pass
	Trailhead No. 17		
8-7	On Spring Creek Rd. from State 89 (6460)	Floating Island	Floating Island Lake. Cathedral Trail* and Lake, Mt. Tallac
	Trailhead No. 18		
8-8	End of Stanford Camp road: Fallen Leaf L. (6380)	Cathedral	Floating Island Trail* and Lake, Cathedral Lake, Mt. Tallac
	Trailhead No. 19		
8-1	Lily L. parking lot. Glen Alpine Rd. (6540)	Glen Alpine	Grass, Susie, Heather, Aloha*, Lucille, Half Moon, Gilmore lakes. Mt. Tallac
	Trailhead No. 20		
8-2	Tamarack trailhead on Glen Alpine Rd. (6540)	Tamarack	Triangle Saddle*, Echo Peak and Basin, Triangle and Lost lakes, Desolation Valley
	Trailhead No. 21		
8-9	Angora Lake Rd.: locked gate (7200)	Angora	Echo Peak*

*principal destination

Distance, climb to Principal Destination		
(Miles)	(feet)	Remarks
4.5	1580	Well-traveled good trail to popular Velmas; easiest eastside access to Rockbound Valley; no stock.
5.1	1650	Climb, distance comparable to Eagle Falls hiker trail, but this is steep, dusty stock trail.
3.0	530	Unofficial, unmaintained, poorly marked, brushy, little-traveled trail into handsome lake basin.
2.6	1080	Pleasant, little-traveled path follows ancient, gently climbing roads through wooded country to Floating Island Lake, Mt. Tallac.
1.8	1160	Steepest, shortest, least interesting route up Mt. Tallac; also shortest route to Floating Island Lake.
6.3	1560	Big, overbuilt, dusty trunk trail offering access to Desolation Valley, Echo, Velmas in addition to Fallen Leaf Basin.
2.5	1700	Poorly marked trailhead; this modest, moderately used trail offers shortest route to Desolation; no stock; wet early.
2.1	1700	Unofficial, vaguely marked, unmaintained; but pleasant and unexposed route up Echo Peak.

Echo Lakes Basin

The easiest and most popular point of access to the Wilderness Area, Echo Basin is reached by 1½ miles of narrow paved road that winds north from Highway 50. The well-signed junction lies a mile to the west of Echo Summit. The Echo road generally has been ploughed free of snow by Memorial Day, and it remains open until the first heavy snowfall, usually in late November. Halfway to the lake the road forks at a signed junction; the old Johnson Pass road continues east to Highway 50, while the Echo road turns north and passes Echo Corral and Pack Station on the left and then Berkeley Camp on the right.

Echo Corral offers all imaginable horse-related services ranging from kiddie rides and barbecue picnics to guided, full-scale back-country pack trips. Write Haven Jorgensen at Echo Lake, Calif. 95721 or call (916) 659-7207 (summers), (916) 622-0736 (winters). Berkeley Camp, with tent cabins, pool and dining hall, offers inexpensive family vacationing for City of Berkeley families. The road climbs through a little pass and descends to a large level flat where visitors planning to remain more than two hours can park free.

From the parking lot the road drops to the lakeshore, past Echo Lake Resort (formerly Echo Chalet) and ends in a short

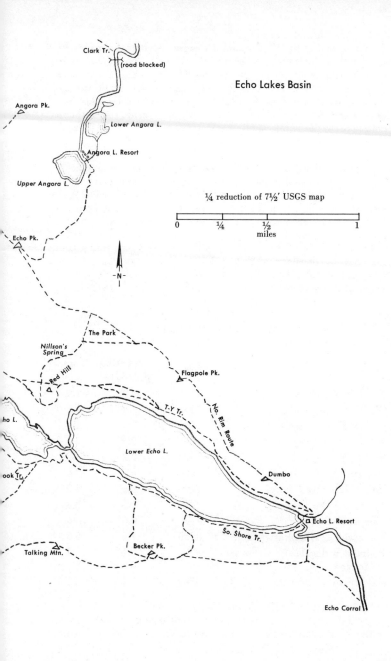

Echo Lakes Basin

Clark Tr.

(road blocked)

Angora Pk.

Lower Angora L.

Angora L. Resort

Upper Angora L.

¼ reduction of 7½′ USGS map

0   ¼   ½   1
miles

Echo Pk.

-N-

The Park

Nillson's
Spring

Red Hill

Flagpole Pk.

ho L.

T-Y Tr.

No. Rim Route

Lower Echo L.

ook Tr.

Dumbo

Echo L. Resort

So. Shore Tr.

Becker Pk.

Talking Mtn.

Echo Corral

frontage road at the boat launching ramp ($2 launching fee) by the trailhead at the dam. Echo Lake Resort offers a fountain, general store, post office, phone booth, rest rooms in the basement, gas station, and housekeeping cabins. Of particular interest to backpackers is the boat-taxi service which for $1.00 per person and 50¢ per pack takes the visitor on a scenic ride through both lakes to the public landing at the far end of the basin, thereby saving the time and energy that would be consumed tramping the intervening 3 miles of trail.

Hikers wishing to return by taxi should make arrangements with the boatman for pickup time in case the somewhat undependable telephone near the public landing is out of order. Also offered at the Echo Marina are several sightseeing excursions led by a USFS ranger each week and boat and motor rentals by the hour, day or week.

In addition to all the territory within Echo Basin, this region includes, on the basis of access, Lost and Triangle lakes in the Fallen Leaf watershed, and the section of the Ralston Peak Trail between the peak and Highway 50 (including Cup Lake).

Sec. 1
Tahoe-Yosemite Trail
(Echo Trailhead to Haypress Pass)

	Elev.	Miles from pt. above	Total miles
Echo Trailhead: dam	7420	0.0	0.0
Old Trail (east end)	7450	1.3	1.3
Old Trail (west end)	7500	0.4	1.7
Red Hill Trail (east end)	7500	0.3	2.0
Spring Trail	7500	0.2	2.2
Red Hill Trail (west end)	7500	0.2	2.4
Public Landing Lateral	7500	0.5	2.9
Triangle Lake Trail	7800	0.5	3.4
Tamarack Lake Trail	7860	0.6	4.0
Tamarack Trail to Fallen Leaf	8250	1.0	5.0
Poopout Ridge Trail: Haypress Meadows	8300	0.1	5.1
Haypress Pass: Ralston Peak Trail	8340	0.4	5.5

Known to the USFS as the Tahoe-Yosemite Trail (abbreviated "T-Y Trail"), this most popular and heavily traveled route in the Wilderness Area is best known to hikers as the Desolation

Trail or the Echo Trail; it is also a segment of the proposed Pacific Crest and Pan-American trails. In recent years it has been straightened, widened, rerouted to yield more constant grades, fitted with water bars and filled with soil. Trees have been uprooted, boulders dynamited, brush cut and slab granite blasted — all of which has cost the trail a good deal of character, though back-country access has probably been improved. The trail is short on shade and running water (by midseason) and there are no campsites before Tamarack Lake (4.3 trail miles from the trailhead or 1.4 miles when a boat-taxi is used).

Echo Trailhead (7420 — 0.0). The trail begins beside a little shack between the launching ramp and the south end of the dam. A sign reads *Tahoe-Yosemite Trail, 17E01, Desolation Wilderness 3 miles, Haypress Meadows 4 miles.* Foot traffic crosses first the curving, sand-topped dam and then a narrow footbridge over the spillway, while stock ford the creek 50 yards downstream. The two trails meet on the north bank and switchback to a point 100' above the water before leveling off and heading northwest above the lakeshore on a broad, sandy boulevard through low-growing huckleberry oak.

We pass beneath cliffs that rise to the rounded summit of a granite hill known locally as Dumbo, on a stretch of trail notable for the disfiguring scar made in 1967 when the USFS trailbuilders blasted a trench across a lovely slanting slab of granite rather than lose 20' of elevation. Beyond Dumbo the trail passes the first 3 lakeside cabins and then the low, flat saddle between Dumbo and the impressive cliffs of Flagpole Peak before passing into light timber to a junction of the

Old Trail, east end (7450 — 1.3). In 1967 the USFS, in the process of rebuilding the trail, decided the section beneath Flagpole was unsatisfactory, so they constructed a new section which climbs well above the old route before dropping to rejoin it. The trail splits at a point nearly opposite a large, attractive older cabin with boathouse, the first to be encountered in $\frac{1}{2}$ mile and the only dwelling shown by the topo map on Lower Echo's eastern shore. A half-hearted attempt has been made to block the old (lower) trail, and it has not been maintained since the new one was built, but it remains perfectly serviceable for walkers allergic to unnecessary climbing.

The new trail makes its way up through waist-high huckleberry oak fields to the cliffs beneath Flagpole, where it levels off for $\frac{1}{4}$ mile and then, blocked by cliffs, drops to an unmarked but not very well disguised junction with the

Old Trail, west end (7500 — 0.3). Located in a patch of forest understoried with willow, the junction lies between cliffs and the easternmost of a row of cabins close to the trail, signed *Kaiser*, *#14*. Arcing imperceptibly toward the west the trail comes out into light timber, passes beneath strikingly colored joint-block cliffs, skirts the top of a wooded draw, and in a clump of trees where a creek bed (dry before midsummer) crosses the trail, we come to an unmarked junction with the locally named

Red Hill Trail, east end (7500 — 0.3). This pleasant path, perhaps ½ mile long, makes an interesting shortcut for the leisurely hiker who doesn't mind climbing and then dropping an extra 100′ in order to see a little more of the country. Once a part of the main trail, this well-marked but unmaintained track ascends a little canyon beside a streambed, climbs through a little saddle behind colorful Red Hill and then descends to the west, crossing the buried pipeline that marks the Spring Trail. It dips through several little dells and returns to the main trail at about the middle of the Upper Lake's north shore.

Returning to the east end of the Red Hill trail, we find the T-Y Trail abruptly turning due south along the base of Red Hill and onto the peninsula that separates the two lakes. As the trail turns back to the west it makes a small loop through a tiny draw tucked under Red Hill. This draw marks the unsigned junction with the

Spring Trail (7500 — 0.2). See Sec. 5 for the route up this trail to the north rim and Echo Peak. About 50 feet beyond the draw the sharp-eyed traveler will note a buried pipeline crossing the trail and a footpath climbing to the north. This is an alternative entrance to the Spring Trail. Several trails may also be noted heading down the peninsula toward the channel that joins the two lakes. It occurs to more than a few homeward-bound hikers that considerable distance might be saved by crossing the channel and following the Lower Lake's south shore back to the trailhead.

Unfortunately the channel, being deep and wide enough to accommodate 20-foot boats, is impractical to wade and most hikers, inhibited from stripping by the heavy boat traffic and the close proximity of cabins, trudge back up the peninsula to the trail. In the fall, however, around the end of September, the lakes have been sufficiently drained to make fording feasible. But the south shore trail (see Sec. 9) is so poor and difficult to follow that any saving of time and energy by this route is negligible.

From the Spring Trail Junction our route continues past Red Hill, and crosses open, tree-studded slopes of pink-brown rock thinly covered with grass. At the western edge of this rolling parkland we re-enter the forest, coming immediately to the

Red Hill Trail, west end (7500 — 0.2). Continuing to the west and well back from the water the trail moves for the first time through mixed pine forest. Numerous small drainages cross the springy trail, and wildflowers last in the cool shade well past mid-summer. A conspicuous pocket of quaking aspen stands out apple-green against the dark pine forest, and in October the yellow leaves, like bright coins, glint in the breeze. The trail climbs through a little gap and a rarely used lateral drops away to the public landing. Fifty yards farther we come to the principal

Public Landing Lateral (7500 — 0.5). A sign reads *Public Pier 300 feet. For taxi service use telephone, Boy Scout Camp ¼ mile,* downhill to the south, *Tamarack Lake 1 mile, Desolation Wilderness 2 miles,* west, and *Echo Chalet 3 miles,* east. About 100 yards south down the rocky gulch, hidden by a fringe of trees along the shore, is the public landing, which serves as the upper terminus of the boat-taxi service from Echo Marina. Probably half the backpackers bound for Desolation Valley (and nearly all the weekenders) take the boat to save hiking the 2.9 miles of trail described to this point.

A little flat behind the pier, though undeveloped for camping and sandwiched between summer cabins and Harvey West Boy Scout camp, nevertheless serves occasionally as an overnight bivouac for improvident hikers. A few yards to the west is the rustic hut containing a not-always-dependable pay telephone. The boat-taxi number (659-7207) is written on the wall. Change can be obtained at the Scout camp. There is also a pay phone in the main lodge of the camp, 100 yards through the trees to the west.

A canteen, reached by following the waterfront trail around the shore and crossing Ralston Creek, is open most of the day and can be a valuable source of such forgotten staples as insect repellent, shoelaces and lip ice. The camp is generally in operation from late June until late August, and during that period a doctor in residence will handle medical emergencies without charge (although donations are gratefully accepted). For emergency transportation down the basin, Scout boats depart for the roadhead at 9 am, 2 pm and 4 pm on weekends; in addition there are sometimes frequent unscheduled trips.

From the signed junction on the T-Y Trail above the public landing the trail turns gradually upward at a carefully controlled grade in broadly serpentining loops that move in and out of the shade of big yellow pines. We cross a culverted creek-bed (drinking water into July), climb through fields of huckleberry oak and after a quarter of a mile emerge onto open rock. Now climbing more steeply, the rocky trail, dynamited out of low cliffs, rises onto a small promontory under a large juniper, which offers an excellent view of the two lakes.

Some 75 yards farther the trail is crossed by a small rill that generally runs to the end of June. Immediately beyond, a faint footpath (shortcut lateral to the Triangle Lake trail) angles up the talus slope toward a little knoll. The main trail continues around the knoll and inscribes a smooth curve into the slope on dead-level, packed earth, in the middle of which lies the important but unsigned (thanks to vandals) and easily missed junction with the

Triangle Lake trail (7800 — 0.5) which serves as access to Echo Peak, Fallen Leaf Lake and Haypress Meadows, in addition to Lost and Triangle lakes. Beyond the junction, the T-Y Trail hooks around a little spur at the end of the sandy flat and a few yards farther re-enters the forest. A USFS trail register on a stand beside the trail requests travelers (for their safety as well as wilderness use evidence) to enter name, hometown, date, time, number in party, means of travel, and destination.

After 1/4 mile through shady forest understoried by a succession of wildflowers, the trail curves back toward the west and forks into two parallel tracks. The upper, official track climbs a few feet unnecessarily but the lower, level, unmaintained route tends to be boggy in early spring and has been partly blocked by rocks on the west end. The two trails rejoin just before coming out of the woods onto a bright, bare slope of blue-white slab and talus. We cross a little hollow on fill from which Echo Lakes again become visible, then turn northwest through a head-high corridor blasted into the rock to the junction with the

Tamarack Lake Trail (7860 — 0.6). Signs read *Tamarack Lake 1/4 mile, Ralston Lake 1/2 mile*, southwest, and *Haypress Meadows 1 mile, Desolation Valley 2 miles*, northwest. In addition to the two lakes named, this trail serves as access to Cagwin Lake, Ralston Peak, various points on the Ralston Peak trail and a cross-country route to Lake of the Woods (see Sec. 8).

About the trail up the canyon to Haypress Meadows there is very little to say. Cut out of the rocky slope, it runs shadeless and straight at a constant grade, with a continuous view down into Tamarack. I generally take the slower but shadier and more interesting old trail (see Sec. 1A).

Near the top of the grade at the main trail's first switchback, the "water trees" and the cold rill that they shade beckon to the upward-trudging hiker and invite him, after drinking, to sit on a conveniently placed log and look out over the country just traversed. The rill behind the two 30-inch lodgepoles normally runs well into August. From the "water trees" the trail, in order to maintain an acceptable USFS grade, embarks upon several long switchbacks. Unfortunately, a majority of hikers, impatient with long switchbacks, climb directly up one of several steep and eroding gullies through tall grass and low willow beside the rill, returning to the trail at a culvert. A few feet above the culvert, at an unmarked and easily missed junction, we meet the

Tamarack Trail (8250 — 1.0) from Fallen Leaf Lake by way of Triangle junction (see Sec. 5, and Region 8, Sec. 2). The trail draws its name from the fact that its original destination was Tamarack Lake; trails have been considerably rerouted since then, and this old and unmaintained but still delightful trail is now little traveled. At this junction the T-Y Trail begins to flatten out through a patch of corn lilies, and 100 yards later it passes into the shade of big lodgepole and red fir that mark the eastern edge of Haypress Meadows. A little farther into the timber the sandy trail levels off to the junction with the

Poopout Ridge Trail: Haypress Meadows (8300 — 0.2). Signs read *Lake of the Woods 1 mile*, *Ropi Lake 3 miles*, pointing west, *Upper Echo Lake 2½ miles*, pointing east, and *Desolation Valley 1 mile*, pointing northwest. The trail heads west through open, brushless timber past a large red fir (felled for some unaccountable reason) and out into a boggy (except in late season) stretch of meadow just below a shallow pool. (This is the source of the "water tree" rill.) The surrounding open meadow, as the season passes, hosts a succession of wildflowers, but it is also thickly infested with lodgepole pine seedlings. The USFS not many years ago cleared the meadow on the north side of the trail; otherwise it would closely resemble the south side, where a dense stand of saplings rises 3-6 feet high.

The lush meadow, which in Gold Rush days was mown and the baled grasses laboriously hauled to Echo Summit to feed hungry stock, seems destined soon to become unbroken forest. At the meadow's west edge a long vista opens through the trees, and we can look south to Ralston Peak and north to Jacks Peak. From the edge of the meadow the trail climbs steeply up a dusty track through red fir and hemlock to the top of the ridge and a junction with the

Ralston Peak Trail (8420 — 0.3). Here on the spine of Poopout Ridge we come suddenly upon a marvelous view of Pyramid Peak and Mt. Price, the climax of the glacially carved, snow-etched Crystal Range. Poopout Ridge takes its name from the condition of the Boy Scouts and their panting parents who must cross it to reach Camp Codor on the shore of Lake of the Woods, just below to the west. Parents traditionally hike over the ridge on Fridays for an overnight visit with their sons.

Back at the junction at the foot of Haypress Meadows, we head northwest on level sand under scattered big trees; the open meadowland, covered with flowers, rolls away to the west toward Poopout Ridge. The trail, wide as a road, passes through a dense, locked stand of lodgepole saplings, then splits into two tracks which skirt opposite sides of a boggy meadow patch. We veer to the west and climb across the top of the grassland, where the two trails rejoin, then enter a corridor through a parklike stand of hemlock that leads to an unmarked junction with the northern end of the

Ralston Peak Trail (8340 — 0.4) at Haypress Pass. There is a campsite ringed with trees (sometimes occupied by a ranger or trail crew) which relies on water from a spring beside the trail (flowing well into August) a hundred yards to the northwest.

Sec. 1A

Old Desolation Trail

Before the present high-speed, carefully graded stock trail was built from the upper public landing to Haypress Meadows there was another trail: a dipping, winding, narrow path that joined these two points in a more interesting if less efficient fashion. Much of the old route still exists and, though sometimes rough or faint, it offers the unhurried, unburdened hiker a shadier and less dusty passage.

First traces of the old trail can be found in a dense patch of ceanothus just below the new trail only a few yards west of the public landing lateral. About 50 yards farther west, as it crosses a small ravine, it becomes distinct enough to follow easily. Paralleling the new trail and never more than 50 yards below it, it climbs over a rotting deadfall, passes under a Scout tent platform and, climbing gradually along the slope, disappears into a large Troop camp. Emerging more distinctly on the far side, thanks to Scout travel, it twists and turns, dips and climbs, then suddenly swoops straight up between two big junipers to touch the new trail for a few feet before dropping once again and running parallel for several hundred yards.

A small cliff forces it to merge with the new trail as it passes the Triangle trail junction but, once it enters the woods beyond, it loops first to one side, then the other. Through this stretch the new trail is simply the old trail straightened. As we turn west the old trail provides a lower (wetter in spring) shortcut to the edge of the woods. A little way out onto the rock it climbs above the new trail and, switchbacking directly to the Tamarack junction, short-cuts the new trail's conspicuous cut and fill. At the junction the old trail heads northwest, bisecting the angle between the new trail and the Tamarack Trail.

From this point onward the old trail follows a winding, shady route of its own up the canyon, keeping well below the new trail. There is a deadfall or two and occasional washouts, but the route is generally discernible, and it offers a character and charm not to be found on the long, straight, dusty boulevard above. As it nears the head of the canyon it begins to climb more steeply, and finally it dwindles away permanently in a pungent sage slope just a few yards below the water tree.

SEC. 2
Ralston Peak Trail

	Elev.	Miles from pt. above	Total miles
Tahoe-Yosemite Trail: Haypress Pass	8340	0.0	0.0
Poopout Ridge Trail	8420	0.2	0.2
Tamarack Pass	8460	0.7	0.9
Ralston Peak Lateral	8800	0.7	1.6
Ralston Peak	9235	0.7	
Cup Lake Lateral	8460	1.0	2.6
Pinecrest Camp: swimming pool	6660	2.3	4.9
Ralston Peak trailhead	6550	0.1	5.0

This trail is something of a maverick, belonging neither to Echo Basin nor to Desolation Valley. For the first 1½ miles it straddles the boundary between them, then drops over the shoulder of Ralston Peak into a drainage of its own. Included here are the lateral trail to Ralston's summit and the cross-country route to Cup Lake. At first glance this trail appears to be a logical access route north into the Wilderness, thus suggesting a description beginning at the highway. But in practice the frequently traveled northern section is generally reached from Echo and the rarely traveled southern section is generally descended, because of its steepness. The drop is 2300′ in 3½ miles through loose sand and brush with little shade or water. Though the trail is virtually unmaintained one can safely wear shorts; in fact they are advisable because of the heat. I have never met anyone coming up.

At 9235′, Ralston Peak is the highest summit on the Echo Basin rim; it is also the only peak with a maintained trail all the way to the top. By trail it lies 7.5 miles from the roadhead at Lower Echo, but this is reduced to 4.6 by taking a boat to the public landing, and to approximately 3.5 (and a climb of only 1800′) by also taking the cross-country route around the north shore of Tamarack Lake to Tamarack Pass (see Sec. 8). The north end of the Ralston Peak trail begins at a junction with the

Tahoe-Yosemite Trail: Haypress Pass (8340 — 0.0). This little-traveled, superfluous, but perfectly pleasant scrap of trail moves dimly south from the unsigned and all-but-invisible junction in Haypress Pass and climbs smoothly up a gravel slope to enter an acre of shoulder-high red fir saplings not unlike a Christmas tree lot. Climbing steadily higher on the open sandy ridge, it finally reaches the top at the intersection with the

Poopout Ridge Trail (8420 — 0.2). Signs read *Lake of the Woods* ½ *mile, Ropi Lake* 2½ *miles,* west, *Upper Echo Lake 3 miles,* east, *Desolation Valley 1 mile,* north, and *Ralston Peak 2 miles,* south. A modest but continuous groove marked by frequent (and occasionally large) ducks, faded orange paint blazes on rocks and blazes cut into the infrequent trees, leads south on a gentle incline up the open, rocky ridge past a sign reading *Motor Travel Prohibited.*

The sign, facing south, marks the boundary of the old primitive area. In elaboration, it states that in . . . *wilderness, wild or primitive areas no motorboat, automobile, jeep, motorcycle or other motorized vehicle may be driven and no airplane or helicopter may be landed.* Trees become scarce and the trail grows dim as we top an unnamed summit, from which Ralston Peak again becomes visible, and head down through Mariposa lilies and marmot rocks into the lightly timbered grassland of

Tamarack Pass (8460 — 0.7). A cross-country short-cut route from Tamarack Lake, directly to the east, passes through this lush saddle on the way to Lake of the Woods (see Sec. 8) directly to the west. The trail dips through the low point of the pass, then slips to the west of the ridgeline as it starts up the northern slope. It passes a little to the east of a shallow pond which abounds in tadpoles, frogs and garter snakes. When the wind and wildlife aren't rippling the surface, it handsomely reflects the summit of Pyramid Peak.

Fed by spring water welling out of the bank just above it, the pool probably was formed (or at least enlarged) by a cheesemaker who early in the century pastured a herd of goats in the Tamarack Pass meadows. Just north of the pond in a clump of lodgepole lie the remains of his two-room log cabin, which once boasted a cast-iron stove, glass windows, a rock chimney serving back-to-back fireplaces, and a square-nailed shake roof. An aqueduct of hollowed split logs once evidently carried water from some point above the pond to the cabin. Just north of the cabin is a section of carefully made rock wall; the camp and ¼ acre of meadow were enclosed within a log corral fence.

Oldtimers at Echo recall the cheesemaker arriving early in the spring with his herd of goats and making his way through Haypress to the cabin on the ridge. All summer he grazed and milked his goats and made his cheese, and when enough had accumulated to justify a journey, he packed it out to the highway to sell. Instead of descending to Echo, he headed directly south, and the trail we follow past his cabin, which climbs over Ralston's shoulder, then drops to Pinecrest Camp, must have been the route he followed — and probably originated.

Beyond the cheesemaker's pond the trail crosses a rivulet (running until midsummer), then enters shady woods where, despite both ducks and blazes, it grows faint and some of the sharper turnings are hard to follow. We climb steeply through timber and come out into a little meadow only 50′ below and 100 yards west of a gap in the ridge. This gap, easily visible from below, is often the target of climbers coming up from Ralston Lake. For the next ¼ mile the trail climbs gently through a strip of timber-fringed meadowland threaded by an all-summer creek, on the western side of the ridge.

All at once we come out onto a lush flat meadow, not unlike a football field, backed by a bare bluff of gleaming white talus. Threading its way through the grasshopper- and grouse-populated meadow, the creek we have been following since the cheesemaker's pond offers the last and highest dependable water on the mountain. A few yards east of the trail, on the edge of the meadow, the remains of a snow-crushed sign spread out on a boulder mark the junction of the

Ralston Peak Lateral (8800 — 0.7). Signs read *Echo Lake 4 miles, Desolation Valley 2½ miles*, north, *State Highway 3½ miles, Camp Sacramento 4 miles*, south, and *Mt. Ralston ¾ mile, Cup Lake 1¼ miles*, southeast. Heading up the mountain to the southeast we skirt the northern edge of the meadow in tall grass that obscures any sign of a path, guided only by ducks visible at the upper end of the meadow. A faint but well-ducked track materializes above the meadow and we angle to the south on a bare sandy slope, crossing the flattened remains of a barbed-wire fence.

The trail leads onto the bluff seen from the trail junction and then turns again to the southeast, climbing directly up the long ridge toward the peak. An easier and less confusing means of reaching this same point involves crossing the meadow, climbing the well-defined switchbacks that mount the bluff, then moving directly up the spine of the bluff for 200 yards. For the next ½ mile the trail climbs steadily through corridors of gnarled, half-prostrate juniper and lodgepole on the narrowing ridge to the summit of

Ralston Peak (9235 — 0.7). The summit is surprisingly broad and flat, and the approach presents no exposure. There is no longer a sign or register on top, but the view is fine in every direction. Like so many peaks, it seems to harbor more than its share of wildflowers, birds and butterflies.

Returning to the junction of the Ralston Peak lateral and turning south, we cross the lush meadow and its cold stream, and switchback up the steep sandy slope of the bluff onto the flattened western shoulder of the mountain. Having reached the highest point on the trail, the traveler may want to reward himself with an exceptional view by walking 50 yards west to the brink of the cliffs. Virtually all of Desolation Valley is visible from this point, including 11 lakes.

As we cross Ralston's shoulder and start down the trail to the south the vegetation changes immediately to dry-climate sage, ceanothus and lupine. From this high, open country there are fine, unobstructed views south to a succession of wooded ridges, including the snow-flecked mountains of Carson Pass. Half a mile down the unmaintained but serviceable trail we pass a small, icy spring. Trees grow more numerous as the trail swings southeast around the mountain, then surprisingly we climb on a long traverse to the top of a little wooded ridge and a sign reading *17E11* which marks the

Cup Lake Lateral (8460 — 1.0). This is the point of departure for an unmarked cross-country route to remote Cup Lake. Due east above this ridge is the little spur that shelters Cup. By climbing toward it the traveler is able to pass through a little saddle and drop to the lake. Like the other routes to Cup, this one is steep and strenuous.

Below the sign on the little ridge, the trail plunges down several steep, sandy chutes and we traverse to the west through a tiny hollow shaded by big red fir. Just above a 15-foot stump there issues from beneath a boulder a small icy spring. Neither this nor the spring higher on the slope should be relied upon much beyond midseason. The trail continues to drop steeply along hot, sandy trenches through the brushfields for another ½ mile, then all at once it drops into the sweet shade of a tall, cool forest understoried with ferns. Tamarack Creek gurgles down the center of a small, steep canyon to the east. The USFS plans, in three or four years, to replace the steepest stretch, between the lush forest and the sign on the ridge, with one giant switchback.

We move down through the forest on springy duff and soon come to a well-trodden trail branching off to the west. This is the first and highest of the many hiking and bridle paths, none of them marked, that serve Pinecrest Camp, below. About 100 yards farther down, another trail branches west. To the east through the trees can be seen a permanent camp furnished with bark-roofed shelters; a trail branches toward it. Some 100 yards farther another trail branches east to a circle of eight covered wagons. And 50 yards farther south the trail takes a deceptive jog and there is another path to the wagons; $\frac{1}{4}$ mile farther we round a bend and find ourselves looking down into the inviting blue water of the

Pinecrest Camp swimming pool (6660 — 2.3). At the southern edge of the pool enclosure we reach a dirt road and a large sign reading *Ralston Trail* with arrows pointing up the trail we have descended. We follow the road downhill to the east beside a corral fence on which there are three more large signs reading *trail*. From the road the trail drops due south under power poles down a broad, cleared right-of-way to the

Ralston Peak trailhead (6550—0.1) at a bend in the paved road at the bottom. A USFS sign reads *Ralston Trail, Lake of the Woods, Desolation Valley*, pointing up the right-of-way. No distances are given. Parking space is scarce. About $\frac{1}{4}$ mile to the southwest the paved road intersects Highway 50 at a painted wooden sign reading *Pinecrest Camp, SDA*, just opposite 45 Mile Campground.

SEC. 3
South Rim Route

	Elev.	Miles from pt. above	Total miles
Ralston Peak	9235	0.0	0.0
Saddle #1: Cup Lake Lateral	9060	0.3	0.3
Saddle #2	9020	0.2	0.5
Peak 9155	9155	0.2	0.7
Saddle #3	8900	0.3	1.0
Saucer Lake Saddle	8880	0.5	1.5
Saddle #4	8700	0.3	1.8
Talking Mountain	8824	0.2	2.0
Becker Peak Saddle	8260	0.6	2.6
Echo Chalet Lateral	7760	1.0	3.6
Echo Corral & Stables	7460	0.4	4.0

The route down Echo's south rim definitely cannot be classified as trail. In places there is a good path, but much of the route, especially across rock, shows no sign of human travel. The route came into being because there are ridgewalkers who like nothing better than to walk a tightrope from peak to peak through the highest, wildest country. The gradually descending ridge from Ralston to Echo Corral also offers a cross-country route home for hikers who have climbed Ralston by trail.

Much of the route is through brush and around cliffs, and hiking in shorts is not recommended. There is no water on the ridgetop, and thirsty hikers will find carrying some liquid preferable to descending to either Cup or Saucer Lake. Distances and elevations given are only approximations. The accompanying map delineates the route, which begins at

Ralston Peak (9235 — 0.0). We move southeast in a gentle arc on a path that follows the ridgeline a few feet back from the cliffs. Below to the northeast lies a seldom-visited high valley in which a charming all-summer brook, fed by springs and snowbanks under Ralston Peak, splashes from pool to pool through lush meadows and into the timber that spreads down to Ralston Creek. This charming little valley, easily the wildest area in Echo Basin, is blocked from below by a series of low cliffs and ledges, and blocked from the rim above by steep talus slopes. Because the brook contains no trout, there are no fishermen's trails or developed campsites. The valley most often is discovered by accident by climbers descending from the ridge above. The going is easy along the tilting sage slope as we drop into

Saddle #1: Cup Lake Lateral (9060 — 0.3). Despite the sign in the meadow at the beginning of the Ralston Peak lateral, there is no trail to Cup Lake. The best approach from the north is down the southern slope from this saddle on talus to a saddle in the barren spur that juts out from the mountain to the southeast. From the saddle there is a 200′ drop on steeper talus to the water's edge. One of the highest, most sheltered and least visited lakes in the region, Cup is among the last to lose its winter ice.

Since the lake remains clear, shows no fluctuation and supports trout, despite the absence of inlet or outlet streams, there evidently is some sort of balance between the springs that feed it and the springs and creeks that it feeds. Standing at the water's edge, beneath towering slopes on all sides, is not unlike standing at the bottom of a well. There is a well-developed, if somewhat bleak, campsite on the bluff to the east in the only timber within the little basin.

Returning to the ridge at Saddle #1 we find the rim rapidly

narrowing and turning to the east. Rather than climb the little knob just ahead we move around it to the south on a descending traverse of the steep talus. Instead of returning to the ridge, which has become a jagged knife-edge with considerable exposure on both sides, we continue to traverse some 20-50 feet south of the ridge, passing beneath.

Saddle #2 (9020 — 0.2). Beyond the saddle the going grows easier as the ridge widens, and we return to the rim and climb to the east. In order to avoid climbing one can contour to the south around peak 9155 but the traveling is easier and there is less exposure in following the ridge up to

Peak 9155 (9155 — 0.2). The summit offers the only point from which both Cup and Saucer lakes can be seen. Also at the summit is a dugout in the rock in which Scouts apparently bivouac. The best route to the east lies a few feet to the north of the ridgeline. This stretch of the crest is rough and narrow in places, but it begins to widen as we come down into

Saddle #3 (8900 — 0.3). From this point eastward, nearly to Echo Corral, the southern slope of the ridge is thickly covered with ceanothus, manzanita and huckleberry oak that extend all the way to the crest and sometimes beyond it. From Saddle #3 eastward the ridge is transformed into a splendid, nearly level, lightly wooded corridor across the sky. There are sheltered campsites, marvelous vistas, caves among the boulders, abundant flowers and birds—everything required for pleasant camping except water.

Surprisingly well-trod paths follow the easiest routes. Immediately beyond Saddle #3 the ridgeline is blocked by brush and boulders, and we follow a sandy corridor along the upper margin of the brush on the south slope for several hundred yards. Once the obstacle is passed, the path climbs to the ridgetop. Directly below to the north are the three black pinnacles that guard the top of Ralston Bowl, another high hanging valley with an all-year stream flowing from its mouth.

Unlike the high valley to the west, Ralston Bowl is largely barren and easily reached from below. This broad and symmetrical amphitheater with the almost vertical headwall shelters snowfields into late summer. In 1967, after a winter of heavy snow, Echo cabin-owners skied a 15-gate slalom course well into August. The generally visible ridgetop trail leads over the top of a little knoll and descends on sand into

Saucer Lake Saddle (8780 — 0.5). To reach the Saucer Lake trail to Echo (see Sec. 10) one simply slides down the steep sandy slope to the lakeshore 200 vertical feet below, then follows the fishermen's trail around Saucer's eastern shore to the end of the trail, indicated by *Echo Lake* written in red paint on a rock just north of the outlet stream. Using the foregoing section of the south rim route, the Saucer Lake trail and one of the several routes up Ralston Peak, it is possible to plan an interesting one-day circuit trip from Echo Basin. In case the rim route above Cup Lake sounds overly forbidding, it should be mentioned that it has been navigated without assistance by a dachshund of my acquaintance.

In Saucer Lake saddle, lying on rocks, are several yellow triangular signs similar to those that mark the Echo Rim Ski Trail, reading *Saucer Lake*. Looking east up the rim from the saddle, we see a small gap in the trees a little south of the crest, and we make our way through it and out onto the broad sandy southern slope beyond. The route passes south below a small summit, then moves back across the ridgeline onto the northern slope and follows a flat, rocky bench with welcome shade to Saddle #4. The south slope is perfectly passable but it crosses shadeless sand to

Saddle #4 (8700 — 0.3). Just beyond, to the east, the ridgeline is blocked by a jumble of brush-encircled boulders and cliffs, and the southern slope becomes steeper and brushier. The north slope, however, offers easy going on sand and rock, and we make our way parallel to the crest but perhaps 50' below it until we are directly opposite the summit. It is then a simple matter to climb directly upward to the south to the undistinguished summit of

Talking Mountain (8824 — 0.2). The echoes that give the basin its name seem predominantly to issue from this high south rim, and this, says the legend, caused the Indians who once fished and trapped in the basin to name the central summit in the ridge Talking Mountain. Another view, however, attributes the name to the roaring avalanches that from time to time cut huge swathes down the mountain's north slope, leaving long vertical scars of brush through the hemlock forest. They have destroyed better than a dozen cabins since 1941.

The topo map suggests that the ridgeline from Talking Mountain to Becker Peak saddle descends in a smooth, gentle eastward arc, the navigation of which should be simple. Unfortunately, more than half the crest here is rocky crags, cliffs and boulders, and unbroken brushfields on the southern slope often spill over the ridgeline to meet the northern cliffs. After the first few hundred easy yards down the crest on open sand, Becker Peak comes into view ½ mile below, the farthest crag on the ragged ridge. The easy going ends at a clump of hemlock as we squeeze past a boulder, cross a little flat and make our way through a brush-field covering the ridgetop. The next obstacle is a small pinnacle, which may be circled to either side: to the south we wade safely but tediously through brush; to the north we clamber more quickly over boulders offering some exposure.

No sooner is the ridge regained than we find it blocked by another crag. The easiest solution is immediately to drop straight down a sandy chute on the north slope which, 50' below, lands us on a narrowing ledge that very conveniently circles beneath the cliffs around the crag and returns us to the ridge. We are now at the highest point that can be reached by horses coming up from Becker saddle. The last of the crags are now behind us but the crest is narrow, steeply descending and well covered with brush. Various stock and game trails tempt us to leave the ridge in hopes of better traveling, but all quickly disappear in the brush. The easiest route runs tight against the brink of the northern cliffs, until the slope eases and the ridge widens, and we step down into

Becker Peak Saddle (8260 — 0.6). Three of the four described routes up Becker Peak pass through this saddle. The 80' scramble up the boulder pile that forms the summit is comparatively easy, and the view it yields of the basin is unexpectedly grand. Lower Echo is revealed as a narrow, deep-blue trench, and majestic Flagpole Peak looms less than 25' above us. Becker Peak is a spur jutting north from the ridge, flanked by a high bowl to the west and a low bowl to the east, each of which offers a cross-country route from Echo Lake to the saddle.

The route to the west drops straight down a steep, sandy, timbered slope into an open, boulder-strewn, flat-bottomed bowl (the high bowl). Snow lies here well into midseason and a trickle of water flows until late summer. From the mouth of the bowl the slope drops away steeply through timber toward the lake, and we angle to the north to escape the willow, alder and aspen thickets and talus slopes that follow the canyon that drains the bowl. Eventually we reach the South Shore trail (see Sec. 9) in the vicinity of a cluster of cabins known as Colony Cove.

On the route to the east, we move south from the saddle along the descending ridge for 50 yards, then drop steeply toward the lake into the top of the eastern (lower) bowl, keeping to the east and threading our way between the widening willow thicket in the canyon and a gleaming talus slope spreading down from the east. Our aim is to turn back to the northwest and cross the stream bed at a rocky gap in the brush where the canyon opens out into a bowl. Once across, we climb over an open slope of ankle-high manzanita, leave the bowl, and descend an open, sandy slope to the South Shore trail.

From Becker Saddle down to Echo Corral there is an easy, more or less continuous groove through gentle country, marked by a few ducks and blazes and a great many triangular *Echo Rim Ski Trail* signs. From either the corral or the Echo parking lot, whether on foot or horse, the journey up the ridge to Becker makes an excellent short trip. As on the route to the lower bowl, we move east from the saddle on a dim track in the dirt, jog south around a patch of brush, and turn back toward the lake to follow the ridge around the head of the lower bowl.

Where the ridgeline starts up toward a crag, we circle again to the south, dropping steeply onto a wooded slope, and returning to the ridgeline in a saddle at the base of the steep crag. For the next $\frac{1}{4}$ mile the ridge runs almost level; a shallow draw, a few feet below to the north toward the lake parallels it all the way. One track drops down into the draw and follows it to the east, while a faint and sometimes rocky track (or tracks) weaves back and forth across the crest. When the draw disappears, the two tracks merge and continue down the flattened western slope, not far from the ridgeline to the

Echo Lake Lateral (7760—1.0). The junction is marked by the top of an old ski tow, an iron rack anchored to a big red fir beside the trail. By descending directly north down the route of the tow (cable and pulleys may still be seen in the trees) on a largely open slope, we come to the edge of the upper parking lot above the east end of the lake. There is no trail down the slope and no sign at the parking lot. From the top of the ski tow a well-defined horse trail leads down through open forest to

Echo Corral & Stables (7460 — 0.4). We emerge at the northwest corner of a railless oval riding ring.

Sec. 4
North Rim Route

	Elev.	Miles from pt. above	Total miles
Echo Trailhead: dam	7420	0.0	0.0
Dumbo Summit	7758	0.5	0.5
Flagpole Saddle	7620	0.3	0.8
Flagpole Peak	8363	0.6	1.4
Spring Trail	8400	0.7	2.1
Angora Lakes Trail	8800	0.6	2.7
Echo Peak	8895	0.1	2.8

The route up Echo's north rim, like its counterpart on the south rim, definitely cannot be classed as trail. Occasionally there are ducks, often there are signs of travel and sometimes there is a highly visible groove. These descriptions represent only the easiest and pleasantest route across country. Where the south rim is characterized by crags and brush, the north rim offers broad and open slopes of granite slab and sand. There is no water except that left in potholes after rains, and a few yards of brush must be traversed on Dumbo, but traveling Echo's north rim, with its beautiful cliffs, rolling sculptured slab and always superb views remains one of the most exhilarating walks I know.

Echo Trailhead: dam (7420 — 0.0). From the boat-launching ramp on the T-Y Trail (see Sec. 1) we cross the dam and the bridge, and mount the switchbacks on the south slope of the brushy granite hill known locally as Dumbo. But when the trail levels off and heads northwest we leave it and, heading straight up the slope, weave through patches of huckleberry oak and buckthorn onto Dumbo's comparatively bare east slope. Both human and game trails are discernible at times as we thread our way on rock and sand along the margin of the brush to

Dumbo Summit (7758 — 0.5). Travelers in shorts should be warned that a certain amount of brush travel cannot be avoided. The high point is a boulder on top of the brushy ridge. For such a modest climb Dumbo offers a surprisingly good view of both Echo Basin and 10,881' Freel Peak to the east. The western (Echo) slope of Dumbo is chiefly brush and steep cliffs and offers no rewarding routes to the summit. There is, however, a fast but steep and sandy path down, really a chute, that threads its way between brushfields and cliffs. Its top is perhaps 50 feet south of the summit boulder.

Continuing along the north rim from Dumbo's summit we drop 50' onto the slabs of the east slope to dodge the brush, and again head northwest, angling back toward the ridgeline as we descend. This slope offers some marvelous specimens of windswept lodgepole and Jeffrey pine and gnarled, prostrate juniper. After unavoidably ploughing through a 50-foot belt of brush, we find the going easy over rolling slab and granite gravel to the center of broad

Flagpole Saddle (7620 — 0.3). Some 100 yards east down gleaming sheets of sculptured granite lies a dramatic stand of weathered lodgepole pine, the windward sides of the trunks devoid of branches and sometimes bark and bleached nearly white. The colorful, soaring cliffs of Flagpole tower impressively above the sandy saddle with a grandeur that would make a set

53

designer smile with envy. Nevertheless the summit is quickly and easily reached by rock climbers willing to traverse steep slab slopes and equipped with boots or sneakers.

From the northern margin of the saddle we make a climbing traverse on slanting slabs, circling up under the cliffs of the southern crag. Our aim is to keep to the ideal footing on slab and make our way to the ridgetop at the jagged saddle between the cliffs of the southern crag and the cliffs dropping from the summit. Once on the ridge, we pick our way over and around small crags to the north, moving slightly onto the eastern slope for the final pitch between large boulders to the windy summit of

Flagpole Peak (8363 — 0.6). The mountain takes its name, simply enough, from the fact that a short section of galvanized pipe set in concrete rises from the summit, and from this staff flies whatever ensign the most recent climbers cared to hang upon it. On one summer day in 1968, for instance, it simultaneously flew an Olympic flag, a plaid scarf, an undershirt, a peace flag and a red wool sock. Though strong winds periodically strip the staff, the pipe itself is visible to the naked eye for more than a mile away, testifying to the clarity of the air.

The view from the top includes the main crest of the Crystal Range, all of Echo Basin, most of Lake Tahoe and the rounded summit of massive Echo Peak (hidden from view from the floor of the basin). Flagpole's summit can be reached in 1-2 hours' walk (by trail to the saddle) from Echo Chalet. Because of its exposure to wind and sun, snow on the mountain melts early, and I have climbed it on bare rock in March and April when the rest of the basin was deeply covered with snow.

Continuing north on Echo's north rim, we drop 50' down the east slope onto sand and traverse to the saddle north of the peak. A more direct but more difficult route involves climbing through boulders down the ridgeline, keeping a few yards east of the crest, until a sandy trail materializes dropping to the saddle. On the north side of the saddle, the trail starts up a short, steep bluff blocked by boulders and brush, but quickly peters out. It is possible to plough up and over the top onto a sandy slope, but the quicker, easier route lies in dropping east out of the saddle far enough to climb north around the base of the bluff and then move up behind it on deep granite sand.

From this point onward an almost continuous groove leads through easy, relatively level country all the way to Echo Peak. We climb, mostly on sand, on the eastern side of the ridge behind the jagged crags visible from Echo. Just beneath the top of the slope the trail forks unobtrusively and a dim branch turns west through a brushy gap in the ridge and down into a handsomely sculptured draw, where it again turns west to join the principal track in a little valley. The main track continues to the top of the slope, then drops into the upper end of a sand- and sage-floored desertlike valley reminiscent of those featured in western movies.

After the forks rejoin, the valley opens into a high, sandy, tree-studded bowl known as The Park and the trail again splits into two somewhat fainter tracks that parallel each other as they dip through the center of the bowl and, gradually diverging, start up the other side. A great many human and game trails cross this sublime little valley (see map), most noteworthy among which are a trail at the bottom along the edge of the cliff which offers fine views across lower Echo, and a delightful trail along the crest which weaves in and out among the crags and offers a view to the north of Fallen Leaf, Mt. Tallac and Tahoe.

Deer and coyote are occasionally to be seen in this flower-sprinkled parkland which has everything except water, and I once surprised a pair of young golden eagles in a snag, late in the spring. The two trails are perhaps 100 feet apart as they begin to climb out of the timber on the west side of the valley, and at this point we intersect the unmarked and only vaguely visible upper terminus of the

Spring Trail (8400 — 0.7). This unmapped but convenient and well-traveled route (see Sec. 5) climbs the western margin of The Park under Echo Peak's southern spur, mostly in deep sand, crossing the lower trail and terminating at the upper. Though the tracks range from faint to invisible, the oriented hiker equipped with map should have no difficulty finding his way through this easy country, with or without trails. Beyond the Spring trail, the lower trail rises through several sandy flats above the spur, tunnels beneath a chunk of suspended slab, and disappears just beyond on the barren sloping sage plain beneath Echo Peak.

The higher trail grows stronger as it climbs out of The Park to the northwest and onto the sage plain. Once the plain is reached, the summit becomes visible as a low crest of rock, ½ mile away. The trail begins gradually to descend across the sage. To reach the summit we can either head directly toward it across the plain, eventually coming upon one of the several paths that lead to the top; or, somewhat more interestingly, we can strike due north a few hundred yards to the nearest point on the crest and make our way up the slightly longer ridgeline trail, which is an extension of the trail around the top of The Park. About 200 yards short of the summit on the ridge, we come to a cairn of rock on top of a boulder marking the arrival from below of the

Angora Lakes Trail (8800 — 0.6). A very pleasant day hike involves walking the ½ mile from the Angora Lake parking lot (see Region 8, Sec. 9) to the lodge on the Upper Lake, enjoying sandwiches, a pitcher of lemonade and ice cream on the veranda, then climbing over Echo Peak and down the Spring Trail (see Sec. 5) to the T-Y Trail and the roadhead at Echo Chalet. From the Angora Trail junction we follow either the ridge or the sage plain to the summit of

Echo Peak (8895 — 0.1). The view from the top is impressive: Angora Peak, Mt. Tallac, Fallen Leaf and Tahoe to the north, and directly beneath the cliffs far below we see the gliding white sails of El Toros on Upper Angora Lake. But the finest view, especially in the spring, is the panorama of peaks running from Ralston in the south through the Crystal Range to Dicks and Jacks in the north. Echo Peak was named for the echoes it produces in the basin below, by the Wheeler survey party in 1877. Like Flagpole, Echo Peak may be climbed on rock very early in the year when Echo Lakes are still frozen and the surrounding country is still covered with snow.

Returning to the point on the sage plain where we left the trail to climb the peak, we move west across the plain, gradually losing altitude as the brush grows thicker and the trail grows fainter (because most hikers are bound for the peak). Reduced to the dimness of a game trail, it dips into the clumps of juniper that border the lower edge of the plain, and after a few hundred yards, during which it splits several times, it drops into a small, stony hollow and for all practical purposes disappears.

The hiker wishing to continue west and descend to the basin floor on the Triangle Lake Trail (see Sec. 6) must drop into the stony hollow, climb high out of its western end, climb still higher (crossing an all-season rill) to skirt the top of a dense willow thicket and make his way through a belt of brush onto the western ridge of the mountain. Here on the crest, if he looks closely, he will find the dim but continuous groove of the Echo Peak Trail (see Sec. 7) descending west to Triangle junction.

Sec. 5

Spring Trail

	Elev.	Miles from pt. above
Spring Trail: Tahoe-Yosemite Trail Jctn.	7500	0.0
North Rim Trail	8400	0.7

Though really a glorified cross-country route, the Spring trail is the shortest, quickest and most popular approach to Echo Peak and Echo's North Rim trail. It takes its name from Nilsson's Spring, which it passes high on the mountain's south shoulder. For half its length the trail follows the buried pipeline that carries spring water to the cabins of the Channel Tract between the two lakes. The T-Y Trail arcs around the base of Red Hill as it crosses the peninsula that separates the lakes. At the southern-most point of the arc it makes a small loop northward into a little draw close under the hill to an unmarked junction with the

Spring Trail (7500 — 0.0) where a faint path leads up the draw. Fifty feet further west on the T-Y Trail a buried pipeline crossing the trail marks a second entrance to the Spring Trail. The two paths join just above a clump of trees and follow the buried pipeline 100 yards up the draw to a pair of redwood water tanks. During the summer the gurgling water can be heard before the tanks become visible. Thirsty hikers can with some difficulty get a drink from the perforated overflow hoses. About 50 feet above the tanks on the faint, unducked path we cross the Red Hill Trail (see Sec. 1) a few yards west of its highest point in the Red Hill saddle.

The trail follows the rock-covered pipeline straight up the steep slope for several hundred yards to the trunk of a weathered, downed tree. At this point we veer east and, contouring across the slope, cross the brush-bottomed ravine (flowing in very early season) through a gap in the vegetation to the base of the steep granite slabs rising on its east bank. Taking care to avoid sand, moss and water seepage, we scramble up the slabs, and pick our way through a pocket of trees growing from crevices in the rock to the bottom of a great sloping bench of monolithic granite as broad as a freeway and almost as flat, known as the "spring ledge."

To the south cliffs drop sheer into Echo Basin; to the north cliffs rise to the craggy south shoulder of Echo Peak. At the base of a narrow vertical cleft in these cliffs, near the upper end of the ledge and just beneath a pair of large yellow pines, lies the aluminum cover of the spring. A 50-yard scramble through boulders and brush brings us to the base of the cleft, where a cup and faucet offer the last chance to drink on the way to the summit.

After following the ledge to its upper limit we dip through a little flat (where boulders and slabs form several sheltering caves) and follow a zigzagging sandy groove up a steep brushy slope 50 yards to the southwest corner of The Park. A faint track and line of ducks branches off to the east along the edge of the cliff on the way to Flagpole, but the Spring Trail turns north directly up the slope, climbing in deep sand around patches of huckleberry oak, past Echo's southern shoulder. About the middle of The Park we cross the lower of the two trails from Flagpole, which climbs above the shoulder and disappears, then 100 feet farther we come to the upper, better-defined

North Rim Trail (8400 — 0.7). For routes to Flagpole and Echo peaks see Sec. 4. It should be noted that travelers continuing up the slope to the crest at the top of The Park will encounter still another trail joining the two peaks.

SEC. 6

Triangle Lake Trail

	Elev.	Miles from pt. above	Total miles
Triangle Trail: T-Y Trail Jctn.	7800	0.0	0.0
Tamarack Trail intersection	8200	0.5	0.5
Triangle Lake	8020	0.5	1.0
Lost Lake	8100	0.5	1.5

Although this is an old and popular trail, serving a considerable area on Echo Basin's north rim, the USFS restored it to the transportation system and began feebly to maintain it only in 1968. Both Triangle and Lost lakes lie within the Fallen Leaf watershed, but since the principal trail access and virtually all visitors come from Echo Basin they are treated in this region. Half a mile above the public landing lateral on the T-Y Trail in a dead level curve arcing through a small hollow is the unsigned, easily overlooked entrance to the

Triangle Lake Trail (7800 — 0.0). The last sign placed at the junction in 1966 lasted less than half the summer before being destroyed by vandals, and the USFS, understandably disheartened, has yet to replace it. From the T-Y Trail, a faint groove on largely footprint-proof scree rises directly up the slope to the north into a rocky watercourse that threads its way through low-growing huckleberry oak and manzanita, and onto a little bluff where it is joined by an equally faint path coming up from a point 50 yards farther east on the T-Y Trail (see Sec. 1).

Once on the bluff and out of the brush, the trail becomes more distinct and almost continuously visible. After climbing through a tangle of partly cut-away deadfalls, it enters the forest and moves on duff and sod up through a series of little hollows filled with wildflowers and birds (and mosquitos to mid-season) beside a miniature cascading brook. The grade abruptly steepens as we move up a steep gravel slope through whitethorn and Indian paintbrush, then the path levels off before again entering timber and climbing along the margin of a boggy, wooded meadow thickly grown with corn lilies.

Gradually the grade diminishes and the track occasionally grows dim as we climb through dense, brushless lodgepole forest. The trail is sufficiently well-defined that I have several times descended it in the dark after fishing too late at Triangle Lake. We come out of the deep woods and into the sandy, open meadows of a saddle in the ridge a few yards before intersecting the

Tamarack Trail (8200 — 0.5). The two trails cross at right angles and old fallen signs read *Desolation Valley*, pointing toward Keiths Dome, and *Triangle Lake ½ mile, Lost Lake 1 mile*, pointing north through the saddle. Gone are signs indicating that Upper Echo lies 1 mile southeast and Fallen Leaf Lake 2½ miles northeast. (The USFS plans to re-sign this junction.) The trail moves north across a tree-studded sandy flat toward suddenly visible Mt. Tallac, then drops gently along flowery meadowland laced with tiny rills running north into several ponds at the bottom of the meadow.

After several abrupt turns to avoid marshy spots, the trail angles to the northwest to the edge of the saddle and onto a small rocky promontory from which Triangle Lake is visible through the trees below to the north. At this point the trail branches, and a sparsely ducked route with no discernible groove contours to the northwest across the rough slope of shattered rock, dips through a draw, curves north around a bluff and follows the line of trees that flank the outlet stream of Lost Lake. Some seasons there are no ducks at all, for there are hikers who feel that a marked trail to a "lost" lake is inappropriate.

The other fork of the trail drops steeply into the canyon leading down to Triangle and likewise disappears in talus before emerging as several faint, intermittent tracks. This is probably explained by the lack of a clearly defined "best" route and the fact that once the goal comes in sight hikers tend to forget the trail and move cross country. I find I tend to use one route going down and another coming up. The upper part of the canyon is steep but dry, except in early season.

Halfway down we come to the runoff stream from the ponds above, which usually runs to midseason. It is most easily crossed in a patch of willow just below a mud-bottomed pool and just above where it enters the willow thickets that block the lower reaches of the canyon. From this point virtually all trails funnel across a rocky side hill above the willows and drop into the prime campsite in a little flat by the southernmost bay of

Triangle Lake (8020 — 0.5). There is usually a grate in the rock fireplace but firewood tends to be scarce. Other comparatively undeveloped campsites are on the northern shore. Walking down the east shore and continuing 100 yards past the lake, we come to the brink of a cliff from which there is an admirable view of Dicks and Jacks peaks, Mt. Tallac, Grass Lake and, in the canyon far below, the cabins at Glen Alpine Spring. Also clearly visible ⅓ mile to the west is the line of willow and lodgepole that stands out like a green arrow on the otherwise barren talus, pointing up to the recess cradling Lost Lake.

In early spring the green is threaded by a booming, frothing cataract of snowmelt water. Lost Lake is most easily reached from Triangle by taking aim upon this green beacon and moving cross-country, trying to lose as little elevation as possible and to avoid cliffs. There are few ducks and fewer signs of foot travel in this jumbled country of shattered rock. After a net climb of less than 100′, we emerge at the top of the outlet stream (dry before midseason) into a tiny wooded flat at the eastern bay of

Lost Lake (8100 — 0.5). Campsites are limited and undeveloped at this attractive, shady, steep-shored little lake. Lost Lake is an excellent point of departure for exploring the seldom-visited gardens fed by all-summer snowbanks on the north side of Keiths Dome, or for making the rough but virtually level traverse west around the dome to Lake Lucille.

Sec. 7

Tamarack, Echo Peak Trails

(Haypress Meadows to Echo Peak)

	Elev.	Miles from pt. above	Total miles
Tamarack Trail: T-Y Trail Jctn.	8250	0.0	0.0
Triangle Lake Trail: intersection	8200	1.0	1.0
Echo Peak Trail	8200	0.1	1.1
Echo Peak	8895	1.3	2.4

The Tamarack Trail, running from just below Haypress Meadows to Fallen Leaf, originally served as access for packers to their cabin at Lake of the Woods. Today, only the concrete floor of the cabin remains. The packers approach from Echo, and the western section of the Tamarack Trail is rarely used except by accident or poor planning, although it offers one of the finest views obtainable of Echo Basin. It remains in the USFS trail system probably because it requires no maintenance.

The Echo Peak Trail, though shown on no maps, gives evidence of considerable age and heavy use. The groove in places is quite deep, and well-decayed deadfalls lie across it. This long-ago heavy use may be explained by the fact that early in the century a shepherd regularly grazed his flock of sheep in summer on the sage plain of Echo Peak and lived in a cabin not far from the trail. It is ironic that the easiest trail to the top of Echo Peak is the least known and least used of the three described in this chapter.

About 150 yards below the bottom of Haypress Meadows, at an unmarked and easily missed junction, just above a culvert on the T-Y Trail, lies the western end of the

Tamarack Trail (8250 — 0.0). A modest path moves east on a gently climbing traverse of a rocky sand slope devoid of vegetation except for sparse grass and clumps of sage. As the path becomes steeper the trail becomes an eroded gully, and there are occasional clumps of lodgepole and fine specimens of weathered juniper. After a vertical climb of little more than 100′ in better than ½ mile, we come out onto a windy, barren knoll just under the east end of Keiths Dome.

The view of Tamarack, Ralston and Cagwin lakes is unsurpassed, and the panorama includes the entire south rim of Echo Basin, the whole of the Crystal Range, Lake Tahoe, Angora Peak, Indian Rock, Echo Peak and Flagpole. From this rocky pass it is only a short scramble onto the mile-long sugarloaf of Keiths Dome, with its birds and wildflowers and prostrate junipers. So seldom is this windy ridge visited that big blacktail deer bed there throughout the summer, assured of feed and water on the dome's northern slope.

Still moving east we descend on shattered rock for several hundred yards before dropping into light timber which obscures the view. The forest cover thickens as we descend but there are pockets of flowered meadow interspersed. After losing 200′ the trail levels off and comes out of the trees to intersect at right angles the

Triangle Lake Trail (8200 — 1.0). A battered sign reads *Desolation Valley*, pointing west up the track we have just descended, and *Triangle Lake ½ mile, Lost Lake 1 mile*, pointing north through the saddle. Neither the trail east to Fallen Leaf nor the trail south to Upper Echo is signed. We continue east through the open sandy flat of the saddle and into the trees to where the trail turns northwest at a big rock cairn that marks the entrance to the dim but discernible

Echo Peak Trail (8200 — 0.1). Just south of the trail and unintentionally marking the junction are orange triangular signs nailed well up in the trees reading *Echo Rim Trail* and *Echo Rim Ski Trail.* The Echo Peak Trail continues to the east and very gradually begins to climb through wooded grassland. In the first ½ mile it climbs gently east-northeast up the centerline of a broad ridge pleasantly forested with lodgepole and red fir.

Occasionally it jumps or skirts a deadfall or harmlessly splits for a few yards but the groove is usually distinct and small ducks help to mark the way. The trail climbs out of the woods onto open, grassy woodland with fragrant clumps of sage growing in the sand, and a little above the trees we pass 50 yards to the north of a remarkable fire- and wind-sculpted large lodgepole log. As the grade increases slightly the trail slips a few feet north of the crest, affording an excellent view across the canyon to the green upper slopes of Mt. Tallac.

We return to the ridgeline climbing a grassy slope studded with occasional trees until all at once we stand on the edge of a precipice, looking down into the boat-dotted waters of Angora Lakes. Southeast along the ridgeline, just beyond a little saddle, Echo Peak rises less than 150' above us. About ¾ mile north and 200' below us lies the summit of Angora Peak (8588).

We turn southeast toward Echo and for the first time the trail becomes faint and poorly marked, probably because the route to the peak is so easy and obvious. The dim path, keeping a few feet back from the cliff, dips through a thickly wooded saddle before climbing on sandy gravel among clumps of windswept pine toward the rocky crest. The route becomes progressively more distinct as we draw nearer and has reached the status of trail as we come to the summit of

Echo Peak (8895 — 1.3). For hikers who have reached the summit by other routes but wish to descend on the Echo Peak Trail, the point at which the trail reaches the precipice can be pinpointed from the summit by locating two clumps of trees on the rim about 100 yards north of the wooded saddle. The nearer clump is dominated by a large western white pine. The farther clump is a group of small hemlock. Midway between the two clumps is the well-ducked trail.

Travelers interested in visiting Indian Rock and Angora Peak or in looking out over Fallen Leaf Basin and Glen Alpine Canyon should walk north up the faint path leading along the broad, flattened ridge to a little knoll from which the view west is exceptional. Beyond this point the ridge abruptly narrows to a jagged knife-edge with sharp dropoffs on either side. About ¼ mile to the north the descending ridge culminates in a tiny plateau, surrounded by sheer cliffs, known as Indian Rock.

Only experienced climbers should attempt this ridge. The view from Indian Rock is breathtaking in every direction, especially straight down. The only flank of Indian Rock that is passable is a steep sandy slope leading down to a wooded saddle from which Angora Peak can easily be climbed.

Sec. 8

Tamarack, Ralston and Cagwin Lake Trail

(plus routes up Ralston's north ridge)

This section treats the trails leading to and among Tamarack, Ralston and Cagwin lakes, as well as the various routes leading up Ralston Peak's long north ridge. There is so little formal trail that the usual elevation-distance summary will be omitted. Two sections of the trail shown on the usually reliable topo map are in error. See the accompanying map for corrections. Because they offer the first campsites on the T-Y Trail and the first attraction inside the Wilderness Area, these three lakes are heavily used by hikers of all stripes. The scenery is handsome and varied, and campsites are plentiful if firewood is not. About 4 miles from the Echo trailhead (1.1 from the public landing) the T-Y Trail curves to the north on bare rock to a signed junction with the

Tamarack Lake Trail (7900). Signs read *Haypress Meadows 1 mile, Desolation Valley 2 miles,* northwest, and *Tamarack Lake ¼ mile, Ralston Lake ½ mile,* southwest. The trail down to the lake (clearly visible below across treeless, shattered granite), though marked by red paint blazes, is rough and often faint, but many hikers feel no need of a trail. It reaches the lake at its northeast corner, where a fishermen's trail branches around the north shore. There are a few rough camps for late-arriving parties when the good ones are taken.

The trail runs south along a fringe of forest near the eastern shore, through a series of large, fine campsites, then dips below the lake through a little wooded hollow to cross the outlet stream on a jumble of logs; it then proceeds across a treeless flat until a little hillock in its path causes it to pinch in close to the water near the lake's southern tip. At this point the well-worn groove of a fishermen's trail turns west around the end of the lake.

At this point the topo map indicates a branch trail heading southeast down a draw to Cagwin Lake. The draw offers a few ducks but no sign of foot travel. The reason for this soon becomes apparent. The draw quickly narrows into a gully and abruptly drops over a 20′ cliff. The nimble hiker, unencumbered by pack, can make his way down safely enough, but it is certainly misleading to represent this stretch as trail.

At the bottom of the dropoff lies a pleasant patch of shady forest sheltering several campsites, and along the southern margin of the timber the all-year stream from Ralston Lake cascades into Cagwin. According to the topo the trail down from Tamarack crosses the woods and joins the trail down from Ralston at the inlet to Cagwin. This stretch of trail, if it existed, would scarcely amount to 300 yards.

Returning to the southern tip of Tamarack, we follow the well-marked Ralston Lake Trail southwest, skirting several snowmelt pools, then climb west 50′ to the top of a low ridge from which Ralston and its rugged basin immediately come into view. The trail drops steeply 100′ to the rock-gated dam built, according to a bronze plaque in its north end, by the Mt. Ralston Fish Planting Club and dedicated to Ross E. Pierce.

The topo map shows the trail down to Cagwin crossing Ralston Creek below the dam, climbing more than 100′ to the south, then looping back to meet Cagwin at the inlet. Such a trail, if it existed, would never be used. The actual well-worn trail down to Cagwin dips through the outlet (or crosses the dam), then makes its way down along the south bank of the stream through light timber. Near Cagwin it forks, the best-traveled branch crossing the inlet to the campsites in the sheltered patch of forest. The other branch moves a few yards to the south and ends at a sign reading *Cagwin Lake, elevation 7740 feet* by the water's edge.

There are two easy routes (not trails) down Ralston Creek to the Scout Trail (see Sec. 9) leading to Echo. The first involves following Cagwin's north shore around to the outlet stream (a handsome cascade in early season), then descending beside the pools and falls and runs, mostly on bare granite, into the bottom of the canyon, where the Scout Trail materializes. The second (more of a trail and easier going) descends from the eastern edge of the patch of timber through a narrow draw, almost a notch, that leads due east between cliffs to the north and talus to the south, emerging onto open granite slopes leading down to Ralston Creek and the Scout Trail. The narrow draw is clearly recognizable from below so this route serves equally well for ascent.

Routes to Ralston Peak and its northern ridge

Ralston Peak's long north ridge, besides providing access to the summit, also forms a barrier between Echo Basin and Desolation Valley. One must go 2 miles north of the peak to find a trail (Poopout, Sec. 1) that crosses it. So there is considerable demand for cross-country routes up the ridge that can reduce the distance from Echo to both the peak and Desolation Valley.

The best and most obvious route up the ridge runs through its lowest point, a gap known as Tamarack Pass, directly west of Tamarack Lake. An apron of grassland fringed with trees clearly marks the saddle. At 8460′ (only 40′ higher than the Poopout ridge crossing) Tamarack Pass offers the best compromise between a direct scramble to the summit from Ralston Lake and the long, all-trail route through Haypress and Poopout. It has the further advantage of lying on a direct line along an easy cross-country route between Tamarack and Lake of the Woods. It saves more than a mile of trail hiking on either trip.

The route begins by circling Tamarack Lake on either side; neither choice offers a distinct advantage. The southern approach follows the fishermen's trail around the south shore through campsites and past snow ponds to the little peninsula pointing out to the lake's lone island. From this point we climb straight up steeply through talus gullies and rocky ledges, past a large snow pond, then edge northwest toward the clearly visible watercourse, plotting a course that will bring us to the lower reaches of the grass apron. Once in the grass the going is easy, except early in the season when bog forces us to the margins, and we move into the saddle to intersect the Ralston Peak Trail.

The route around the north end of Tamarack is slightly more direct but possibly more rigorous. About 50 yards east of the lake we pick up a trail that parallels the north shore about 25 yards back (the fishermen's trail beside the water is inferior). We follow the faint track west behind a rocky peninsula, and then behind a large alder thicket extending some 50 yards up the inlet stream. After crossing the stream we turn south and climb very steeply across a talus slope for several hundred yards to the top of a little spur. The pitch lessens at this point and the bottom of the grass apron becomes visible just above. We make our way up to it through light timber and proceed to the top.

Another popular route up the ridge involves following the trail to the low ridge separating Tamarack and Ralston lakes, then following the broad, lightly timbered bluff, which is an extension of the low ridge, due west into the southern margin of the Tamarack Pass saddle. This is the least steep and best shaded of the three routes so far suggested. The grade is consistent and there is drinking water trickling through patches of flowered meadow into midsummer. The last stretch of the climb is through a Christmas tree lot of red fir and lodgepole seedlings, and it is necessary to veer to the north to avoid crossing the ridgeline above the saddle.

Another route, farther south and more direct, follows the Ralston Lake Trail over the ridge and then takes the fishermen's trail to the western end of the lake, keeping close to the water to avoid cliffs and brushfields. We then scramble up the steep, bright, bare, talus slope, cross the inlet cascade (dry before midseason) and angle southwest toward a low point in the ridge just south of summit 8690, immediately beyond which lies the Mt. Ralston Trail. This is a rough, steep, shadeless rock scramble of some 900 vertical feet. Snow lingers on the ledges almost to midseason.

SEC. 9
South Shore Trail
(Echo Chalet to the Public Landing) .

	Elev.	Miles from pt. above	Total miles
Echo Trailhead: dam	7420	0.0	0.0
East Becker Creek	7414	0.7	0.7
West Becker Creek	7450	0.3	1.0
The Channel	7414	0.5	1.5
Dartmouth Cove: "Upper Echo Trail"	7420	0.2	1.7
Saucer Lake Trail	7450	0.1	1.8
Brook Trail	7470	0.1	1.9
Trail's End	7414	0.4	2.3
Camp Harvey West: 3 Flagpoles	7420	0.4	2.7
Public Landing	7420	0.2	2.9

Although a more or less continuous path skirts the south shores of both lakes and connects with the T-Y Trail via the public landing lateral, it by no means should be considered an alternate route to the back country. Haphazardly built to meet the needs of cabin-owners, and largely unmaintained, it fights its way through willow thickets, slips through bog, clambers over deadfalls, climbs foolishly, detours to outhouses and watertanks, and sometimes joins the back door of one cabin with the front door of the next.

Essentially a cabin-owners' and day-hikers' trail, it exists only for its own sake, providing no real access except to such points along the way as Becker Peak, the Channel, Dartmouth Cove, the Brook and Saucer trails and, ultimately, Camp Harvey West and the public landing. An extension of the trail continues from the Scout Camp up Ralston Creek to meet cross-country routes coming down from Cagwin Lake. In the fall the water level in the lakes drops sufficiently for the channel to be easily forded or jumped, opening a route of doubtful value between the north (T-Y) and south shore trails.

Echo Trailhead: dam (7420 — 0.0). The frontage road that runs south around the harbor narrows to a trail beyond the big piers and heads west along the shoreline. Just beyond the breakwater it climbs in an unsuccessful attempt to avoid a dense willow thicket, and we thread our way beneath the canopy in a half crouch for 100 yards. The trail descends across a steep open slope, then climbs 100′ above the water to cross a small patch of willows. It then gradually descends through steep, open woodland thickening into forest for ¼ mile before dropping to the water's edge to cross, on stepping stones,

East Becker Creek (7414 — 0.7). The trail climbs out of the willows onto a pleasant, lightly timbered slope and levels off a little above the water for nearly ¼ mile. It is from this open woodland that the ascent of Becker Peak, whether via the eastern bowl or the direct route up the northeastern face, is best begun.

After crossing a 40-foot slab of granite close to the water, the trail turns sharply uphill and, marked by ducks, climbs onto a glacially polished bench. Failure to make the abrupt turn quickly leads us to an impassable barricade of cliffs, boulders and brush, from which we must backtrack to the trail. Beyond the granite bench the trail climbs again through trees and brush to pass about 75′ above the first cabin. It grazes a corner of the second cabin, then weaves its way through a cluster of cabins, where red-painted arrows are designed to keep us from visiting a series of outhouses. Beyond the trees it enters a broad willow thicket, in the middle of which we cross

West Becker Creek (7450 — 0.3). Just beyond the creek the trail forks, the left branch dead-ending at a water tank. The right branch crosses a stony brush slope and then drops toward the lake to squeeze between a mammoth willow thicket and several cabins. The boardwalk leading uphill into the willows serves a private outhouse. Just beyond we come into the maze of cabins, outhouses and trails known as Colony Cove. The ascent of Becker Peak through the western bowl should be started just south of the cove.

By keeping to the deepest rut on the logical route, and by avoiding any sharp turns, we make our way on a comparatively straight course through the little settlement and out onto a grassy flat 100′ above the lake. Blue-green daubs of paint on rocks and trees mark the trail for a short stretch but quickly disappear as the path drops into an open corridor between two parallel rows of cabins.

We are guided down this boulevard by a series of garish red arrows painted on the granite. At the end of the corridor the arrows abruptly turn west, but by continuing straight for another 50 yards we reach

The Channel (7414 — 0.5). During spring and summer the channel runs nearly waist-deep at its shallowest point and is consequently not fordable except by the most determined hiker. In the fall, however (usually late September), it can easily be forded or jumped. Its condition can be determined in advance at the marina. The best place to ford is at the narrow point immediately above the big oxbow pool.

Backtracking to the corridor, we follow the vivid red arrows back to the south behind the upper row of cabins and zigzag between boulders to cross the rocky barrier that separates the two lakes. At the summit the red paint ends and a line of more sedate orange dots leads us gently down into Dartmouth Cove. A swath of willow runs down an avalanche chute on Talking Mountain and levels off into a meadow threaded by a little stream which empties into the shallow cove with a white sandy bottom.

Wading, swimming and picnicking are good when the persistent Echo wind is not blowing. The trail, marked by orange dots and a faint groove, crosses the meadow about 200 feet back from the water but a trail along the water shows greater signs of wear. At the west edge of the meadow, on the orange-dotted trail, we come to a flat rock on which is printed in brown and orange

Upper Echo Trail (7420 — 0.2). We climb abruptly up a rocky slope marked every few yards in orange and brown, traversing to the northwest into a shallow draw. After passing behind the still-intact floor of a cabin that was destroyed by avalanche in the winter of 1967, we pass into the trees about 30 yards above Admiral Riebe's dam, then cross a rill and follow an exposed water pipe a few yards to the junction of the

Saucer Lake Trail (7450 — 0.1). An arrow pointing uphill to the southwest is labeled "Waterfall, Saucer Lake." This well-marked trail and its delightful subsidiary the Brook Trail are described in Section 10. On another rock is painted "Upper Echo," to indicate the continuing South Shore Trail, which now is marked by orange dots that occasionally sport brown circles. Blue dots denote the path of the waterline. We traverse the slope to the west, climbing gradually to the somewhat hidden junction of the

Brook Trail (7470 — 0.1) in a little rill (dry by midsummer). One rock reads "Brook Trail to Saucer Lake" with an arrow pointing uphill to the southwest. Another rock says "Echo Trail" with an arrow pointing across the slope to the west. Both the Brook and Saucer Lake trails rise to a waterfall (often dry by midseason) directly up the slope. There the Brook Trail ends and the Saucer Lake Trail continues to climb. See accompanying map.

From our junction, the Brook Trail and the blue-dot-marked waterline climb across the slope while the South Shore Trail, still marked by orange and brown dots, moves nearly on the level across the slope, passing about 100′ above a shingle cabin. Once past the cabin we dip down on a well-worn groove to pass through and under a willow and alder thicket and cross an all-season brook.

Descending on a traverse across a steep, forested slope we drop into a little hollow on the edge of a large avalanche chute where we find painted on a flat rock *Upper Echo Trail* with arrows pointing east and west. Still following a profusion of orange dots we enter the treeless brush and almost immediately cross a little stream and several pipelines. The trail then leaves the brush to mount a long, straight ridge of rock that runs on a long, gentle incline toward the water. The orange markers, now weathered and faint, run straight down the ridge's bare spine, passing two outhouses, all the way to the water's edge before again jogging west across a stream-bed and up the shore a few yards to the

Trail's End (7415 — 0.4) marked by a rock faintly inscribed with "To Lower Lake" and an arrow pointing back to the east. From here to the Scout Camp the route is unmarked and often vague; much of it is cabin-owners' and fishermen's trail, and it is only presented here to complete the South Shore route to the T-Y Trail.

The path moves west up the shore beside the water, threading between a pier and stairway, skirting a clump of willow, then jogging inland to pass behind a boathouse before returning to the shoreline. It passes below a gray waterfront cabin, crosses a miniature peninsula, then climbs up a little draw, moving away from the water and over a ledge some 25 yards behind a green-roofed cabin.

From this point there is only the rarest sign of a path. Moving diagonally away from the lake in order to get behind the row of cabins, we climb over several small ledges to a longer, more open ridge about roof-high. This we descend to the north for perhaps 100 yards, passing an ancient outhouse and aiming for an old stump about 100 yards behind the gray Sproul cabin, last in the row.

Beneath the stump our route crosses an all-summer creek, and as we move into Boy Scout territory we encounter a great many paths. Immediately across the creek we come to a long, low ridge of granite running to the north across the camp. By following the trails paralleling the ridge for $\frac{1}{4}$ mile, we would intersect the Scout trail up Ralston Creek. Since we are headed for the public landing to complete our circuit of the lake, we follow the ridge only 25 yards before encountering a well-traveled trail crossing it.

On this trail we turn east toward the lake and descend between "Spotted Fawn" printed in red paint on the ledge and an abandoned cabin at the edge of a meadow. The muddy trail skirts the shoreward side of the meadow for 100 yards before the meadow gives way to a barren, stony parade ground sporting

Three Flagpoles (7420 — 0.4). At the northeast corner of the parade ground (during the summer) is a drinking fountain, which marks the junction of the Ralston Creek (Scout) Trail with the North Shore Trail. Continuing to the north we follow the latter past the craft lodge where, more road than trail, it winds through the willows, twice crossing Ralston Creek on wooden bridges, before returning to the lake shore in the heart of Camp Harvey West. After passing the main lodge, the trail enters a forest of young lodgepole, passing the doctor's house and the public telephone before reaching the

Public Landing (7414 — 0.2). The total distance to this point via the South Shore Trail is a tortuous 2.9 miles, identical to the distance via the streamlined T-Y Trail; the traveling conditions are not to be compared!

To walk the Scout Trail up Ralston Creek we return to the three flagpoles and from the drinking fountain head west along the northern margin of the rocky field, aiming for a large sign reading *A Scout is Helpful*. The dusty trail climbs over a rocky knoll on which at intervals we pass signs reciting the remainder of the Scout Law. At the top is an open-air chapel, and on the far side we drop into a wooded dell sheltering an often-occupied troop encampment. The trail skirts the camp and drops to cross the creek on a rickety bridge after which it forks.

To reach the T-Y Trail we head north past a sign *Painted Rock* and into a wooded hollow sheltering another troop camp. On the north side of the camp a line of stones leads up into an occasionally ducked gully that runs some 200 yards north up the slope. At the end of the gully we climb 25 yards to the old T-Y Trail and follow it another 200 twisting yards to the T-Y Trail, coming out about 100 yards below the Triangle Lake Trail junction.

To head upstream on the Scout Trail we return to the fork in the trail by the bridge, head west up the north side of the creek on well-marked trail for several hundred yards, and enter a third troop camp, this one equipped with a drinking fountain and a permanent shelter. At the camp's upper end the Scout Trail ends and a faint fishermen's trail moves upstream, dodging willow thickets and crisscrossing the stream to find the easiest terrain.

To reach Cagwin Lake (see Sec. 8) we cross to the south bank below where the all-summer creek from Cagwin Basin joins Ralston Creek and, keeping south of the brush that chokes the watercourse, climb over the easiest, most open country toward either the cataract of the Cagwin creek, where it drops out of the lake basin, or the steep draw just to its north. Both lead up to the lake.

Sec. 10
Brook and Saucer Lake Trails

From Dartmouth Cove (the southeast bay of Upper Echo) the Saucer Lake Trail climbs 1200′ in approximately 1¼ trail miles to provide the only trail link between the basin's floor and its long south rim. Though rarely shown on maps, impassable to stock, signless, unmaintained and unofficial, this modest track is thoughtfully located and exceptionally well marked. Its unrelenting steepness is compensated for by its directness, so that Saucer can be reached in as little as an hour.

Almost from the first the view into and across the basin is unusually good, and the lush vegetation on this shady north slope, though rich and varied, does not prohibit hiking in shorts. Water is available at several points in all seasons. Campsites are nonexistent along the steep trail and scarce at the lake, but the steepness and shortness of the trail make day hikes far more practical than overnight camping.

Both the Saucer and Brook trails branch from signed junctions on the South Shore Trail (see Sec. 9) but are more swiftly reached by boat from Dartmouth Cove or the channel (make arrangements with the resort's boatmen). From the western margin of the meadow in the cove we climb west up a rocky draw and within 50 yards intersect the orange paint blazes that mark the South Shore Trail. The trail passes above Admiral Riebe's dam, dips to his pipeline and moves a few yards to a rock inscribed "Waterfall, Saucer Lake," with an arrow pointing uphill. This rock marks the beginning of the Saucer Lake Trail which branches uphill to the south.

The narrow path switchbacks steeply upward on pine needles through fern- and flower-floored forest, marked approximately every 10 feet by small, well-placed red paint blazes. We make a climbing traverse to the west through damp grassy woodland for several hundred yards before coming out of the trees and clambering over a ledge into a verdant hollow at the foot of a 30′ waterfall (unfortunately dry by midsummer). Wildflowers thrive in the hollow, and the view across the basin is excellent.

This is the upper terminus of the Brook Trail, which is nothing more than a loop of trail beneath the willows beside the brook leading back to the South Shore Trail. Signs painted on the rock read "Saucer Lake," pointing south up the ledge to the east of the falls, "Dartmouth Cove," pointing down the trail we have ascended, and "Brook Trail, Down," pointing west into the willows that spill out of the hollow.

We move up along the ledge, then turn west and climb steeply through brush and flowers behind the waterfall, beside a thicket of young aspen. The trail traverses westward through deep grass, ducks under a canopy of willow to cross the brook, and climbs beside it a few yards before again heading west on a long traverse across a dry slope of lupine and sage. At the end of the traverse we switchback up steeply under a rocky knob, finally climbing to its top through waist-high willow.

This is the only point at which the trail is hard to follow. It makes a right-angle turn to the west at the top of the knob, and hikers coming down often overshoot the turn. As a consequence there are several extra tracks through the brush which can be temporarily confusing. From the knob the trail switchbacks up a very steep slope through scattered big trees, the first we have seen since below the falls. We climb between two boulders, touch briefly at a mossy spring, then swing away to the east on a long, gently climbing traverse across another steep slope.

A series of short, steep switchbacks lead up through woodland into the mouth of a small, rocky bowl, where shaded snowbanks on the north wall provide a trickle of water past midsummer. Immediately upon entering the bowl the trail swerves west and climbs out of it on short, steep switchbacks up a rocky bluff. Here we find some minor disagreement between the sharply zigzagging groove and the paint blazes. At the top of the bluff the trail again swings west on a 200-yard, gently climbing traverse that moves from an extremely steep slope into rolling woodland.

The trail dips through a little draw, then climbs around the western end of a boulder-strewn ridge, passes a campsite and comes over the top some 50 feet from the northern shore of Saucer Lake. The blazes end halfway to the water at a rock reading "Echo," with an arrow pointing back the way we have come. Across the lake a narrow sandy slope leads to a saddle in the south rim. After circling the lake to the east on the fishermen's trail, we make an easy 200′ climb to the top. Travelers headed west toward Ralston Peak should leave the sand three quarters of the way to the top and make a climbing traverse westward to the ridgetop.

Returning to the top of the Brook Trail, at the bottom of the little hollow beneath the waterfall, we find the trail immediately plunging into willow thicket and we move down steeply on the damp, winding path, crouched low under a canopy of willow, never more than a yard from the little cataract. After a hundred twisting, turning yards through a dim, green, noisy, delightful tunnel (more easily navigated by children than adults) we emerge onto open rock at a little dam where Admiral Reibe's waterline begins.

In addition to brown and orange dots, the pipeline and its blue dots lead gently down to the east across an open rock avalanche slope for 100 yards to a junction, somewhat concealed in trees, with the Upper Echo (South Shore) Trail. Painted on rocks at the junction we find "Brook Trail to Saucer Lake," with an arrow pointing up the trail we have descended, and "Upper Echo," indicating the South Shore Trail, which runs roughly east-west (see Sec. 9 and accompanying map).

Desolation Valley

Though Desolation Valley itself occupies less than a tenth of the Wilderness Area that bears its name, there are many who believe that this beautiful little basin, with its blue water and white granite, represents California Sierra at its finest. This hanging valley runs roughly north-south, and the accumulated runoff from its glaciated surfaces is all channeled into a torrent that cascades from the valley's mouth over Horsetail Falls and drops to the American River as Pyramid Creek.

The eastern rim of the valley is very low, almost flat, and along it runs a network of the basin's only trails. The western rim is the nearly 10,000′ crest of the Crystal Range — tall glistening slopes of polished granite virtually devoid of vegetation and signs of man. Of every hundred visitors to the valley, probably seventy come in from Echo and twenty from Fallen Leaf, the remaining ten being divided between Twin Bridges and Rockbound Valley. These proportions reflect ease of access.

Included in this region on the basis of access, though outside its drainage, are Lakes Margery, Lucille, Jabu and Le Conte, all of which drain toward Fallen Leaf. Though the trail system is limited to the eastern edge of the valley, cross-country travel in almost every direction is relatively simple for the oriented hiker with a topographical map. Water is plentiful, as the map suggests; in fact, the principal obstacle to cross-country travel, especially in early season, is Pyramid Creek.

Despite the scarcity of vegetation, the little pockets of forest along the watercourses and beside the lakes shelter ample if not

75

abundant campsites. In the most popular areas they are well developed, but firewood is almost always scarce. Travelers who like to hike in shorts will find no brush, but mosquitoes enjoy a long season in this well-watered valley.

Sec. 1
Haypress Pass to Mosquito Pass

	Elev.	Miles from pt. above	Total miles
Ralston Peak Trail: Haypress Pass	8340	0.0	0.0
South Lake Lucille-Lake of the Woods Laterals	8320	0.2	0.2
Aloha (PG & E) Dam Lateral	8300	0.3	0.5
North Lake Lucille Lateral	8300	0.1	0.6
Lake Aloha	8140	0.6	1.2
Lake Le Conte Lateral	8140	0.6	1.8
Glen Alpine Trail	8140	0.8	2.6
Mosquito Pass	8420	1.1	3.7

The combined Pacific Crest/Tahoe-Yosemite Trail from Echo Lake (sec Region 1, Sec. 1) climbs northwest through Haypress Meadows to an unsigned junction in Haypress Pass with the dim northern terminus of the

Ralston Peak Trail (8340 — 0.0), at a campsite in a small grove of large hemlock and fir trees. From the junction we descend northwest across a patch of meadow (with a fine view of Jacks Peak) 100 yards to a pair of culverts from which icy spring water issues, usually until beyond midsummer. Another 100 yards brings us to an intersection with the

South Lake Lucille — Lake of the Woods laterals (8320 — 0.2). Signs read *Margery Lake,* 1/4 *mile, Lake Lucille* 1/2 *mile,* north, and *Lake of the Woods* 1/2 *mile,* south up a faint track that climbs dwindling Poopout Ridge. This track is also known as the Old Fallen Leaf Trail (see Sec. 3 for both trails). Beyond the junction the trail dips north through a little hollow of jagged rock on fill from which Lake Margery is visible 100' below to the northwest. A section of the old trail loops around a little outcropping above the lake. Beyond the hollow, the trail gradually climbs to the northwest until, at the extreme northern end of Poopout Ridge, we encounter the

Aloha Dam Trail (8300 — 0.3) descending through the trees to the southwest (see Sec. 3). Hopefully this major trail junction is only temporarily without a sign. At this point we leave the Fallen Leaf watershed and for the first time enter Desolation Valley proper. Thousands of fishermen every year take this lateral to the dam to angle for brook trout. We continue to the northwest across flat, open woodland to the

North Lake Lucille Lateral (8300 — 0.1), which makes its way through the trees to the east (see Sec. 3). A sign at the junction reads *Mosquito Pass 3 miles,* northwest, *Upper Echo Lake 3½ miles,* southeast, and *Margery Lake ¼ mile, Lucille Lake ½ mile,* indicating the lightly traveled lateral to the east. Due north of this junction rises the southern end of a naked spur known as Cracked Crag; in a hollow on the ridge nestles chilly Jabu Lake. This junction offers an excellent point of departure for the cross-country scramble to the 8480′ lakelet, known before it was planted with trout as the "ladies' swimming lake."

Still heading northwest the trail threads its way through flat, lightly wooded country dotted with snowmelt ponds (usually dry by midsummer). After ¼ mile the forest thickens, and as Cracked Crag draws closer the trail begins to drop toward Aloha. We move down a wooded canyon and come out of the trees at the lakeshore to a junction with the

Lake of the Woods Trail (8140 — 0.5). Signs read *Lake of the Woods 1 mile, PG & E dam 1 mile,* south (see Sec. 3), and *Glen Alpine Trail, Rockbound Valley,* north up the shore. This junction, too, is a good jumping-off point for the climb to Jabu Lake. The last of the lateral trails from other parts of the valley is now behind us, and we move up the lakeshore on the one strand of trail linking Echo Basin and Desolation Valley to Rockbound Valley. Though it generally follows the Aloha shoreline, the trail manages to dip and climb and wind excessively. There are stretches of deep sand and others of mud; and the almost total lack of shade, added to the monotony of the drowned shoreline, makes this a long stretch for the backpacker. Halfway to the north end of the lake, in a horseshoe bend, we come to the

Lake Le Conte Lateral (8140 — 0.6). A sign reads *Lake Le Conte ¼ mile,* indicating a path leading north. A short walk over hilly, boulder-strewn ground brings us to the charming if somewhat barren little lake. Though only a few yards above Aloha, Le Conte lies beyond the eastern rim of Desolation Valley and drains, via Heather and Susie lakes, to Fallen Leaf. A rather dim trail scrambles along the steep eastern shore to a lovely little bay and the outlet stream. Campsites are poor and unsheltered and wood is always scarce. From the outlet we can look down on—and easily reach —- Heather Lake in its dramatic setting of red rock.

From the Le Conte Lateral the T-Y Trail continues up the desolate, windy shore of Aloha to a major junction with the

Glen Alpine Trail (8140 — 0.8). At this point the T-Y Trail drops east past Heather and Susie before starting the long climb to Dicks Pass, while the Pacific Crest Trail turns west around the top of the lake toward Mosquito Pass and Rockbound Valley. Signs read *Heather Lake ½ mile, Susie Lake 1½ miles, Glen Alpine Springs 4 miles*, east, *South End Desolation Valley 2 miles, Echo Lake 5 miles*, south, and *Mosquito Pass 1 mile, Rockbound Valley 1 mile*, west.

We turn west and, following Aloha's north shore, cross a broad, treeless, open plain on alternating stretches of gravel, grass and rolling slabs of glacially smoothed granite. The route is marked by rows of small rocks and occasional red paint blazes on the otherwise trackless slab. Though not unlike the dreary trail up the northeast shore, this stretch has a pleasant feeling of openness.

The trail climbs very gradually for almost a mile, then turns abruptly north and switchbacks up a moderate slope into light timber. A trail crew in 1968 set the waterbars too high and filled behind them with such loose material that it has either washed or blown away, and the waterbars have become hurdles for the hiker. But the climb is mercifully shady and short (about 200 vertical feet), and it is easy except in early season, when deep snow blocks the slope.

Mosquito Pass (8420 — 1.1). A sign in the pass gives the elevation as 8760, an exaggeration of 340 feet! The pass marks the northern end of Desolation Valley and the southern end of Rockbound Valley. For the descent into Rockbound, see Region 5, Sec. 3.

Sec. 2

Desolation Trail

(Twin Bridges to Lake Aloha)

	Elev.	Miles from pt. above	Total miles
Twin Bridges: Pyramid Peak trailhead	6100	0.0	0.0
Desolation Valley Rim: opposite Avalanche Lake	7500	2.0	2.0
Ropi Lake (east end)	7620	0.7	2.7
Lake of the Woods (south end)	8060	0.8	3.5
Fallen Leaf-Echo Lakes Trail	8060	0.6	4.1
Lake Aloha: double junction	8160	0.6	4.7
Aloha (PG & E) Dam	8116	0.7	5.4

Located 2 miles above Strawberry, at the point where Highway 50 crosses Pyramid Creek, Twin Bridges offers a small general store, bar, restaurant and gas station, overnight lodgings, and Greyhound bus service. Parking for hikers is permitted behind the gas station. Though it is the lowest trailhead in this guidebook, Twin Bridges offers quicker access to the Wilderness than any paved road except Highway 89 at Emerald Bay. From the highway the white plume of Horsetail Falls can be seen cascading from the mouth of Desolation Valley 1½ miles (airline) to the north; the Wilderness boundary lies only half that distance up the valley.

Most maps show no trail from Twin Bridges to Desolation Valley, and those that show one are vague about its location (see map). Strictly speaking there is no trail — just a dimly marked, often difficult route up the canyon. It is impossible for horses and pack animals, and not recommended for Sunday hikers, children, dogs or heavily laden backpackers. Because it is particularly difficult to find from above, it is not recommended as an exit trail for a loop trip.

If this sounds overly forbidding it should be reported that one day while I was lunching at Avalanche Lake a fresh-looking backpacker came over the rim from below, walked down to the lake, and looking at his watch reported that the ascent from Twin Bridges — though he had finally lost the trail — had taken him less than an hour. To summarize, then, the distance is short and the route direct, but the trail is vague and the climb considerable.

Twin Bridges (6100 — 0.0). The trail begins at the west end of the highway bridge (there are no longer two bridges) and climbs 100 yards up the west bank of Pyramid Creek on unmarked granite slab before first becoming visible as it enters a clump of trees. Almost immediately it forks: a well-trodden track (route A) continues to the northeast through the trees, and a dim track (route B) branches off to the north onto granite slabs.

Route A follows a black plastic waterline and parallels an overhead power line for 50 yards before forking again. The east fork continues up the power and water lines to dead-end at the Twin Bridges power house, while the north fork comes out of the trees onto slab granite and climbs a faint drainage into an old stream-bed (dry by early summer). Following occasional ducks, we make our way upstream for nearly ¼ mile until the ducks abruptly climb out of the stream-bed and strike west to the middle of the valley, where at an unmarked junction we join the groove of route B.

From the lowest fork, route B inconspicuously leaves the better-worn route A and moves directly up the middle of the valley

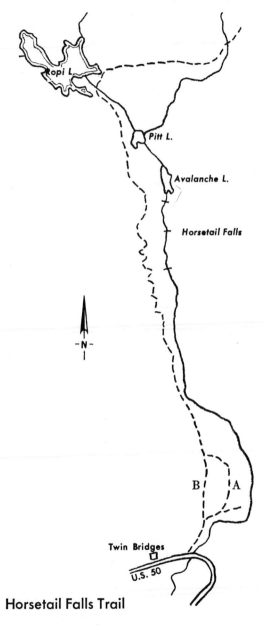

Ropi L.

Pitt L.

Avalanche L.

Horsetail Falls

–N–

B   A

Twin Bridges

U.S. 50

Horsetail Falls Trail

Same scale as 7½′ USGS map

0   ¼   ½   1
              miles

toward the falls for 100 yards on granite slabs, marked only by an occasional duck or candy wrapper. Beyond this stretch of granite the trail becomes a generally visible groove winding up through the sage- and stone-studded sandy floor of the valley. In summary: route A is the easiest route to find and follow going up, while route B is the natural choice for descending travelers.

Above the junction the trail moves up the center of the valley on the west side of Pyramid Creek, through an open woodland of mixed conifers (notably incense cedar), bush chinquapin and manzanita. For the following mile in the narrowing valley the route is usually distinct: a groove is evident where the terrain is impressionable, and ducks fill in most of the gaps. In a glade at the head of the valley the trail splits harmlessly for a few yards and rejoins; then it crosses a smooth slab of granite and starts climbing more steeply through fields of huckleberry oak and manzanita.

Following overgrown (but dry) watercourses the trail passes under the west side of a cabin-sized boulder and moves up the brushy western slope between the wreckage of a small plane and a patch of charred brush, apparently burned in the crash. Through this section the height of the brush and the absence of both trees and large rocks keep the route poorly marked and hard to find. Above the plane ducks begin to reappear as the trail, to avoid cliffs, swings to the northeast toward the bottom of booming Horsetail Falls.

From its nearest approach to the stream, just above the bottom of the falls, the trail climbs north up steep granite slabs and rocky chutes through the brush, where it is marked by widely spaced ducks, to the base of a huge Jeffrey pine. This is the most difficult and vague part of the route. Above the Jeffrey pine the route zigzags steeply up the canyon's west wall, seeking the easiest going. Ducks become more frequent as we leave the brush and move up into a scattering of gnarled junipers growing miraculously in the steep talus.

Occasional splashes of white paint, not unlike seagull droppings, begin to appear, and if recognized are helpful. Above the junipers, ducks become more regular and reasonably spaced, and the sharp-eyed traveler can depend on them from this point to the top. The trail unexpectedly tops out on a shoulder of granite about $\frac{1}{4}$ mile west of, and perhaps 100' higher than, the top of the falls. This is the southernmost rim of

Desolation Valley (7500 — 2.0). It is certainly unfortunate that the haphazard route up Horsetail, constructed by random usage, has not been developed by the USFS to at least the stature of a well-marked knapsack route — especially inasmuch as it is represented as trail on various USFS maps. The Placerville Ranger District, into whose jurisdiction it falls, claims that a special appropriation of at least $10,000 would be required to build a trail that would meet present USFS minimum standards. But I feel sure that in the space of a few days a trail crew could easily double the usability and identifiability of the present route, thus justifying its representation on USFS maps.

From the edge of the rim a line of ducks leads north down a gently slanting ledge, over a hummock and into the bottom of the valley. Keeping well to the west of Avalanche Lake and a network of snowmelt ponds and channels nearby, the trail climbs the west side of the broadening valley, skirting the west shore of Pitt Lake on a bench and moving closer to Pyramid Creek above the lake. Both Avalanche and Pitt are more wide pools in the creek than lakes, but the lower reaches of the valley offer abundant water, fine vistas, ample firewood and excellent campsites. Unfortunately there is also a great deal of litter.

Although the great open slabs of granite and the creek leading up to Ropi make trail markers almost superfluous when ascending, there are occasional ducks leading up toward the fringe of timber that marks the lake. Passing a snowmelt pond that nearly joins with a narrow southern bay of the lake, we come to a battered old bridge of stout, hand-hewn timbers spanning the outlet stream. Crossing to the eastern bank for the first time, we pick up a line of faint red paint blazes leading north-northeast across the granite slab to a series of campsites at the eastern end of

Ropi Lake (7620 — 0.7). This is the beginning of the official, maintained stock trail — the southern end of the Desolation Trail as shown on most maps. We climb gently uphill to the east through a joint in the granite (where a softer vein of rock has weathered away to leave a groove). After several hundred yards, we climb out of the joint, dip through a marshy dell, climb east over a little knoll and settle into another joint parallel to the first. Although comparatively little used, this stretch of trail between Ropi and Lake of the Woods is well-marked by ducks and paint blazes and easy to follow.

We pass beneath the cliffs of the blocky knoll between Lake of the Woods and Desolation Lake and climb due east across an area of open rock offering an excellent view over Avalanche Lake out the mouth of the valley to the ranges beyond. About $\frac{1}{2}$ mile above Ropi we swing northeast to enter a charming wooded valley, and walk beside the meandering stream that joins Pitt and Lake of the Woods. We cross the stream and move $\frac{1}{4}$ mile

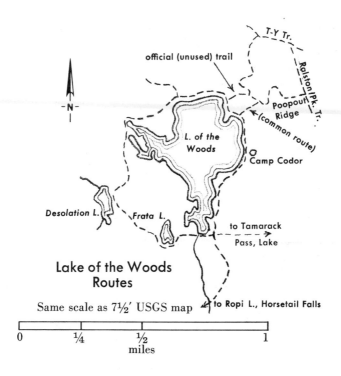

official (unused) trail

T-Y Tr.

Ralston Pk. Tr.

Poopout Ridge
←(common route)

L. of the Woods

Camp Codor

Desolation L.

Frata L.

to Tamarack
Pass, Lake

Lake of the Woods Routes

Same scale as 7½′ USGS map

to Ropi L., Horsetail Falls

| 0 | ¼ | ½ | 1 |

miles

-N-

through the woods before climbing around the edge of a sandy knoll and moving gently down to the southernmost bay of

Lake of the Woods (8060 — 0.8). Suddenly the trail is broad and heavily used, and at times there may be two or more tracks. We climb a slight rise, return to the lakeshore for several hundred yards, then swing behind a small peninsula on which there is a campsite. The trail splits as it crosses a small all-summer rill. One branch crosses on a culvert at the water's edge; the other, used mainly by stock, pushes through a patch of willow. Both are muddy.

Immediately after the trails rejoin we move through Camp Codor, which is occupied during the middle of the summer by several dozen Boy Scouts. The camp's storage cabin has been dismantled in accordance with Wilderness Area regulations but its four boats remain. North of the camp the trail is a broad boulevard on springy duff beneath a shady forest beside the lakeshore. We pass a small block of granite to the east of the trail on which is inscribed *Laid by C.C.H. Club, July 17, 1933*, and come out into a roughly triangular meadow that fans out from a dry creek-bed to the lakeshore.

The Scouts habitually short-cut up the steep bank at the head of the meadow to intersect the trail to Poopout Ridge about two thirds of the way to the top, thus saving perhaps ¼ mile of trail. Above the north end of the meadow are several excellent camp-sites, and the trail passes near the concrete-slab floor of a cabin once used by packers from Fallen Leaf. On the northern margin of the meadow the heavily traveled trail from Poopout descends through the trees to intersect our trail at an unsigned and unofficial but commonly used junction.

Beyond the campsites the slope grows rocky and the trail splits into several tracks. Most hikers, being inclined to take the lower of any two given trails, dip between the rock pile and the water. The official trail, however, climbs above the rock pile, and 50 yards from the water we come to the official, signed but little-used junction with the

Fallen Leaf-Echo Lakes Trail (8060 — 0.6). A battered sign reads *Ropi Lake*, south, and *Fallen Leaf Lake 7 miles, Echo Lake 3 miles*, east. About 150 yards up the slope to the east is the signed junction of the old Fallen Leaf and Echo Lake trails, to which this sign refers (see map). The USFS agrees that this interweaving of old and new, signed and unsigned trails is unnecessarily confusing and plans some sort of consolidation.

Beyond the junction, the Desolation Trail again dims as it circles above a pair of wind-thrown pines and drops through a verdant dell below an aspen thicket to the lake's north shore, to run along the edge of a white sandy beach (submerged until late summer). Though this glorified fishermen's trail squeezes between trees and climbs along slippery rocks and is therefore avoided by packers, who detour behind it, it is perfectly passable to hikers.

We follow the shore around the north end of the lake and, about 50 yards short of the western shore, in a cluster of campsites, the trail makes an abrupt and invisible turn away from the water and to the north. We move uphill through the campsites to where a rocky path, marked by a few ducks, climbs steeply over a bluff about 100 yards east of a big cracked dome. At the top of the bluff we come into a little green draw between the dome and a narrow belt of dark forest. We move gently down the draw on grass to the southern terminal of

Lake Aloha: Double Jctn. (8160 — 0.6). About 100 yards from the southeastern corner of the lake a lateral from the T-Y

Trail arrives from the east. Signs read *Echo Lake 4 miles, Fallen Leaf Lake 5 miles,* east, and *South End Desolation Valley ¼ mile,* southeast. Less than 100 yards northwest we come to the northern terminal of Double Junction, where signs read *PG &E dam, Waca Lake 1½ miles, Pyramid Lake 2 miles, Pyramid Peak 3⅝ miles,* west; *Lake Le Conte 1 mile, Glen Alpine Trail 1¾ miles, North End Desolation Valley 2 miles,* north; and *Lake of the Woods 1 mile,* southeast.

What could have been a clearly signed, simple intersection of two crossing trails has unfortunately been divided into two confusing, poorly signed junctions standing in sight of each other. On any summer weekend puzzled hikers can be found staring perplexedly at the jumble of signs. The trail to Aloha Dam (better known as "The PG & E Dam") heads roughly northwest along the lake's southern shore.

Until 1917 when the dam was built, the broad flat valley that is now filled by Aloha was a series of lakelets known as "Medley Lakes." The valley floor returns to that state every fall when PG & E opens the dam to drain Aloha—except that a crust of cracked mud now covers the basin and the trees have become drowned gray snags. It is only thanks to man's manipulations that Desolation Valley lives up to its name.

The trail moves northwest along the lakeshore, often on sand-topped check dams, swings behind a granite-slab peninsula, then crosses a dam separating a small deep bay in Aloha from a string of lakelets to the south. We climb almost 100' above the water to pass around the northern end of a bare granite bluff, then descend, arcing to the west through gullies and around snow ponds in monolithic rolling granite. The trail is vague at best and often disappears entirely, but by keeping to the west we cannot fail to strike either the lake shore, the dam or the stream below it. In fact, once the bluff has been left behind the sound of rushing water will in most seasons guide us to

Aloha (PG & E) Dam (8116 — 0.7). The dam itself is a fairly remarkable structure. It was built, in a single month in the fall of 1917, of beautifully faced granite blocks quarried — as can readily be seen — from the west bank of the damsite. The face is nearly as smooth as poured concrete, although a minimum of mortar was used. The back is a series of seven tiers built of two- to three-foot granite blocks. Only the regularity of outline and the chained gate valve sitting on a five-foot turret on the dam's center keep it from merging altogether with its granite surroundings. The spillway elevation is given at the dam as 8210' but subsequent surveys have placed it more accurately at 8116'.

Poopout Ridge to Lake of the Woods to Lake Lucille to Lake Aloha (double junction) to Lake Aloha (Tahoe-Yosemite Trail)

(The lateral trails between and around the Desolation and T-Y trails)

	Elev.	Miles from pt. above	Total miles
Poopout Ridge: trail Jctn.	8420	0.0	0.0
Old Fallen Leaf Trail: Lake of the Woods	8180	0.4	0.4
T-Y Trail (Jctn. South Lucille Trail)	8320	0.4	0.8
Lake Lucille (Jctn. southwest end)	8180	0.3	1.1
T-Y Trail (Jctn. North Lucille Trail)	8300	0.5	1.6
Lake Aloha: double junction	8160	0.5	2.1
Lake Aloha (Jctn. T-Y Trail)	8140	0.7	2.8

The descriptions that follow are not so much those of a single trail or recommended route as they are a collection of short laterals that link the two principal trails (T-Y and Desolation) to each other, and also to Lakes Lucille and Margery. The zigzagging result, though not exciting in its own right, is indispensable to hikers from Echo who wish to reach Desolation Valley by trail. Furthermore, knowledge of these paths and junctions makes it possible to plan more interesting trips. A lateral from the T-Y Trail at the foot of Haypress Meadows (see Region 1, Sec. 1) leads west 0.3 miles to an intersection with the Ralston Peak Trail (see Region 1, Sec. 2) at the top of

Poopout Ridge (8420 — 0.0). Signs read *Upper Echo 3 miles,* east, *Ralston Peak 2 miles,* south, and *Lake of the Woods ½ mile, Ropi Lake 2½ miles,* west. Taking the latter trail we head west across the open sandy ridge toward prominent Pyramid Peak and, as the trail begins to drop steeply, swing north to traverse the slope for 50 yards before switching back to the south to a large fallen red fir bucked into three sections.

About 50 yards below the fir on another traverse to the north, at an unmarked junction, the little-used but official trail takes off to the north through sage and tall grass. The deeply worn rut of the unofficial trail (used by virtually everyone) continues down to the lake, coming out into a string of campsites just north of the triangular meadow, where it joins the Desolation Trail (see Sec. 2). Not far from the junction lies the concrete slab floor of a cabin once maintained by packers from Fallen Leaf. Back up on the sage slope, the dim official trail drops gently through sand and low brush to a junction with the

Old Fallen Leaf Trail (8180 — 0.4). A battered sign reads *Tamarack Trail 1 mile, Echo Lake 2⅜ miles*, east toward Poopout, and *Lucille Trail, Glen Alpine 4 miles*, northeast up the ridge. From this junction the combined trails drop straight west through the trees 100 yards to a junction with the Desolation Trail (see Sec. 2) a little above the lake.

Heading east up the Old Fallen Leaf Trail, we climb on a dim traverse to the north, then switchback steeply to the east before swinging less steeply to the north. The slope begins to level off, and we cross the ridgetop and drop a few yards down the sandy northside to cross the

T-Y Trail: South Lucille Jctn. (8320 — 0.4). The Old Fallen Leaf Trail to this point is faint and little traveled, but east of the intersection it suddenly becomes clear and heavily used. Signs at the intersection read *Lake of the Woods ½ mile*, south, and *Margery Lake ¼ mile, Lake Lucille ½ mile*, north. We cross 50 yards of meadow and move down into the woods, where after a winding 100 yards we pass the ducked but easily missed junction with a fishermen's trail from Margery (described below from its other end).

A little farther into the woods we see the first glimmering from Lucille through the trees, and switchback down toward the lake on well-shaded, springy duff. Near the bottom of the wooded slope the trail forks. The left branch is shorter, steeper and dryer than the right, which dips into a patch of meadow that remains boggy into midsummer. The two branches rejoin at a big western white pine 100′ above the lake. A few feet farther north the trail reaches the stream-bed (dry by midsummer) joining the two lakes and a sign reading *Lake Lucille, elevation 8180 feet* which marks the trail junction at

Lake Lucille (8180 — 0.3). A variety of paths, loops and short-cuts sort themselves out as follows (see map). Several tracks run southwest up the stream-bed and combine into a well-worn trail up to Margery; other paths either continue down the stream-bed to Lucille's south shore or cross the stream-bed to join and continue north along the lake's northwestern shore. The branch along the shore is the continuation of the Old Fallen Leaf Trail which is treated, beyond this junction, in Region 8, Sec. 3.

The remaining tracks merge into the poorly-marked but mapped and official North Lucille Trail, which crosses the stream-bed and, turning almost due west, enters the woods on a course that brings it to the northern tip of Lake Margery. From this point a fisher-men's trail follows the eastern shore of the lake, crosses the out-let stream and continues past the south end of the lake, where it starts to climb. Forced by boulders to veer to the east, it climbs gradually through needle-floored forest and, by now quite dim, makes its way to an unmarked junction with the South Lucille (Old Fallen Leaf) Trail about 100 yards below the north edge of the meadow.

Back on the North Lucille Trail at the northern tip of Lake Margery, we wind through a pretty little wooded creek bottom and climb abruptly up a rocky bluff and out of the Margery basin. At the top of the bluff the land levels off and the trail wanders through pleasant, rolling, open woodland to a junction with the

Tahoe-Yosemite Trail (8300 — 0.5). Signs read *Mosquito Pass 3 miles*, northwest, *Upper Echo Lake 3½ miles*, southeast, and *Margery Lake ¼ mile, Lucille Lake ½ mile*, east. To reach the lateral leading toward Aloha Dam we move southeast down the T-Y Trail 0.1 mile to a junction with the unsigned but well-trodden lateral leading gently downhill to the west. After skirting a snowmelt pond the trail wanders through open sandy wood-land, winding in and out of grassy hollows and coming out through meadowland to the southern terminal of

Lake Aloha: Double Jctn. (8160 — 0.5). For a full descrip-tion of the many signs and trails at this confusing crossroads see Sec. 2. At the junction we turn northwest toward the lake and walk 100 yards to the northern terminal of Double Junction, where the relevant signs read *Lake Le Conte 1 mile, Glen Alpine Trail 1¾ miles, North End Desolation Valley 2 miles*, north.

The trail descends a few feet toward the corner of the lake, then turns up the eastern shore and passes a sign reading *Aloha Lake 8180 feet* and a camping area equipped with metal stoves and grills. The trail splits into several tracks in vain efforts to escape early-season mud as we skirt a stagnant (by late season) lily pond kept filled by seepage from the east. We climb to the edge of timber and pass through Lake Aloha's best, and perhaps only decent, camping area.

At the edge of a little grove of lodgepole that shelters a big campsite, a shortcut trail heads east 150 yards up the slope to join the T-Y Trail coming down. We follow the lakeside trail past the little grove to the signed, official junction with the

T-Y Trail (8140 — 0.7). Signs read *Lake of the Woods, 1½ miles, Ropi Lake 3 miles*, south, *Mosquito Pass 2½ miles*, north, and *Upper Echo Lake 4 miles*, southeast. For descriptions of the trail continuing north around Aloha see Sec 1.

Sec. 4

Miscellaneous Routes: Desolation Valley
(including routes up Pyramid Peak)

One of the greatest pleasures of wilderness travel is cross-country wandering, and that pleasure can be enhanced (and misfortune avoided) by knowing a little about the country to be wandered. Desolation Valley divides itself into three sections: an upper basin occupied by Lake Aloha, a central section with three separate and roughly parallel drainages, and a lower basin containing Toem, Ropi, Pitt and Avalanche lakes.

Upper Basin

Lake Aloha is without trail from the main dam around the western shore to the foot of Mosquito Pass. The shoreline is largely barren, but in early season there are waterfalls that one can walk behind, and in the autumn, when the water is down, it is possible to cross the middle of the lake by jumping a few channels. Benches under Mt. Price offer exhilarating walking; and there is a wrecked plane to be inspected above the westernmost bay on the northeast shoulder of Mt. Price.

Central Section

In the central section the easternmost drainage (Lake of the Woods, Frata Lake) is easily the best known, because of the trails described in Secs. 2 and 3. There are several shortcut routes from Tamarack Lake (see Region 1, Sec. 8) through Tamarack Pass in the north ridge of Ralston Peak, to Desolation Valley. From the saddle one can make an easy descent by heading due west (directly toward Pyramid Peak) through pretty, wooded, well-watered country until Frata and Lake of the Woods appear below, and then heading directly toward them.

To reach Frata and continue west to Desolation Lake, in the middle drainage of the central section, we take the fishermen's trail west around the bottom of Lake of the Woods, cross the dam at the outlet, take a sight on Pyramid Peak and walk west about 200 yards up a gently rising slope of granite. Because Frata's watershed is tiny, it warms quickly and provides hikers with probably the earliest and warmest swimming to be found in the basin.

To reach Desolation from Frata we follow the distinct fishermen's trail around the south end of the lake and halfway up the west shore until the way is blocked by cliffs. Then we climb west about 60' to cross the low ridge in a saddle (there are occasional ducks), from which we can look down on Desolation about 250 yards northwest. A gentle, lightly wooded granite slope leads

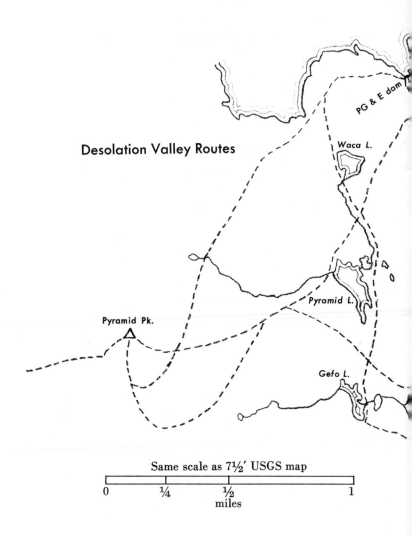

Desolation Valley Routes

PG & E dam

Waca L.

Pyramid L.

Pyramid Pk.

Gefo L.

Same scale as 7½′ USGS map

0	¼	½	1

miles

down toward the lake, and we skirt a large pond to reach the foot of the falls on the northern shore.

To reach Desolation from the north end of Lake of the Woods, we continue west past the trail turnoff to Aloha Dam and follow the fishermen's trail through several campsites and onto the low.

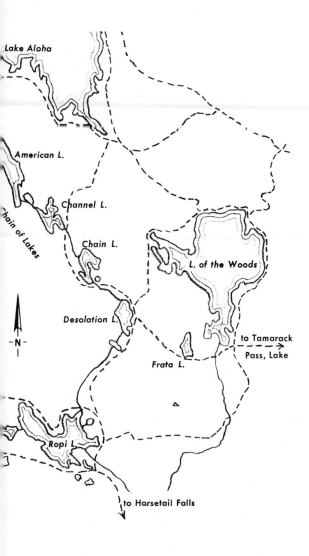

parklike peninsula on the western shore. The trail gradually grows dimmer, and disappears entirely before we reach the lake's western bay. We continue to the west, climbing awkwardly over a large lakeside boulder beneath cliffs, then circle south around the bay, threading our way among several snowmelt ponds.

After crossing an almost imperceptible ridge we move gently south down a wooded draw toward the clearly visible lake, past a boulder and slab slope studded with spectacularly formed junipers, to the mediocre campsites near the falls. This middle drainage of the central section embraces the "chain of lakes" (American, Channel, Chain and Desolation) running from Aloha Dam to Pyramid Creek between Desolation and Ropi.

The topo map fails to name Chain and mistakenly shows its gauging station at the outlet of Desolation. A well-defined fishermen's trail runs down the eastern shore of Desolation and past a series of beautiful pools and channels before hurdling a pocket of deadfalls and coming out on open slab. The easy, pleasant traveling on this bright granite beside the frothing cascade leads directly to Ropi Lake in the lower basin.

Ascending the chain of lakes from the head of Desolation, we climb on slab east of the falls, passing one of the few points (where the flow divides) at which it is possible to jump across, even at early-season high water. Still on the east bank we climb past 200 yards of pools and cascades to the gauging station at the outlet of Chain Lake (also known as Lower Channel Lake). This small, square rock building has an iron door on the front and a shuttered window at the back; inside are waterflow measuring and recording devices owned by PG & E.

The flow of water through the chain of lakes fluctuates wildly (playing havoc with the fishing) depending on PG & E's need for water. Chain Lake is most easily passed on the west, and it is possible to jump the creek a little below the gauging station. We then skirt a little bay and climb onto a ledge to pass above cliffs that drop into the water. By climbing a little higher, to the top of a low ridge, we discover an unusually fine view across the lower basin to Pyramid Peak.

The $\frac{1}{4}$-mile stretch of stream between Chain and Channel lakes, known to Echo cabin owners as the Japanese Gardens, is one of the loveliest spots in the basin. The stream spreads out into a number of channels that cascade gently through a series of tree-shaded pools in the polished granite, making this an idyllic place to rest, eat lunch or bathe. Above this point the traveling is easiest on the eastern bank, and the Japanese Gardens offers the last easy crossing for some distance.

From the east shore of Channel Lake a line of ducks leads northeast, across nearly level, rolling granite pocketed with a thick concentration of ponds and lakelets, to the southern end of Lake Aloha at Double Junction. Though there is no trail, the traveling is easy and the route passes a number of good campsites. Heading north from Channel we find the country flattening out into a plain of broken rock, where trees and campsites are scarce and the wind often blows. At the head of American Lake there is a stream crossing on boulders, but it is only a few hundred yards farther to the more easily crossed Aloha Dam.

Opposite the middle of American Lake to the west, there is a low (8200') pass leading to Waca Lake. Except for the longer route along the Aloha shoreline west from the dam, this is the only easy access from the middle to the western drainage. The western drainage—Waca Lake through Pyramid Lake to Ropi— lies close under Pyramid Peak, and because of its comparative remoteness and lack of trails it sees far fewer visitors than the other two drainages.

Timber is sparse at both Waca and Pyramid, but there are a few campsites in scattered clumps of trees. The routes to Pyramid Lake from both American and Aloha lakes are comparatively easy and obvious in the rolling open granite; so is the walk downstream to Pyramid. Pyramid Lake offers the most popular point of departure for the 9983' summit of Pyramid Peak, first climbed in 1863 by William Brewer of the Whitney Survey party. As the highest point in the Wilderness Area, it is the premier attraction for many climbers.

Climbing Pyramid Peak

There are as many routes to the top as there are hikers, and none of the routes is marked. Probably the easiest climb is from Lake Sylvia in the west (see Region 3, Sec. 1), but the most popular routes begin in Desolation Valley. The principal point of departure from a maintained trail is at Aloha Dam. At the northern terminal of Double Junction, at the southeastern corner of Aloha (see Sec. 2), a sign reads *PG & E dam, Waca Lake 1½ miles, Pyramid Lake 2 miles, Pyramid Peak 3⅝ miles.* (Surely the author of that last absurdly precise distance was joking!)

From the dam the northernmost route up the mountain follows the shore to the southern tip of the western bay and climbs southwest into the mouth of the basin between Pyramid and Mt. Price, well below the little lake. From here one can with difficulty climb directly to the summit, or more easily traverse to the south across talus and ascend the gentle south ridge. Probably the most popular route begins by crossing the dam, drops downstream to American Lake, climbs through the 8200' saddle to Waca Lake, then goes downstream to the west end of Pyramid Lake.

From this point routes vary. It is not very difficult to climb due west up talus to the summit, but the easiest, gentlest route heads west-southwest, then loops about ½ mile to the south and ascends via the south ridge. There are also several routes from Toem Lake, in the lower basin, although the climb is greater by some 400'. From the south end of Toem one can with difficulty climb steeply southwest nearly 1200' onto a flat, sandy meadow, and from there climb the gentle south ridge to the summit.

From the north end of Toem one can climb northwest through gentle country to a point due east of the peak and then follow one of the Pyramid Lake routes to the top. The easiest way to make the ascent is to spend the night camped at Pyramid Lake, so that the entire following day is available for the climb and return to camp. Climbers making the ascent and the return in a single day from the trailhead at Echo Lake or Twin Bridges should be strong, experienced hikers, well acclimated and oriented.

Amateur climbers should realize that while the lungs strain only on the way up, knees, thighs and ankles, already fatigued by climbing, suffer their greatest strain on the way down. Talus slopes are more dangerous in descent, and most climbing accidents occur on the way home. Climbers from the trailheads should plan to be on the trail soon after sunup (and a good breakfast) and should double the size of their usual trail lunch.

From Pyramid Lake there is no reasonable route east into the middle drainage; the ridge in between is easily climbed from the west, but cliffs form a barrier on the eastern slope. Neither should one attempt to follow the outlet stream from Pyramid down to Ropi Lake because the cliffs are high and jagged. The only easy descent is due south, where sloping granite slabs lead gently down to Gefo Lake. From here it is comparatively easy to descend along the north shore of Upper Toem and Toem lakes to Ropi in the bottom of the basin.

Lower Basin

As has already been indicated the lower basin is reached by a good trail from Lake of the Woods, a knapsack trail from Twin Bridges, and a cross-country route down the outlet stream from Desolation Lake. Twenty-year-old maps show two poor trails coming east from Upper Forni (see Region 3, introduction), suggesting that this unlikely route was once used to some extent. The lower basin offers more campsites and more wood than the remainder of Desolation Valley, and the comparatively low altitude and southern exposure open it to early-season hiking and camping when the west of the valley is still buried under snow.

Chapter 8—Region 3

Wrights Lake

Wrights Lake and the road that serves it constitute the principal access to the trails that enter the Wilderness Area from the west. The Wrights region is bounded by the crest of the Crystal Range in the east, Highway 50 in the south, Wrights Lake road and its extension, the Barrett Lake Jeep Trail, in the west, and the junction of the Lake #3 and Red Peak trails in the north. From this area flow the headwaters of the Silver Creek watershed.

Visitors accustomed to dense forest on the Sierra's western slope will be surprised to discover the Crystal Range comparatively bare in the west—in places utterly treeless. The resulting rugged vastness and space recall the timberline slopes of the southern Sierra high country. Visitors likewise will be surprised to find that most of the streams, despite exposure to the hot western sun, flow through the summer and into the fall.

Though fourth in popularity as a point of entry into the Wilderness (after Echo, Emerald Bay and Fallen Leaf) Wrights Lake offers no store, gas station, telephone or pack station. There are, however, three large campgrounds administered by the USFS clustered near the southwest corner of the lake. Private summer cabins (guarded by a resident patrolman) line the remaining shore. Motorboats are prohibited on both Wrights and Dark lakes.

The entrance to the Wrights Lake road on the north side of Highway 50 lies five miles east of Kyburz, somewhat hidden on a bend in the road. The motorist must be alert for a small blue sign reading *Wrights Lake 8 miles*. On winding, pitted asphalt, which soon gives way to rocky dirt, we climb 1300′ in 3.4 miles to Chimney Flat, where a dirt road enters a California gate to the east.

Shown on the topo map as jeep trail, this high-standard, private and generally closed road leads 4 miles east past the barns of Lower Forni to the cabin and sheds of Upper Forni in a meadow by a stream.

Climbing the Forni road we quickly pass a second California gate and a corral and come to a locked iron gate set in concrete 0.3 mile up the road from Chimney Flat. A sign reads *No motorscooters.* Other signs at various points farther up the road read *No motor vehicles allowed, No trespassing* and *Area Patrolled by John Forni.* The dusty, rocky logging and cattlemen's road passes across private land for the most part, and although foot travel has been permitted in the past, this policy is subject to change.

Upper Forni, located in rolling, wooded grazing land on Peavine Ridge, offers good access to fishless, shallow Forni Lake and to a comparatively gentle route up the south shoulder of Pyramid Peak. Old maps show two trails from Upper Forni running east across the ridge and dropping into Desolation Valley below Ropi Lake, and another trail descending Forni Creek to Highway 50. During gold rush days a dairy at Upper Forni produced butter and milk for immigrants descending the American River Canyon. Another trail linked the dairy to its nearest neighbor, the Lyons Dairy, on Lyons Creek.

Returning to Chimney Flat we drive north through a little saddle and, 0.6 mile from Forni Road, reach the Lyons Creek road and a sign reading *Lyons Creek Trail, 16E13* (see Sec. 1). The road crosses all-season Lyons Creek, then swings to the west in a big half circle that passes Wilson Ranch and crosses Silver Creek. We come out of the woods 7.7 miles from the highway by a road leading east into a meadow signed *Bloodsucker Trail 16E14* (see Sec. 2).

This meadow, known as "Horse Camp," has been set aside as a campground for horsemen and their animals. We pass a weather station on the edge of the meadow and drive 0.1 mile north across a cattleguard to a three-way fork in the road at the southern tip of Wrights Lake. The road branching east crosses the outlet stream on a stout bridge, near which relics from a once-large Indian encampment were discovered in 1961, and passes a large public campground and several dozen cabins before ending at the eastern end of the lake.

The middle road continues north along the lake shore from the fork, passing a campground to the west and lakeside picnic area to the east.

After 0.3 mile it forks again. The lower, eastern fork hugs the shore and gives access to the cabins that line it. The higher, western fork climbs onto a low ridge and runs parallel to the lake shore behind and above the cabins. Both forks are of considerably poorer quality than the Wrights Lake road, and passenger cars, especially those with low clearance, should be driven with care. The two roads rejoin at the northern end of the lake and lead east several hundred yards to a signed junction with a cabin-owners' road that branches southeast. A sign here reading *Willow Flat Trail, Twin Lakes Trail* points up the road branch to the northeast.

About 100 yards beyond a California gate, the road comes over a little knoll and drops to the edge of a meadow, where it ends in a large parking area between two trailheads (see Secs. 3 and 4). At the southern trailhead a sign reads *Grouse Lake 2 miles, Twin Lakes 3 miles, Island Lake 4 miles,* east. About 100 yards north a sign reads *Willow Flat Trail, Maud Lake 4 miles, Tyler Lake 4 miles, Rockbound Pass 5 miles,* pointing north up the track. This double trailhead lies 1.2 miles above the three-way fork and 9.0 miles from Highway 50.

Returning to the three-way fork, we this time take the ½ mile western branch, which leads around the bottom of the campground and turns north to the east end of Dark Lake, where the road forks at a large sign. The road to the west serves half a dozen cabins; the road to the north, known as the Barrett Lake Jeep Trail, continues 5.0 miles to Barrett Lake (see Sec. 5). Much of the road is good, but the bad spots require four-wheel drive and high clearance. The sign reads *Red Peak Trail, Rupley Cow Camp, Tells Peak, U.C. Cow Camp, Barrett Lake, Lawrence Lake,* north up the jeep trail. No distances are given.

Sec. 1
Lyons Creek Trail

	Elev.	Miles from pt. above	Total miles
Lyons Creek Road	6900	0.0	0.0
Lyons Creek Trailhead	6920	0.5	0.5
Lyons (site): Bloodsucker Trail	7020	1.4	1.9
Lyons Lake Jctn.	7960	2.7	4.6
Lake Sylvia	8060	0.4	5.0
Pyramid Peak	9983	1.5	6.5

The Lyons Creek Trail, in addition to its other virtues, offers the closest trail approach and the easiest climb up Pyramid Peak. To most hikers, however, the modest, gently rising, well-shaded trail offers a pleasant walk beside a pretty trout stream to a pair of attractive lakes. In early season the track is apt to be damp, and mosquitos are often thick until midseason. From Highway 50 the Wrights Lake road climbs 4.0 miles to a signed junction with the

Lyons Creek Road (6900 — 0.0) leading east. A sign at the road junction reads *Lyons Creek Trail, 16E13*, and 50 yards east up the road a second sign reads *Lyons Lake 5 miles, Sylvia Lake 5 miles, Wrights Lake 5 miles*, east. Less than 100 yards farther east we come to the first of half a dozen signs reading *Private Property, trespassing permit required. Apply Wilson Ranch.* (Foot and horse traffic and overnight camping are generally permitted, although most of the lower stretch of the trail is on private land. The Wilson Ranch lies 1½ miles up the Wrights Lake road to the northwest.) The Lyons Creek road ends at a number of good campsites close to the creek and we come to the

Lyons Creek Trailhead (6920 — 0.5) marked by a sign reading *No jeeps, scooters or other motorized contrivance allowed beyond this sign. George Wilson, owner.* The trail heads a little north of east to pass through wooded meadow along the south bank of the all-year creek, virtually on the level, along what once was a road. There is an excellent, continuous groove; blazes were freshened and deadfalls removed when the trail was reworked in 1968. The modest but high-speed trail comes out into a meadow from which Pyramid Peak becomes visible for the first time and we come to a junction with the

Bloodsucker Trail (7020 — 1.4) at what the topo map calls "Lyons (Site)". A sign reads *Wrights Lake 3 miles*, north, and *16E13, Sylvia Lake 3 miles, Lyons Lake 3 miles*, east. All that remains of the century-old Lyons Dairy, which supplied early immigrants, are several low rock walls that run 50 yards north to the creek. We return to the shady lodgepole and red-fir forest, and gradually the trail begins to climb. Occasionally there are harmless multiple tracks that rejoin.

As the valley floor rises more steeply the trees begin to thin, and 2 miles above Lyons we come out of the woods to climb a rocky slope beside a beautiful stretch of pools and falls in marble-tinted slab granite. Pyramid Peak again becomes visible directly above to the east, and for the first time the trail is marked with ducks. We climb back into forest, and some 200 yards after crossing the creek we come to the junction with the

Lyons Lake Trail (7960 — 2.7). A sign reads *Lake Sylvia ½ mile*, east, and *Lyons Lake ½ mile*, north. The Lyons Lake Trail circles across wooded meadow to the outlet stream, then climbs steeply up a rocky wooded canyon on the western stream-bank

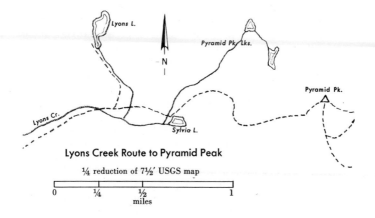

Lyons Creek Route to Pyramid Peak

¼ reduction of 7½′ USGS map

```
0        ¼        ½                    1
              miles
```

to the granite cirque in which the lake rests, a climb of 400′ in ½ mile.

From the trail junction the Lake Sylvia trail makes multiple crossings of the Lyons Lake outlet, dips down across the edge of a wet meadow, crosses a stream from Pyramid Peak Lakes, and leads up through trees to

Lake Sylvia (8060 — 0.4). Mosquitos last into late season at this shallow but attractive lake directly under Pyramid's west ridge. There are good campsites on the north and west shores. Standing at the lakeshore one can see to the northeast a wide swath of willow thicket sloping up from the lake, bordered by light forest to the north and a talus slope to the east.

The easiest and most direct approach to the peak follows the fishermen's trail around the lake's north shore, then climbs up through the light forest near the edge of the willows. When the slope begins to level off the willows thin out and we circle to the southeast above them to the foot of a steep talus-and-slab slope. Moving directly to the southeast, up the steepest slope on this ascent, we climb some 400′ onto the mountain's western ridge.

Keeping to the gentler slope just south of the ridgeline, we move up on rock, rubble and talus, plotting a course that avoids loose, sandy soil. Neither Lyons nor Sylvia Lake is seen again, but various lakelets become visible below, and as we near the summit the cabins of Upper Forni at the top of a long meadow come into view.

At about 9600′ the western ridge levels off, and we move to the edge of the cliffs on the north side for a spectacular view of the semipermanent snowbanks under the summit cliffs, the sawtooth spine of the Crystal Range running north and Pyramid Peak Lakes below to the northwest. From here it is a short climb through boulders and talus onto the flat southern ridge and up to the summit of

Pyramid Peak (9983 — 1.5). At the top we find two four-foot-deep rock-walled enclosures where one can bivouac or eat lunch out of the wind, two bench marks dated 1940, a flagstaff flying various ensigns and undershirts, and a small metal box with a wing-nut-secured lid concreted into a crack. The lid is inscribed "Register, Contra Costa Hills Club, 1927"; inside are (usually) pencils, notes, lists of climbers and their comments.

The view to the east is marvelous. Desolation Valley in its entirety is spread below like a relief map, and nearly all its lakes are visible. To the northeast we look down on Heather, Susie, Gilmore and Tahoe. To the east are Jabu, Lucille, Fallen Leaf and Lower Echo. And to the south beyond Forni Lake lie successive ridges of the Carson Range and the main Sierra crest.

Sec. 2
Bloodsucker Trail

	Elev.	Miles from pt. above	Total miles
Bloodsucker Trailhead	6960	0.0	0.0
Bottom of Horse Camp Road	6940	0.4	0.4
Bloodsucker Lake Lateral	7320	1.3	1.7
Lyons Creek Trail	7020	0.8	2.5

Though never in the Wilderness Area and running partly on logging road, the Bloodsucker Trail offers an easy, short walk through pleasant country. Bloodsucker Lake is a shallow, fishless lake on cutover private land, but there is an excellent view across it to Blue Mountain and Pyramid Peak. Most of the traffic on the trail is between Horse Camp and the lake since Lyons (Site) is more easily reached by the Lyons Creek Trail. Originally the Bloodsucker Trail linked the early Lyons dairy to that of the Wright brothers north of Wrights Lake. The trail officially begins at a sign 0.1 mile south of Wrights Lake on the east side of the Wrights Lake road, 7.7 miles north of Highway 50.

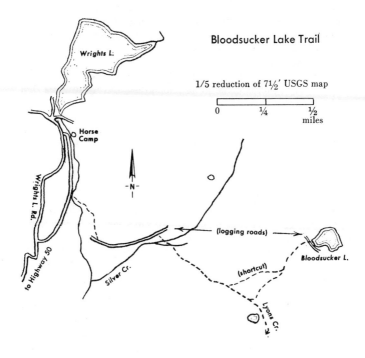

Bloodsucker Lake Trail

1/5 reduction of 7½′ USGS map

Bloodsucker Trailhead (6960 — 0.0). The sign on the edge of the meadow reads *Bloodsucker Trail, 16E14.* We drive into the meadow known as "Horse Camp" where horses graze among the tents, pass a weather station and turn south to the meadow's end, where we weave our way among rocks and trees down a sandy slope to the creek and a sign that marks the actual beginning of the Bloodsucker Trail at the

Bottom of Horse Camp Road (6940 — 0.4). The sign reads *Bloodsucker Lake 2 miles, Lyons Creek 3 miles, Lyons Lake 6 miles, Lake Sylvia 6 miles,* southeast across the creek. There is no satisfactory parking area nearby, although a single car can be squeezed off the road. Though somewhat deteriorated and little traveled, the road from Horse Camp eventually finds its way back to the Wrights Lake road, but it is not recommended for passenger cars.

The trail immediately crosses the all-season creek on rocks and follows a good groove down the east bank 100 yards through open lodgepole and red and white fir forest before turning away

101

from the stream. We dip through a patch of dense woods and climb out of the trees to a barricaded old road and a green and white sign reading *Trail* with an arrow pointing northwest along the route we have ascended.

We turn east up the road, dip through a shallow hollow and, after nearly ½ mile, come to another green and white *Trail* sign with an arrow that leads us southeast into a corner of private land that once was logged. We quickly cross two branches of all-season Silver Creek, and about 100 yards past the second crossing we come to a confusing fork in the trail. One groove leads several hundred yards up an old skid road to the east before petering out, while the blazed, slightly more distinct Bloodsucker Trail goes southeast up a steeper slope.

Some 100 yards above the fork a USFS sign reads *Two-wheel vehicle route.* After a 350′ climb from Silver Creek through open mixed-conifer virgin forest (we have temporarily left the cutover private land) the excellent trail (reworked in 1968) reaches the top of a little ridge and a signed junction with the

Bloodsucker Lake Lateral (7320 — 1.3). A sign reads *Lyons Creek Trail, Wrights Lake 2 miles,* northwest, *Lyons Creek 1 mile,* southeast, and *Bloodsucker Lake,* with no distance, east. We turn east on the lateral and gradually descend on a more modest but continuous track into a lush wooded meadow under large red firs. The hiker may realize at this point that both distance and elevation would have been saved by leaving the trail ¼ mile below the junction and ascending a wooded draw to the meadow.

Now heading northeast, we climb out of the meadow on a gradually steepening slope and once again exchange virgin forest for brutally clear-cut, slash-littered private land. The trail wades upward through the debris, among a sometimes confusing maze of skid roads, and climbs onto a ridge along which a road runs. Immediately across the road lies shallow

Bloodsucker Lake (7420 — 0.5), which probably takes its name from the small, bloodsucking leeches that are often found in warm, fishless ponds. The Department of Fish and Game estimates a maximum depth of three feet for the lake. There is a fine view to the east of Blue Mountain and Pyramid Peak. The climb from the trail junction is 100′ (net) in ½ mile.

Returning to the junction we move southeast through parklike timber across the level top of the ridge dividing Silver Creek from Lyons Creek, pass trail sign *16E03* (incorrect) and a shallow, pretty all-year pond, then descend to the southeast on a good but little-used track through handsome mixed-conifer forest. At the bottom of the slope we come out of the forest and cross a rocky meadow to all-year Lyons Creek, which we cross on rocks. The trail turns south across another patch of meadow to the signed junction with the

Lyons Creek Trail (7020 — 0.8) (see Sec. 1).

Sec. 3

Twin Lake and Smith Lake trails

	Elev.	Miles from pt. above	Total miles
Twin Lake Trailhead	6940	0.0	0.0
Smith Lake Trail	7540	1.1	1.1
Grouse Lake	8140	0.7	1.8
Hemlock Lake	8380	0.5	2.3
Smith Lake	8700	0.5	2.8
Twin Lake	7980	1.4	2.5
Island Lake	8140	0.6	3.1

About a mile east of the trailhead the trail divides. The eastern branch climbs a wooded canyon leading to Smith Lake, at 8700′ one of the highest lakes in the Wilderness Area. The northeastern branch climbs more gradually into the almost barren but lower Twin Lake-Island Lake basin, just to the north. From Island Lake there are excellent cross-country routes up Mt. Price and through a saddle in the Crystal Range to Clyde Lake and Mosquito Pass (see map). A narrow road leads up the west shore of Wrights Lake and turns northeast to end at the

Twin Lake Trailhead (6940 — 0.0). A trail descends near the stream from the trailhead to the cabin-owners' road at the east end of Wrights Lake. A sign reads *Grouse Lake 2 miles, Twin Lakes 3 miles, Island Lake 4 miles*, east. Almost immediately the trail crosses the creek (flowing from the above-mentioned three lakes) on a flat-topped log and comes out of the woods into an open meadow where a sign reads *Ed Wright Cabin Site. Near this site stood the homestead cabin of Ed Wright from which he operated his dairy ranch from about 1850 to 1900*. Ed and his brother Bert sold butter to the immigrants and the inns along what is now Highway 50. From the east end of the meadow a sandy, ducked groove begins to climb across open rocky slopes, which gradually give way to woodland. On this climb we meet a trail coming up from the east end of Wrights Lake. We come to a signed junction with the

Smith Lake Trail (7540 — 1.1). Signs read *Twin Lakes 1 mile, Island Lake 2 miles*, north, and *Grouse Lake 1 mile, Hemlock*

Lake 2 miles, Smith Lake 2 miles, east. The actual distances for the latter lakes are more nearly 0.7, 1.2 and 1.7 miles. Heading east toward Smith Lake we find a modest but well-marked trail climbing steadily and then steeply through pleasant, open mixed-conifer forest. At the top of the steepest pitch the trail suddenly swings north near the all-year outlet from Grouse, climbs beside it for 50 yards before crossing on stepping stones, then leads east 50 yards to the marshy foot of handsome little

Grouse Lake (8140 — 0.7). At a sign reading *Grouse Lake* the trail splits. The lower, lakeside track (wet in early season) moves through several campsites into a little meadow at the northeast end of the lake, then climbs steeply to the northeast out of the little bowl beside the all-year outlet from Hemlock Lake. The other branch, useful in early season, climbs dimly onto a little ridge along the north side of the lake and rejoins the main trail as it climbs out of the bowl. At the top of the steep slope the well-ducked trail levels off to pass through thick red fir and hemlock forest to sterile-looking

Hemlock Lake (8380 — 0.5), which takes its name from a dense forest of slender, blue-green mountain hemlock along the southern shore. A bone-white talus slope drops dramatically from summit 9318 to the north shore of the lake. The trail, by now somewhat faint, makes its way along the edge of the dense hemlock stand, turns southeast in a long, gently climbing traverse, comes out of the forest onto bare rock, and then switchbacks up a steep slope to the east, crossing and recrossing the stream from Smith Lake. Just to the south, sweeping slabs of thin-layered exfoliating granite provide an unusually fine example of onion-skin jointing. At the top of the slope we climb into a high, barren, windy bowl to

Smith Lake (8700 — 0.5). From the gated rock dam we look southeast to a gap in the ridge which suggests a feasible cross-country route to Lyons Lake, just on the other side.

Returning to the junction we now turn northeast on the Twin-Island Lake Trail, which moves gently up inclined slabs of monolithic granite. We move up ramps through rolling granite, guided by prominent ducks and paired, painted arrows of faint gray and faded red. In more than a few places, for no apparent reason, the trail splits into two well-constructed routes which after a few yards merge. We cross a small creek, climb over the top of a broad bluff and make our way through a bare granite valley to the all-year stream from Twin Lakes. The trail climbs gently along the south bank of the pleasant stream for $\frac{1}{2}$ mile before crossing on the dam at

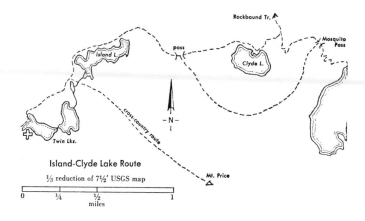

Island-Clyde Lake Route

⅓ reduction of 7½′ USGS map

0   ¼   ½   1
miles

Twin Lakes (7980 — 1.4). The trail turns northeast along the north shore of the lake and we notice, just across the western-most bay on a flat slab of granite, a bright orange, black-bordered cross painted on the rock, evidently some sort of checkpoint for aerial mapping. At the north end of a little bay the trail leaves the lakeshore, and we cross rolling fields of rubble before coming to Boomerang Lake, the first in a series of lakelets and ponds. The gradually dimming trail picks its way among low, rocky ridges, and officially ends on the west shore of

Island Lake (8140 — 0.6). As we continue on a faint fisher-men's trail along the jagged north shore, we soon pass the last of the sparse timber. No tree grows beyond the middle of the lake, giving the illusion of great elevation. From the middle of the lake an easy and direct route to the summit of Mt. Price (9975) is clearly visible. A continuously green spring-fed mead-ow at the head of the lake is a favored feeding ground for the white-faced cattle that graze this country in the late summer and fall.

The headwall of the basin, known to Wrights cabin-owners as the "gray wall," looks formidable at first, but there is a saddle to the southeast, and careful inspection reveals a long, slanting ledge climbing toward it. From the northeast corner of the lake a well-defined ravine runs perhaps a third of the way up the head-wall. When the ravine ends in cliffs we turn southeast onto the broad ledge that makes a long climbing traverse up the headwall, nearly to the saddle. When the ledge disappears we climb onto another (invisible from below) that carries us into the windy saddle. The 650′ climb to the pass (8860) is surprisingly easy and safe, with a minimum of exposure, and can be made (with packs) in less than an hour.

There is an excellent view to the east, straight down into deep blue Clyde Lake and off through Mosquito Pass to distant Freel Peak, at 10,881′ the highest mountain in the area. To complete the crossing of the Crystal Range crest (see Region 5, Sec. 3) we either descend a steep, grassy drainage directly to Clyde Lake or contour between Clyde and Mt. Price in such a way as to drop directly into Mosquito Pass.

Sec. 4

Willow Flat and Tyler Lake Trails

	Elev.	Miles from pt. above	Total miles
Willow Flat Trailhead	6940	0.0	0.0
Tyler Lake Trail	7220	1.4	1.4
Tyler's Grave Lateral	7860	1.8	3.2
Tyler Lake	8220	0.3	3.5
Willow Flat: Cattleman's Lateral	7460	1.9	3.3
Maud Lake	7660	0.3	3.6
Rockbound Pass	8550	1.4	5.0

The Willow Flat Trail, better known as the Rockbound Pass Trail, is the only official, maintained trail across the Crystal Range to Rockbound Valley. As such it sees a great deal of use. Designed for use by stock, the trail is big, highly developed, well-maintained and somewhat monotonous. The country through which it passes tends to be dry and unexciting, and there are few good campsites before Maud Lake. The Tyler Lake Trail offers more interesting country, far fewer travelers and better camping in the upper reaches. A narrow road leads up the west shore of Wrights Lake and turns northeast to end just beyond the signed

Willow Flat Trailhead (6940 — 0.0). The sign at the northern trailhead reads *Willow Flat Trail, Maud Lake 4 miles, Tyler Lake 4 miles, Rockbound Pass 5 miles*, north. We move north through level, open woodland on an old road beside the meadow. In ¼ mile the road ends and the dusty boulevard, reworked in 1969, climbs gently on a weaving course to the north through jumbled, rolling country and descends to a signed junction with the

Tyler Lake Trail (7220 — 1.4). Signs read *Willow Flat Trail, Maud Lake 2 miles, Rockbound Pass 4 miles*, north, *Wrights Lake*

2 miles, south, and *Tyler Lake Trail, Tyler Lake 2 miles, Tyler's Grave 2 miles,* east. We turn east onto a modest, well-ducked track that quickly begins to climb up a shadeless slope through fields of huckleberry oak. A rocky watercourse leads through a sandy saddle and we drop again into brush before turning abruptly north and climbing a steep rocky ravine through brush to the flat top of a ridge.

The trail turns east through a lush little flat fed by a spring (until midseason) and, growing dim in the rank growth, again turns abruptly north to climb through a little saddle east of summit 7984 and drop 100' into a large, wooded hollow cut by several rills. Better marked through this pleasant hemlock parkland, the trail begins to climb to the east, and once more on dim trail we come to a signed but easily missed junction with the

Tyler's Grave Lateral (7860 — 1.8). A broken white signpost in a pile of rocks by the trail marks the junction. About 25 feet north a green-and-white enameled sign on a tree reads *Tyler's Grave 125 yards.* We look down a corridor through the vegetation to the northwest and see in the distance the glittering white marble headstone. A path leads down to the grave. In a shield carved into the headstone we read *Wm. W. Tyler, Company B, Fourth California Infantry.* Tyler, a hand on one of the very early cattle ranches, froze to death while rounding up cattle near the lake that bears his name.

Beyond the broken signpost the faint, ducked groove climbs east to the edge of the forest, where travelers bound for curiously shaped Gertrude Lake should leave the trail and head due north 200 yards to the outlet. At the edge of the forest the ducked Tyler Trail turns southeast and climbs a bare, sandy slope onto a little bench to barren-looking, rock-rimmed

Tyler Lake (8220 — 0.3). A few trees at the northeast corner shelter the only good campsite.

Returning to the Tyler Lake Trail/Willow Flat Trail junction, we this time follow the big dusty trail north, crossing two small bridges and climbing several hundred feet through brush slopes and pockets of pine before crossing a granite ridge in which better footing for stock has been arranged with dynamite.

The trail drops 100' to cross pretty, all-year Jones Fork of Silver Creek on rocks, then turns northeast up the canyon and, following gray and yellow paint blazes, passes through unimpressive Willow Flat in a corridor beneath willows growing 15 feet high. At the upper end of the flat we come to an easily missed junction with the

Cattlemen's Lateral (7460 — 1.9). This faint trail slips in at an angle through a pocket of lodgepole, marked only by trail signs reading *16E08* (Willow Flat) and *16E11* (Cattlemen's Lateral). Immediately our trail begins to climb on waterbar staircase, which on bare rock gives way to rock-and-concrete masonry. After a steep stretch of trail, which owing to the smoothness of the rock is difficult for animals, we level off into meadow and pass through a California gate in a barbed wire range fence to the lower end of

Maud Lake (7660 — 0.3), where the imposing 900′ barren headwall of rust-red rock comes suddenly to view. The trail skirts the north shore on meadow interspersed with clumps of trees. There are a number of sheltered campsites, but fireword is scarce. Maud Lake, while attractive, is gradually filling in and its transformation into meadow is everywhere evident. For ¼ mile beyond the lake we climb gently on rolling meadow, then abruptly the green ends and we begin to climb through shattered red rock.

The trail dips tantalizingly through a last patch of meadow, then turns north in a frontal attack on the wall, remorselessly climbing halfway up in a switchbacking trench before swinging northeast in a steep furrow traversing the wall. Near the top we pass an arrow painted on the rock, pointing upward, and beneath it the word "tired," expressing the predominant thought. Eventually the trail moves onto the windy, barren crest and 100 yards through the flat saddle comes to a sign marking

Rockbound Pass (8550 — 1.4). The sign, overlooking Lake Doris and Rockbound Valley, reads *Entering Desolation Valley Wild Area, no motorized vehicles permitted.* A few yards east in a clump of trees sheltered from the wind, a weatherbeaten sign reads *Rockbound Pass, elevation 8650,* an exaggeration of 100 feet. For an account of the eastern side of the Willow Flat Trail, leading past Lake Doris to the Rubicon River, see Region 5, Sec. 6.

SEC. 5
Barrett Lake Jeep Trail

	Elev.	Miles from pt. above	Total miles
Dark Lake Roadhead	6900	0.0	0.0
Beauty Lake Lateral	7020	0.3	0.3
Mortimer Flat: Rupley Jeep Trail	7100	1.7	2.0
Rockbound Stock Driveway	7660	1.9	3.9
Barrett Lake: Road's End	7620	1.1	5.0
Lawrence Lake Lateral	7760	0.2	5.2
Lake No. 5	7940	0.8	6.0
Red Peak & Lake No. 3 Trail Jctn.	8160	0.6	6.6

The Barrett Lake Jeep Trail is, unfortunately, a road, and as such it finds little favor with backpackers, who need at least the illusion of wilderness. Though portions are rough enough to require four-wheel drive and high clearance, the route is never faint and never anything but a road. Beyond Barrett Lake a section of trail through seldom-visited country links the road to the Red Peak Trail climbing up Bassi Fork of Silver Creek (see Region 4, Sec. 4).

The USFS has ordered new signs for this jeep trail, but the texts are inaccurate and contradictory, and neglect the junction most needing a sign. To provide for all contingencies I include the texts of both the signs existing in 1969 and the signs projected for 1970. From the three-way fork in the road at the foot of Wrights Lake we take the westernmost branch, which after ½ mile ends at a sign at the

Dark Lake Roadhead (6900 — 0.0). The existing directory-like sign reads *Red Peak Trail, Rupley Cow Camp, Tells Peak, U.C. Cow Camp, Barrett Lake, Lawrence Lake*, with no distances. The sign scheduled for erection is to read *Red Peak Trail, Barrett Lake 5 miles, Lake No. 5 6½ miles, Lake No. 3 7½ miles.* Parking for passenger cars at the roadhead is limited. Despite a row of cabins on the north shore, Dark Lake offers no facilities.

There is very little to be said for wilderness hiking on roads, but as roads go this one is modest and passes through pleasant if unexciting country. Unfortunately the obstacles to passenger cars (boulders, steepness, loose sand, etc.) are also obstacles to hikers. The road is blocked to two-wheel drive vehicles immediately behind the sign by a steep, boulder-studded slope covered with loose dirt. The road quickly levels off and we turn northeast to the

Beauty Lake Lateral (7020 — 0.3). A sign pointing down a modest trail to the east into the woods reads *Beauty Lake*. The jeep trail wanders north through level, unexceptional lodgepole forest for ¾ mile, turns sharply west to dip through the bed of an intermittent (early season) stream flowing from Fourth of July Flat, then immediately fords all-year Jones Fork of Silver Creek, which in early season can be a torrent. Beyond the ford we turn northwest, and climbing gradually, never far from the stream, we move to a California gate in a barbed-wire fence at the southern end of

Mortimer Flat (7100 — 1.7). A sign on the fence reads *Wrights Lake*, with an arrow pointing south. A little way up the meadow the unsigned Rupley Jeep Trail intersects from the northwest. At the upper end of the flat we pass through another California gate. A trail leads east down the north side of the fence 50 yards to a rock on which is painted "Trail," pointing across the fence to the road. Apparently, southbound travelers unfamiliar with the road have hesitated to enter the gate and have moved down the fence looking unsuccessfully for a way around it.

Above the flat the jeep trail for the first time begins to climb, arcing to the north, heading northeast across a bluff, then turning back to the north to climb gently but continuously through nondescript lodgepole forest. At the top of the slope the road levels off, and just before it starts down the far side we come to an easily missed, no longer signed junction with the

Rockbound Stock Driveway (7660 — 1.9). A cairn on the eastern side of the road and a faint groove in the loose dirt are all that mark the entrance to one of the highest, wildest trails in the region. Unfortunately, the USFS neglected to include this junction while ordering new signs for the Barrett Lake Jeep Trail. Fortunately the junction sits squarely in the center of the only ridge crossed by the road for a considerable distance, and consequently it can always be found.

We drop down the ridge to the north ¼ mile, into a meadow, to a naked signpost on the west side of the road and a sign reading *16E11* nailed to a tree on the east side. A faint but continuous and charming little trail (removed from the USFS trail inventory and no longer on the maps) leads east through a wooded meadow frequented by deer, and intersects the Rockbound Stock Driveway (see Sec. 6) at a signed junction with the lateral to the Willow Flat Trail (see map). The naked signpost once marked the continuation of this trail westward to Upper Bassi Ranch.

We leave the meadow and descend to the north through forest ½ mile to a tiny meadow valley extending to the west and stoutly fenced with barbed wire. At the southern margin of the meadow a sign reading *16E11* marks a well-worn (principally by cattle) trail west to Upper Bassi, which replaces the track shown on the topo map and marked by the naked signpost. The little meadow marks the University of California Cow Camp.

Beyond the meadow the road turns northeast and climbs over a wooded ridge, dropping a few yards north to ford the all-summer outlet stream from Barrett Lake. Part of this stretch can also be traversed on a loop of trail that offers no great advantage over the jeep trail. Beyond the stream (formidable in early season) the road winds northeast into a parklike hollow and ends on the northwest shore of

Barrett Lake (7620 — 1.1). In the late 1920's campers fond of the lake carried in a big galvanized box in which to store their

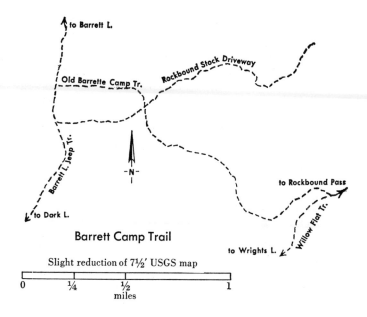

to Barrett L.

Old Barrette Camp Tr.

Rockbound Stock Driveway

Barrett T. Jeep Tr.

to Dark L.

-N-

to Rockbound Pass

to Wrights L.

Willow Flat Tr.

Barrett Camp Trail

Slight reduction of 7½′ USGS map

0   ¼   ½   1
miles

gear during the winter. Reportedly it is still there, well-hidden. The cascade from Lawrence Lake gurgles into the north edge of the hollow. Near a sign reading *Barret Lake* (one of three different spellings to be found on USFS signs) the road narrows into a trail that climbs a steep, shady slope to the northeast and soon reaches a signed junction with the

Lawrence Lake Lateral (7760 — 0.2). A sign on a tree reads *Red Peak Trail, Camp Lakes*, north, and *Lawrence Lake*, northeast. About 50 feet up the Lawrence Lake Trail we come to a sign reading *Lake No. 5*, north. In the triangle between the two forks are several connecting and sometimes confusing paths. The scheduled sign is to read *Lawrence Lake ¼ mile*, northeast, and *Lake No. 5, 1 mile, Lake No. 3, 2 miles*, north.

Taking the Lawrence Lake Lateral we continue northeast ¼ mile on springy, shaded trail to a series of large camps on the handsome lake's northwest shore. Across the gated rock dam there are additional fine campsites, and across the lake to the east can be seen two streams coming down a long, monolithic apron of bare granite from Lake No. 9 and Top Lake.

Returning to the junction, we climb north through a saddle into a little hollow with several snowmelt ponds and move through open, level forest to

Lake No. 5 (7940 — 0.8), a shallow, marshy, uninviting pond in a scrap of meadow. One sign reads *Lake No. 5,* another *Lake No. 3,* pointing north. Still nearly level the trail wanders northwest through well watered, grass-floored forest, then climbs onto a rocky ridge to a saddle where the trunk of a red fir sapling slotted to hold a (missing) sign marks the junction of a mysterious trail, shown on no maps, leading to the northwest toward a shallow, heart-shaped lake with a fringe of meadow.

The reason for the trail becomes obvious when we reach the east end of the little lake, for there lies the wreckage of a World War II B-26 Army bomber. A large red cross placed by the Civil Air Patrol on one wing is dated July 12, 1969. The trail ends at the plane, and there is no reasonable shortcut route north to the Red Peak Trail. Returning to the slotted red fir trunk, we turn northeast and, following ducks and a faint groove, climb steeply up a barren, rock-studded, sandy slope that levels off into a little meadow. On the edge of the meadow, marked by two faint grooves branching around a sawed-off-tree signpost, we come to the seldom-used junction of the

Red Peak and Lake No. 3 trails (8160 — 0.6). A scheduled sign should read *Lake No. 3, ½ mile,* northeast, *Bassi Fork 4 miles,* north, and *Barrett Lake 2 miles,* southwest. "Bassi Fork" refers to the beginning of the Red Peak Trail at the end of a dirt road on the Van Vleck Ranch (see Region 4, Sec. 1).

Sec. 6
Rockbound Stock Driveway

	Elev.	Miles from pt. above	Total miles
Barrett Lake Jeep Road	7660	0.0	0.0
Willow Flat Trail Lateral	7700	0.4	0.4
Rockbound Stock Driveway Pass	9180	2.6	3.0

The Rockbound Stock Driveway, also known as the Cattlemen's Ridge Trail, was built by stockmen in order to bring cattle over the Crystal Range to graze the lush meadows in Rockbound Valley. The grazing permit allows no more than 150 animals to visit the Wilderness Area between August 1 and September 20. As a matter of practice cattle are not brought over the pass before Labor Day, and prior to their journey the trail shows fewer droppings than the Willow Flat Trail.

Spring fishing on Pyramid Creek at the inlet to Desolation Lake.

A popular stop on the T-Y Trail for Wilderness-bound hikers from Echo.

Spring runoff pours from Avalanche Lake into Horsetail Falls.

Looking northwest from North Tells Peak Saddle to Loon Lake.

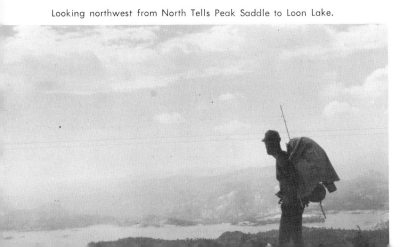

Looking west across Island Lake from the pass between Island and Clyde.

A weary 12-inch brook trout about to be lifted from Pyramid Creek.

A hiker and his dog move west toward Rockbound Stock Driveway Pass.

Ralston Peak reflected in the still waters of thawing Tamarack Lake.

When the Corn Lily blooms the blossoms often stand six feet high.

Looking south from Mosquito Pass across Lake Aloha to Ralston Peak.

Looking south from the T-Y Trail across Middle Velma to Dicks Peak.

Fording the stream draining Horseshoe, McConnell and 4-Q lakes.

Looking west across Half Moon to the saddle between Dicks and Jacks.

Looking west from Poopout Ridge across Lake of the Woods.

Hikers halfway up Flagpole Peak look out over Lower Echo Lake.

Corn Lily blooms in Haypress Meadows beneath Poopout Ridge.

Drowned lodgepoles rise from Lake Aloha under Pyramid Peak.

A comfortable camp on the western shore of Rubicon Reservoir.

Looking east across Tamarack and Upper and Lower Echo Lakes.

This corniced snowbank clings to the western face of Pyramid Peak.

Pits weathered in the smooth surface of glacially polished granite.

Looking east across the calm surface of Lake Zitella before a storm.

The floating slice of turf that gives Floating Island Lake its name.

An Eastern Brook trout from Ropi Lake.

Looking south from summit 9155 into seldom visited Cup Lake.

Looking from Cracked Crag across Lake Aloha to Mt. Price.

The vast majority of hikers crossing from the west into Rockbound Valley take the direct, maintained Willow Flat Trail, which has the added virtues of starting at a roadhead and ending at a river. By comparison, the Stock Driveway leads from nowhere to nowhere over an unmaintained, largely unsigned route that runs 600′ higher and several miles longer than its competitor. But the hiker with the time and inclination will find that it traverses some of the highest, wildest, most beautiful country in the Wilderness Area. The trail begins at an unsigned junction on the

Barrett Lake Jeep Road (7660 — 0.0) nearly 4 miles north of the roadhead at Dark Lake (see Sec. 5). Though apparently marked only by a rock cairn and a dim footpath, the junction fortunately occurs at the highest point in the only ridge to be crossed by the jeep trail for several miles. The faint but continuously discernible trail leads due east through light forest along nearly level ground, descending slightly to a signed junction with the

Willow Flat Trail Lateral (7700 — 0.4). There is also, surprisingly, a trail shown on none of the maps going north from the junction. Old, probably forgotten signs read *Rockbound Stock Driveway*, east, *Two Peaks Trail*, west, *Old Barrette Camp, Upper Bassi*, north, and *Willow Flat, Rockbound Pass, Wrights Lake*, south. The trail to the north (see Sec. 5) though virtually untraveled, offers a modest groove and plentiful ducks. It soon turns west and intersects the Jeep Road about ¼ mile north of the Stock Driveway trailhead.

At the junction we turn south on a little-used but well-marked (blazes and ducks) trail that leads down through open forest, swinging gradually to the east as it passes a pair of connected, marshy, shallow lakes. Despite the absence of fish there are several old camps. We climb a few feet out of the meadowed hollow through a saddle onto a barren, brush-dotted slope and then drop 100′ down a draw to the edge of Willow Flat. To conserve elevation for eastbound travelers, the trail swings around to the northeast and moves up the canyon ¼ mile before turning south to intersect the Willow Flat Trail in a pocket of lodgepole where signs read *16E08* and *16E11* (see Sec. 4).

Returning to the signed junction, we this time head east-north-east on the Stock Driveway through nearly level forest. As might be expected on a trail built for cattle drives, signs of travel cover a swath 5-15′ wide instead of being concentrated in a narrow groove, and where passage is constricted there are multiple tracks. As a consquence the trail seems somewhat dim until the traveler learns to recognize the signs that mark the route. About 200 yards east we pass a yellow section-corner marker, and shortly there after we begin to climb.

In the next ½ mile the steepening trail climbs 600' from nondescript rolling forest to the nose of a high, narrow, lightly wooded ridge. Without question this is the steepest, poorest section of the Driveway. The loose earth of the steep north slope has been badly torn up by cattle, and instead of a trail we climb a rocky swath where snow lies to midseason and dust lies deep thereafter. Once we reach the nose of the ridge, however, scars disappear in the rocky open country and we make our way northeast up the gently rising spine of the ridge through corn lilies and lupine and a fringe of timber.

At the top of the ridge the trail swings east around a little knob and we move into a lush meadowed hollow from which an all-year spring gushes. At the top of the hollow we climb out onto another ridge, where the land drops away steeply to the north and we look out across Top Lake, Lake No. 9 and Lawrence Lake to the long, wooded canyon containing Bassi Fork of Silver Creek and the Red Peak Trail. The ridge quickly widens into broad upland meadow filled with wildflowers and watered by springs.

Through fields of lupine we move upward on a gentle grade through vast, treeless, exhilarating high country, sometimes on slab but more often on boulder-strewn sage plain interspersed with pockets of lush, flowered meadow. As we go higher the slope flattens, and near the top there materializes a marvelous view to the south along the highest crest of the Crystal Range to Mt. Price and Pyramid Peak. By moving a few hundred yards to the south one can look 500' straight down into the rusty notch of Rockbound Pass. The trail levels off in a windy gap between low hills to unmarked

Rockbound Stock Driveway Pass (9180 — 2.6), second only to Dicks Pass in elevation. For the thoroughly charming route up from Rockbound Valley, see Region 5, Sec. 6.

Chapter 9—Region 4

Loon Lake

Loon Lake is unlike the other seven regions in that it is traveled more by lumbermen and ranchers than by vacationing hikers. The scarcity of hikers is due largely to the remoteness of the region from a well-traveled highway, the meager trail system and the tracts of private land that tend to block access. The quality of the Wilderness has been somewhat modified by jeep, construction and logging roads, and ranches, cattle and cutover timber.

This modification in quality, however, is found principally at lower elevations and outside the Wilderness proper. The high country — around Tells, McConnell, Silver and Red peaks — offers a rugged wilderness and solitude unexcelled in the Wilderness Area. In fact, the only country of comparable wildness lies just across the crest of the Crystal Range, high on the western slope of Rockbound Valley (Region 5).

The USFS, in a large-scale effort to open this area for recreation, has in the past few years paved the road to Loon Lake, built campgrounds, and erected countless new signs, all in the low country. Its efforts are now being extended into the Wilderness, where a new trail from Loon Lake was opened late in 1969 and new signs have been ordered for all the principal west-side trails. Projected sign text is provided below along with that of the few existing signs.

Region 4, which provides access to the northwest corner of the Wilderness Area, is bounded in the north by the Wentworth-Rubicon Springs Jeep Trail as far east as Big Sluice Box; in the east by the spine of the Crystal Range as far north as the junction of the North Tells Peak Trail and Rubicon Dam Road; in the west by Loon Lake and the Van Vleck Ranch; and in the south by the junction of the Red Peak and Lake No. 3 trails.

Access to the region is from Riverton on Highway 50 via the Loon Lake Road to Van Vleck Ranch, Loon Lake Campground and Wentworth Springs Campground; from Wrights Lake via the Barrett Lake Jeep Trail; and from Georgetown via the 42-mile road to Wentworth Springs. The Loon Lake Road begins just east of the bridge over the American River on Highway 50 at what used to be Riverton (before the river washed it away). Big illustrated billboards facing both east and west read *Riverton, Ice House Reservoir 12 miles, Union Valley Reservoir 17 miles, Loon Lake 27 miles*. Green highway signs read *Crystal Basin Recreation Area*.

Exactly 20 miles up the climbing, winding, newly paved, pleasant road just beyond a sign reading *Robb's Saddle, elevation 5745*, a sign at a dirt road descending toward the east reads *Van Vleck Ranch, Cheese Camp Rd*. Just 3.1 miles farther north the paved road forks. The branch to the east passes Schlein Ranger Station and climbs Chipmunk Bluff to reach, in 4.9 miles, a sign at another fork in the road reading *USFS Recreation Area, Loon Lake*.

Returning to the first fork in the paved road and taking the other branch, we continue north 2.6 miles to a point just south of the highway bridge over Gerle Creek, where there is a dirt road leading east, signed *Wentworth Springs 6 miles*. This is the longer, rougher road to the springs; travelers are advised to continue north across the bridge for another 3.3 miles to a dirt road heading east signed *Wentworth Springs 4 miles*. Helping to mark the junction is a sign just across the highway reading *Deer Creek Trail 14E11, Gerle Creek 3 miles. U.S. #50 25 miles*.

SEC. 1
Wentworth Springs Jeep Trail

	Elev.	Miles from pt. above	Total miles
Wentworth Springs	6013	0.0	0.0
Wentworth Springs Campground	6160	1.0	1.0
Big Sluice Box	6680	5.0	6.0

About ¼ mile east on the dirt road is an unsigned crossroad. We continue across it and pass several other junctions (always choosing the better-traveled track to the east) to Wentworth Springs, 4.1 miles from the highway. The not-quite-abandoned settlement in the lush, tree-shaded meadow still boasts a sagging,

116

boarded-up three-story hotel (dated 1873) that once bulged during the summer months with guests eager to sample the supposedly therapeutic mineral water that still flows from two springs.

There are a variety of other buildings of varying ages, some of them in danger of being washed away by Gerle Creek. The Upper American River Project of the Sacramento Municipal Utilty District, by means of a series of tunnels and dams, diverts most of the runoff from Rockbound Valley away from the Rubicon River and into Loon Lake, from which it is dumped into Gerle Creek, turning that once-quiet little stream into a deep, swift river. Conventional passenger cars are advised to go no farther, so the jeep trail begins at

Wentworth Springs (6013 — 0.0). Jeeps, pickups and other sturdy two-wheel-drive vehicles will find a passable road leading east up the meadow. As the road begins to climb we pass an easily-missed spring in rusty rock about 50 yards north of the road. At the top of the rocky slope we pass the signed entrance to a trail to Loon Lake and level off near Gerle Creek to approach

Wentworth Springs Campground (6160 — 1.0), which offers tables, stoves, outhouses, garbage cans, etc. At the campground's eastern end the road forks at a sign. The southern branch goes a mile up Gerle Creek to the Loon Lake Dam. The eastern branch is the beginning of the jeep trail that passes Buck Island Reservoir and Rubicon Springs on the way to Chambers Lodge on Highway 89 at Lake Tahoe (see Region 5). The sign reads *Four wheel drive only. Ellis Creek Trail, Spider Lake, Rubicon Springs,* east.

There is a difficult spot just behind the sign on the eastern branch, but vehicles able to pass it can easily drive another ½ mile through level forest before the road starts up a rocky ravine and becomes passable only to four-wheel-drive vehicles. This is borne out a few yards up the slope by the remains of a World War II Army ambulance beside the road. The rocky jeep trail turns steeply north up a brush slope and splits into two tracks. Hikers will pick their way north on the rough shorter track; jeeps will more likely switchback to the southwest and take the loop around the hill.

After the two tracks rejoin the road turns east, climbing more gently, and after ¼ mile it levels off and turns north to a ford of Ellis Creek. For a mile the road runs level across moderately sloping forest beneath Devil's Peak; then it dips to the south to traverse a rocky, open slope to Little Sluice Box, just north of Spider Lake. Again the road forks. The southeastern branch up the narrow, rough, sluicelike canyon offers the most direct route for hikers; the northeastern loop provides passage for jeeps.

Where the tracks rejoin, a road branches south to Spider Lake. The main road circles above aptly named Mud Lake and gradually turns to the south, following the ridge and climbing slightly. We ford the outlet stream from Spider and follow a good road, with a view southeast to Buck Island and Rockbound lakes, along the ridge to another fork in the road (this one faint) just north of

Big Sluice Box (6680 — 5.0). The fork is at the point that the well-marked road turns abruptly east down the slope onto open granite slab. Close inspection reveals that an old road once continued south 100 yards through an old camp (iron stove and bed springs) to a little hollow where several ducks mark the beginning of the North Tells Peak Trail (see Region 5, Secs. 1 and 2) at the top of the narrowing, no-longer-passable canyon that is Big Sluice Box. A scheduled sign is to read *Buck Island Reservoir*, east, and *Tells Peak Trail*, south. At the beginning of the trail or thereabouts a second sign will read *Lake Winifred 1 mile, Tells Peak 5½ miles, Forni Lake 6½ miles*, southwest.

SEC. 2

Loon Lake Trail

	Elev.	Miles from pt. above	Total miles
Trailhead: Loon Lake Campground	6420	0.0	0.0
Boy Scout Camp	6420	2.0	2.0
Loon Lake Tunnel, Road	6420	1.5	3.5
Pleasant Campground Lateral	6500	0.5	4.0
Spider Lake Lateral	6760	0.8	4.8
North Tells Peak Trail	6700	1.1	5.9

The most recent USFS effort to develop the area north of Highway 50 for recreation is the construction of the Loon Lake Trail to the Wilderness Area, opened September 1969. While most trails into Rockbound Valley labor over some rocky pass, this one slips around the north end of the Crystal Range at a maximum elevation of scarcely more than 6800′. Only the trails leaving the difficult-of-access Wentworth-Rubicon Springs Jeep Trail in the mouth of the valley are lower.

Because it offers easy, nearly level access to the Wilderness from a paved road, the Loon Lake Trail seems destined to become popular and heavily used. Unfortunately, the USFS, in a weak moment, acceded to pressure and opened the trail from the outset to two-wheel-vehicle travel on the specious reasoning that there

118

was little to lose in the way of wilderness experience since part of the trail followed an abandoned road.

More logical reasoning suggests that wilderness ought to be kept as wild as possible, and since the backpacker is obliged to follow a road, greater — not lesser — pains should be taken to spare him the added indignity of having to dodge motorcycles. The Pacific Crest Trail from the Jeep Trail south to its intersection with the Loon Lake Trail also permits two-wheeled vehicles, so that motorcycles from two directions are allowed to drive right up to the northwest corner of the Wilderness boundary!

This is without precedent and clearly an unnecessary violation of the "No sight or sound . . ." prerequisite for wilderness. To protect wilderness quality it would seem the USFS has the obligation to prohibit all vehicles on trails destined for heavy traffic of hikers, horses and pack animals. The USFS has agreed to reconsider the appropriateness of motorcycles on a trail to the wilderness. Hikers should make sure their views are known.

In the late 1950's a crushed-granite road was built from the roadhead at the south end of Loon Lake up the southwest shore and over the hill past Spider Lake to Rockbound Valley and Buck Island Dam. It then turns south into the Wilderness (under power withdrawal rights established in 1875) to end at the dam on newly built Rubicon Reservoir. In the early 1960's a new dam on Loon raised the surface elevation 58' to 6410', flooding the portion of the road along the shore but leaving the remainder intact.

The walk to the Wilderness boundary can be reduced from 6½ trail miles to 3 by launching an outboard motorboat at the USFS roadside facility and cruising to the new boat camp (Pleasant Campground) at the north end of the reservoir. Other facilities at Loon include a picnic ground, floating dock, bathrooms, a rocky beach, dressing rooms and a large new campground. Unfortunately, fees, though modest, are charged for nearly everything, even parking.

From Highway 50 a paved road (see introduction to this region) climbs 28.0 miles to a fork just below the lake, where a sign reads *USFS Recreation Area, Loon Lake*. The northern (left) branch goes about 2 miles up the northwest shore, turns to gravel, and ends at the north end of the dam. The eastern (right) branch goes ½ mile through the trees before turning north past campground units to a large parking area by the lake above the launching ramp, floating dock and alleged beach. A road forks to the east several hundred yards, then turns northeast to another parking area serving the dressing rooms, bath-

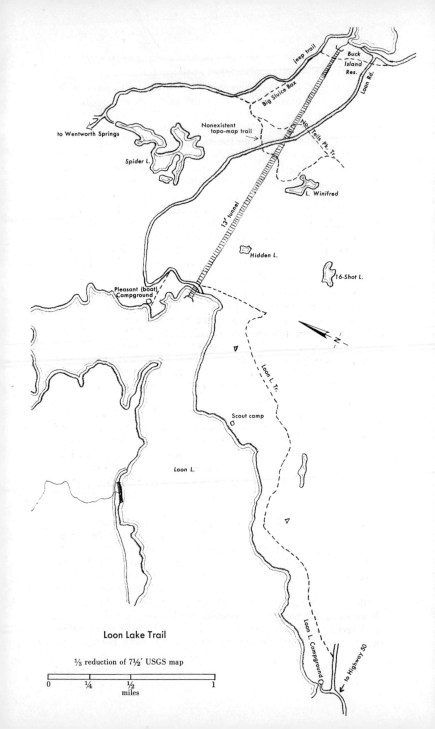

to Wentworth Springs

Spider L.

Jeep trail

Big Sluice Box

Buck Island Res.

Loon Rd.

Nonexistent topo-map trail

No. Tells Pk. Tr.

L. Winifred

13' tunnel

Hidden L.

16-Shot L.

Pleasant (boat) Campground

N

Loon L. Tr.

Scout camp

Loon L.

Loon L. Campground

to Highway 50

Loon Lake Trail

⅓ reduction of 7½' USGS map

0   ¼   ½   1
miles

rooms, picnic area and more campground. In the turn, halfway between signs reading *Camping Units 1-12 . . .* and *Picnic Units, swimming beach,* an old road blocked by a cable departs to the east. This is the

Loon Lake Trailhead (6420 — 0.0). A temporary sign in 1969 read *Trail to Buck Island Lake, Rockbound Lake, Rubicon Reservoir, Spider Lake. Not for 4-wheel vehicles.* A scheduled sign should read *Loon Lake Trail, Scout Camp 2 miles, Pleasant Campground 4 miles, Buck Island Reservoir 6 miles.* Hikers relying on the topo map should be reminded that the surface of Loon Lake has risen (at high water) some 58'. The 6400' contour line quite accurately represents the new shoreline.

The route winds gently uphill through trees on the old road for several hundred yards to a sign reading *Trail to Boy Scout Lodge, Buck Island Lake, Spider Lake, Rockbound Lake, Rubicon Reservoir,* pointing north down the slope. We leave the road and descend northeast on a big, high-standard trail requiring neither ducks nor blazes through dusty forest and a scattering of bucked deadfalls. When the lake again becomes visible through the trees, it is evident that the trail has taken us on a climbing loop to the southeast in order to detour well behind the campground on the south shore.

We move northeast through rolling, wooded country well back from and often out of sight of the lake, climbing occasionally through ravines and over low bluffs. We pass a sandy knoll where the brush has burned and the fallen trees have been turned pink by the borate dropped to put out the fire. We pass under a cliff to the east on which sits a water tank and come to the

Scout Lodge Lateral (6420 — 2.0) marked only (in 1969) by the black plastic waterline from the tank, emerging from beneath the trail, and signs of foot travel. A path follows the waterline west ¼ mile into Loon Lake Scout Camp, dominated by a large lodge completed in 1965. In 1969, the first year of full operation, 700 boys used the camp. At the north end of the lake the trail makes its greatest climb through a saddle (under summit 6636) and we look down to the northeast corner of the lake, where the construction road can clearly be seen emerging from the water.

Just beyond it at low water we see the black hole in the rock that is the mouth of the 1½ mile long, 13' diameter tunnel from Buck Island Reservoir to the east. The trail starts down toward the road and tunnel, then, reaching a small ravine, detours ¼ mile upstream to maintain elevation, and descends the east bank to finally intersect the

Construction Road (6420 — 1.5). The tunnel mouth is reached by dropping down the road and turning north up the rocky beach. Spelunkers contemplating using the tunnel as a shady shortcut to Buck Island should not venture inside unless a circle of light at the far end reveals that the water level is down in Buck Island. Five tunnel walkers in 1968 were engulfed by a suddenly released head of water from Buck Island and washed all the way into Loon. From the junction with the trail the crushed-rock road climbs north under a steep slope to the east, winding through jumbled country, and just beyond a sharp, dipping turn to the west we come to an unmarked junction with the

Pleasant Campground Lateral (6500 — 0.5). A scheduled sign should read *Buck Island Reservoir 2 miles*, pointing west up the road, and *Pleasant Campground ½ mile*, pointing also west down the trail. The lateral trail winds its way down a sandy slope through clumps of trees and brush for ½ mile to the new boat camp in a narrow bay in what once was Pleasant Lake. A sign at high water reads *Camp Units 6-10*. Beneath it, in the water, a small raft joined to the shore by a plank serves as a floating dock.

At low water the bay is ringed with rocky islands and could be quite difficult to find, especially for the first time, by boatmen from the campground at the roadhead. Facilities at uncrowded Pleasant Campground include secluded camps in the light timber with grilled concrete fireplaces and picnic tables, garbage cans and an elegant white-interiored outhouse.

Returning to the lateral junction we climb steeply west on the road for several hundred yards, then abruptly turn to the east and follow a little ridge on bare rock up onto a gradually leveling plateau. In the second dip in the road after reaching the plateau, several ducks on the north shoulder mark the beginning of the

Spider Lake Lateral (6760 — 0.8). The route is not well marked but the traveler should have no difficulty finding his way ¼ mile down the lightly wooded, gentle slope to the clearly visible lake below. The road continues east across sandy, rolling open country, and about ¼ mile beyond the Spider lateral we find ourselves in a good position to begin the cross-country climb ½ mile southwest into the little basin between two prominent peaks to Hidden Lake. The road reaches its highest point before descending to the east past a pond screened by trees and a huge snag felled to block the road. At the foot of steep switchbacks it passes through a thickly wooded hollow and under a tiny knob which marks the ducked crossing of the

North Tells Peak Trail (6700 — 1.1). The topo map, which shows the trail looping to the west to cross the road on the top of the ridge on the way to Lake Winifred, is mistaken. No such trail exists, though the route is easy enough.

Sec. 3
Tells Peak-Highland Trail

	Elev.	Miles from pt. above	Total miles
Van Vleck Gate	6200	0.0	0.0
Van Vleck Ranch Road	6600	1.6	1.6
Red Peak Road	6600	1.0	2.6
Highland Trail	6700	0.2	2.8
Landing Strip	6693	1.2	4.0
Logging Road	7000	0.4	4.4
Tells Peak Trail	7200	0.3	4.7
Highland Trail	7250	0.8	5.5
Forni Lake	7950	1.0	6.5
South Tells Peak Pass	8550	1.2	7.7
Tells Peak (9135)	8872	0.5	8.2

Spread along the northwestern boundary of the Wilderness Area are half a dozen cattle ranches ranging some 2000 head of cattle. Their grazing rights extend on public land up the western slope of the Crystal Range into the Wilderness, and in some instances spill over the Cattlemen's Ridge Trail into Rockbound Valley. The Van Vleck Ranch, consisting of some 3400 acres, is the northernmost of the six ranches, and two important trails into the Wilderness from western roadheads (Tells Peak-Highland Trail and Red Peak Trail) either originate on or pass over Van Vleck property.

Unfortunately the Van Vlecks (father and son), for sufficiently good reasons based on experience, do not welcome the public unless it is afoot or on horseback, which means cars are not welcome beyond the Van Vleck gate. If the Van Vlecks' wishes were heeded, a great hardship would be worked upon the backpacker, who would be obliged to walk nearly 5 miles of dusty, dreary logging-ranch road to the Tells Peak-Highland trailhead and 3½ miles to the Red Peak trailhead. But the Van Vlecks have placed their gate more than a mile outside their lands and therefore cannot legally lock the public out there.

As a matter of practice the gate usually is not closed (except on weekends during deer season) and in 1969 neither it nor the land beyond it was posted against trespass. Travelers deciding

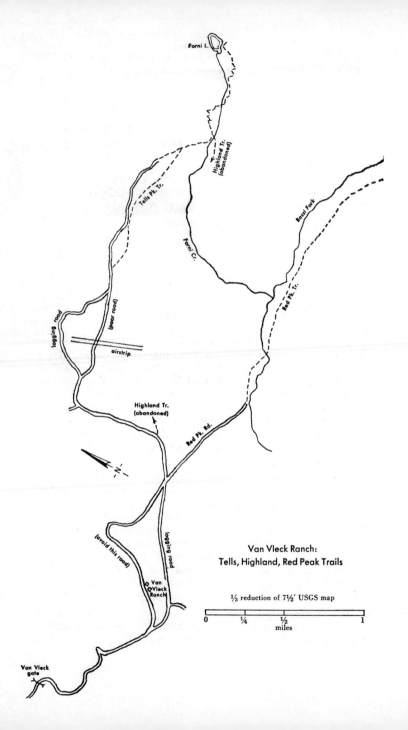

Forni L.

Highland Tr.
(abandoned)

Tells Pk. Tr.

Bassi Fork

Forni Cr.

Red Pk. Tr.

logging road

(poor road)

airstrip

Highland Tr.
(abandoned)

Red Pk. Rd.

N

(avoid this road)

logging road

Van
Vleck
Ranch

Van Vleck Ranch:
Tells, Highland, Red Peak Trails

⅓ reduction of 7½′ USGS map

Van Vleck
gate

0   ¼   ½   1
miles

to drive in should realize that at some point they must cross private land (see map) although very little need be crossed to reach the Red Peak Trail. Visitors should, out of courtesy, avoid the fenced farm buildings in the middle of the meadow and otherwise behave like guests; there are no other gates to cross. The USFS has tentative plans to run a public road around Van Vleck land to the trailheads, but that may take 2-3 years.

The usefulness of the 7½′ topo map is somewhat reduced on the Van Vleck Ranch by the maze of ranch and logging roads which do not appear on it, and by the destruction, by loggers and cattle, of the trails that are shown. The lower reaches of the trails shown are neither interesting nor wild; the Tells Peak Trail from the Van Vleck landing strip to the junction with the Highland Trail below Forni Lake does not appear on the topo map at all; and the upper ends of both trails (Tells Peak and Lake No. 3) can be reached from other trails.

The Van Vleck Ranch Road begins 20.0 miles north of Highway 50 on the Loon Lake Road at a sign reading *Van Vleck Ranch, Cheese Camp Rd.* on the road's east shoulder. Just south of the road junction a sign reads *Robbs Saddle, elevation 5745 feet*. The largely one-way dirt road to the east is passble to passenger cars but drivers should watch carefully for logging trucks from both directions. After 3.2 miles we come to the

Van Vleck Gate (6200 — 0.0) in a drift fence which extends only 100 yards to either side. In 1969 it was neither signed nor posted. There is parking room for perhaps three cars, no place to camp and no water. Beyond the gate the road winds uphill onto a low ridge from which the mountains (Tells, McConnell, Silver and Red peaks, north to south) first come into view. The white Van Vleck Ranch buildings can also be seen in a meadow below to the east. Branching off toward them is the

Van Vleck Ranch Road (6600 — 1.6) which should be avoided, even by hikers and horsemen. The main road (which from this point onward we will call the "logging road") continues south past the junction, then gradually swings to the east around the bottom of the meadow. We pass an unsigned road branching south (to Upper Bassi Ranch), ford Tells Creek (a problem for passenger cars in early season) and continue northeast to a junction with the

Red Peak Road (6600 — 1.0) which leads southeast a mile to the Red Peak trailhead. Just north of the junction, about 20 yards up an old road leading to the ranch, is a somewhat hidden USFS sign reading *Red Peak Trail, Bassi Fork 2 miles, U.C. Cow Camp 9 miles*. Returning to the logging road we again cross Tells

Creek (this time on a culvert) at the corner of a little meadow and swing to the north up a steep hill to the signed entrance to the

Highland Trail (6700 — 0.2). The sign on the east side of the road reads *Highland Trail, Tells Peak, Forni Lake, Highland Lake, Rockbound Valley,* east; there are no distances. A good groove takes off to the east, but it dwindles to nothing long before intersecting the new Tells Peak Trail 2½ miles later. The Tells Peak Trail was built to replace the Highland Trail and the latter has been largely abandoned. Now that a good logging road leads nearly to the upper junction of the two trails, the largely overgrown and forgotten Highland Trail serves little purpose.

The road continues north uphill ¾ mile into a little meadow to a junction shown on the topo map as bench mark 6812. We turn abruptly east into the trees and when the road branches again (the logging road turns north), we continue east through the trees to the mile-long Van Vleck private

Landing Strip (6933 — 1.2). We cross the rocky raised bed just north of the red windsock and immediately come to old USFS signs reading *15E05* and *Shadow Lake,* pointing east up a faint road across the meadow through the trees. The road emerges through badly battered, freshly logged forest to rejoin the

Logging Road (7000 — 0.4) which, since we left it at the last fork, has looped around the north end of the landing strip and now heads east-northeast up a gently rising slope of light forest. From here on the Tells Peak Trail is virtually obliterated by recent heavy logging and the passage of deer and cattle. Though parts of it can be found, the hiker is better off keeping to the dusty logging road, known on the ranch as the Shadow Lake Road (a jeep trail shortly branches to the northeast and climbs toward that lake). We trudge uphill through the dust into a sandy meadow and at the meadow's eastern edge we return to the trail, leaving the road (which ends within a hundred yards) for the last time at what serves as the

Tells Peak Trailhead (7200 — 0.3). Visible from the road a few yards to the south, on the top of a reddish boulder sticking out of the meadow, are two large ducks which mark the passing trail. To the west it crosses butchered forest and meadow, marked by widely spaced but freshly blazed trees, on the way down to the landing strip. To the east a nearly continuous groove marked by fresh blazes and strips of scarlet plastic (the latter marking the boundary between ranch and Forest Service land for the logging crews) moves east along the fringe of the destruction, passes an old salt lick and enters a meadow to leave ranch land, roads and logged-over forest behind.

The meadow narrows and after passing a yellow section marker we cross a small creek. The trail climbs over a low wooded ridge and moves into denser forest, where we hear the sound of running water (from Forni Creek hidden under willows) as we come to a second yellow section marker, which serves to mark the return of the

Highland Trail (7250 — 0.8). This is the end of the new Tells Peak Trail and from this point eastward the fresh blazes we have been following are replaced by the old blazes of the Highland Trail. Exploring the Highland Trail to the west we find a faint, overgrown, unmaintained track, marked by old blazes, disappearing into a maze of game trails in less than 100 yards. We continue east a few yards before switchbacking steeply on heavily used dusty trail up a 300' high brush slope.

The trail dips into a little hollow, crosses all-year Forni Creek (the first remotely drinkable water we have passed) and climbs another 350' steeply (the ranch buildings in the meadow are now plainly visible to the west) up a brushy, dusty slope to

Forni Lake (7950 — 1.0), a very shallow but clear lake offering limited camping. The well-ducked, heavily traveled groove ends at the outlet and only a fishermen's trail leads around the shoreline. The route shown on the topo map climbing steeply east from the lake unfortunately passes across a sodden meadow that is either covered with snow or streaming with water until after midseason. Consequently the path is difficult to find.

Fortunately, the general route is fairly obvious and the objective (Tells Peak) close at hand. We move up out of the shaded, snowy basin onto dry open slopes, where the trail again becomes well-defined. The track switchbacks through woodland up a broad sandy canyon to a ducked junction 100' west of and below

South Tells Peak Pass (8550 — 1.2). A ducked route continues east through the pass and ends. The USFS maps show 0.8 mile of trail joining the pass with the trail that ends at Highland Lake, but there is no such trail, and the 750' drop is difficult and steep, and hazardous for laden backpackers, especially in early season, when the shaded boulders and cliffs are still covered with ice and snow.

A ducked, steep trail switchbacks northward below the ridgeline on loose sand, coming up onto the flat and surprisingly wooded summit ridge which runs northwest to the top of

Tells Peak (8872 — 0.5). A sign reads *Tells Peak, elevation 9125*, which unaccountably is 253 feet higher than the topo map's more reliable estimate. A trail runs north from the summit (North Tells Peak Trail, see Region 5, Sec. 2) crossing the new Loon

Lake Trail on the way to the Wentworth-Rubicon Springs Jeep Trail at Big Sluice Box.

SEC. 4

Red Peak Trail

	Elev.	**Miles from pt. above**	**miles Total**
Red Peak Road	6600	0.0	0.0
Red Peak Trailhead	6600	1.0	1.0
Lake No. 3-Barrett Lake Trail Jctn.	8140	4.0	5.0
Lake No. 3	8220	0.3	5.3

From Highway 50 the Loon Lake Road goes 20.0 miles north to the Van Vleck Ranch road, on which we drive 3.2 miles to the Van Vleck Ranch gate. See the introduction to Sec. 3 for the considerations involved in driving the remaining 2.6 miles (partly across private land) to the Red Peak Road, where a somewhat hidden sign on an old road 20 yards north of the junction incorrectly reads *Red Peak Trail, Bassi Fork 2 miles, U.C. Cow Camp 9 miles.* (The distances are closer to 1.0 and 7.3 miles.)

Curiously enough a trail begins at the junction and runs parallel to and north of the Red Peak Road for 100 yards to a bench mark and copiously marked witness trees, after which it grows dim and turns south to the road with which it merges. Reopened in 1968 after many years of neglect the road (passable to passenger cars) climbs east-southeast through a shallow saddle, passes through a usually open California gate and drops to Bassi Fork of Silver Creek to end at the

Red Peak Trailhead (6600 — 1.0). A scheduled sign should read *Lake No. 3, 4 miles, Barrett Lake 6 miles, Dark Lake 11 miles.* The trail, reworked in 1968 for the first time ever, heads east along the north bank of pretty, all-year Bassi Fork through meadow and trees. The dim, little-traveled track is often obscured by the trampling of cattle. After nearly ½ mile we pass a yellow section-corner marker and make a dry (except in early season) crossing of the creek in a narrow channel through slab granite at a poorly marked ford.

For the next several miles the trail leads up a broad, nearly level meadowed valley under a light predominantly lodgepole forest. The groove is often vague although fresh blazes and bucked deadfalls help to mark the way, and the route is never far from the creek. Cattle are plentiful at times and deer outnumber hikers. There are ample potential campsites but little evidence of human use.

128

At the end of the valley we move away from the stream to climb up a shallow canyon beside a dry (except in early season) creek-bed parallel to Bassi Fork. After a 500′ climb we emerge into a smaller wooded valley and return to Bassi Fork. We make an easy crossing at the ford and leave the creek to ascend a small canyon that parallels it, coming out onto a bare granite slope and returning to the creek at the foot of a steep, narrow canyon. We move up Bassi Fork along its north bank on a poorly marked track across monolithic granite to a last crossing, after which we circle around the base of a cliff-rimmed outcropping and make our way up a draw into a flat meadow south of the stream. The trail follows ducks and a dim groove southeast through the meadow to the

Barrett Lake—Lake No. 3 Trail Jctn. (8140 — 4.0) which is marked by a sawn-off tree trunk that once held a sign. A dim track moves up out of the meadow and onto rock southwest toward Barrett Lake (see Region 3, Sec. 5) and an equally dim path climbs northeast across lush meadow toward 9307′ Red Peak. The trail gradually arcs around to the north, enters timber, crosses the creek and moves up to the west shore of

Lake No. 3 (8220 — 0.3). This is one of the remotest, least visited lakes in the Wilderness Area, though it offers good camping. There is a cross-country route to the northeast through a shallow saddle between Red and Silver peaks to Leland Lakes.

Rockbound Valley

By far the largest of the regions into which the Wilderness is divided, Rockbound Valley encompasses all of the Rubicon River watershed from the headwaters beneath Mosquito Pass in the south, to the Miller Lake Jeep Trail in the north. It is bounded on the west by the crest of the Crystal Range, and on the east by an undistinguished ridge running south through Lost Corner and Middle mountains to Dicks and Jacks peaks.

As might be expected, this region offers more than the usual diversity: the last remaining stretch of the Rubicon as a wild river, a dozen high lakes on the western side of the valley, and in the northwest probably the most remote, least traveled section of the Wilderness Area. There are also, unfortunately, two reservoirs complete with dams, gauging stations, tunnels and channels, and an abandoned construction road joining them.

Water storage and development rights in this area pre-date its designation as a Primitive Area, and consequently the Sacramento Municipal Utility District was able, in 1957, to build a 15-foot-wide, crushed-granite construction road from the highway at Loon Lake around the northern end of the Crystal Range, to Buck Island Reservoir and Rockbound Lake, and south to Onion Flat. Dams were built in the early 1960's which flooded Onion Flat to create 146-acre Rubicon Reservoir and raised the levels of Buck Island and Loon lakes, converting them into reservoirs.

Once a world-renowned trout stream, rising beneath Mosquito Pass, the Rubicon now runs wild for less than 9 miles before emptying into Rubicon Reservoir. Its waters then flow northwest through a tunnel blasted through granite, and empty via a bull-dozed channel into Rockbound Lake. From Rockbound they cascade down to Buck Island, then drain west down a bulldozed channel and into a 1½ mile tunnel under the Crystal Range to Loon Lake, west of the Wilderness.

As a result of all this water-storage development, much of the original Rockbound Trail has been flooded, and most of the indestructible construction road remains. To restore its transportation system, the USFS has patched together a network of new scooter trails, construction roads, old trails and vaguely ducked cross-country routes — all of which it represents on its maps as trail. From the Miller Lake Jeep Trail to the upper end of Rubicon Reservoir the country, though in places quite handsome, has ceased to be wilderness, and the laden backpacker may find it more than irksome to walk where cement trucks so recently rumbled.

Because of the considerable alteration to the country, the usually reliable topo map is of limited use. Though the newest USFS maps fail to distinguish between trails, roads and paths, they do represent the transportation system with reasonable accuracy, and show the expanded dimensions of the three reservoirs.

Although the low elevations in the lower reaches of Rockbound Valley invite early-season travel, visitors are warned that the two trail crossings of the wild Rubicon between Camper Flat and Rubicon Reservoir are dangerous or impossible, due to heavy run-off, before the 4th of July following a light winter, or the first of August following a winter of heavy snows. A glance at the map suggests that this difficulty can be overcome by keeping to the river's west bank for 2 miles of cross-country travel between the two crossings. But in early season the booming cascade coming down the cliff from 4-Q, Horseshoe, McConnell and Leland Lakes from the west presents an almost equally formidable obstacle, forcing the cross-country traveler to ford or retreat.

Access to the Rockbound Valley region tends to be difficult. From the west and the south the passes are high, and the climb from the east is considerable. In the north, passenger cars from Lake Tahoe will get little farther than Miller Lake, necessitating a 6 mile hike south to the Wilderness boundary at Buck Island Reservoir. Winch-equipped, four-wheel-drive jeeps can navigate the trans-Sierra Miller Lake Jeep Trail from Miller Lake, via Buck Island, to Wentworth Springs in the west. The new Loon Lake Trail (Region 4, Sec. 2) offers by far the easiest access to the North Tells Peak and Pacific Crest trails (Secs. 2 and 3).

Sec. 1
Miller Lake Jeep Trail to Big Sluice Box

	Elev.	Miles from pt. above	Total miles
Richardson Lake Rd. Jctn.	7150	0.0	0.0
Private road branching south	7050	1.4	1.4
Miller Creek Ford	6020	2.0	3.4
Rubicon Soda Springs	6063	1.3	4.7
Old Rockbound Trail	6380	1.4	6.1
Buck Island Hill Trail Jctn.	6520	0.5	6.6
New Rockbound Trail Jctn.	6420	0.6	7.2
Big Sluice Box (jctn. North Tells Peak Trail)	6680	0.7	7.9

Between Homewood and Tahoma on state Highway 89, a paved road leads southwest from Lake Tahoe. A street sign on the north corner reads *Rubicon Rd.* On a tree at the south corner, beneath a large sign advertising *McKinney Estates*, a small sign reads *Miller Lake Jeep Rd.* About ¼ mile west through a sub-division a sign reads *Miller Lake 5 miles, Richardson Lake 7 miles, Rubicon Springs 11 miles.* Six tenths of a mile farther the pavement ends. A paved road turning south is inconspicuously signed *This is NOT the way to Miller Lake.* We enter an unsigned, narrow, rocky road that climbs gradually up McKinney Creek. This is the easternmost stretch of the old Indian Trail between Lake Bigler (Tahoe) and Georgetown.

The road occasionally branches and most junctions are signed, but at those that are not, it is safe to choose the better-traveled track. The road passes north of McKinney, Lily and Miller lakes, all visible and full of lilies. Between Lily and Miller we cross an almost imperceptible divide, and the Miller Lake outlet flows west toward the Rubicon. Just beyond Miller an unsigned but conspicuous road turns south past a cow camp on the way to Richardson Lake. Beyond this turnoff the road crosses boggy Miller Meadows, and since most passenger-car drivers will wisely balk at the first mudhole, it is at this junction that we begin the trail.

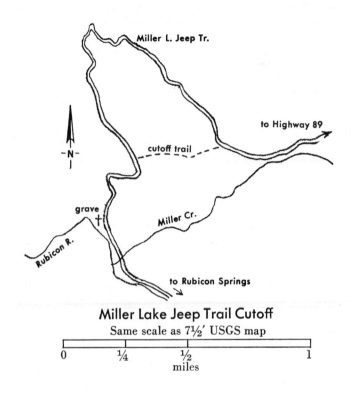

Miller Lake Jeep Trail Cutoff

Same scale as 7½' USGS map

0   ¼   ½   1

miles

Richardson Lake Road Jctn. (7150—0.0). The road, with some detours, wanders from one mudhole to the next in the wooded meadow north of Miller Creek, fords North Miller Creek and climbs over a little knoll to

Private road branching south (7050 — 1.4). Just downhill to the west is a little grassy flat where most two-wheel-drive jeeps park. Beyond, the road drops down a wash of dusty boulders, then levels off and starts down a sidehill close above Miller Creek. About ¼ mile farther, the road starts uphill to the north, but a small black-on-pink sign reading *cutoff* points to a trail leading downhill west through the trees (see map).

This ½-mile shortcut trail, which must once have been the road into Rubicon Canyon, cuts 1½ miles off the jeep road for the hiker. It comes out of the woods above cascading Miller Creek Falls onto an open, steep slope with a fine view south, including the aluminum roof of the streamflow measuring station at Rubicon Springs and the summits of Tells, McConnell, Silver and Red peaks.

The trail now drops steeply west just under the crags circled by the modern jeep road, returning to the road at another black-on-pink *cutoff* sign. The rusting remains of a heavy car, probably built in the 1920's, lie just below the road, and the rear axle and block of another lie a few switchbacks lower. At the foot of the grade (a drop of about 1100' from Miller Lake) just inside the woods, we come to the grave of *S.S. Mainwaring, 1909-1965*. About ¼ mile south through the trees we come to

Miller Creek Ford (6020 — 2.0), which can be crossed dryly, except in very early season. The road-trail winds through timber across the valley floor, passing beneath a new, locked trolley and car with several calibrated poles for measuring water depth which, sitting well above and out of sight of the river, strongly suggest the possibility that the dam-builders mean to flood this canyon.

The road climbs out of the forest, picking its way among old rock slides through the valley bottom, and eventually drops down into a little parklike flat by the river, once famed throughout the west as

Rubicon Soda Springs (6063 — 1.3). The two springs, about 100 yards apart and each issuing a trickle of cold, carbonated, strongly mineralized water, were probably known by Indians using the trans-Sierra trail through this canyon several centuries ago. The flat was not settled by whites until 1867, but by 1880 bottled water was being exported by pack animals to the outside world to improve appetites and cure virtually all human ills. By 1890 the four-horse Rubicon Flyer was hauling hundreds of health-seekers down an improbable trail-road from Tahoe to sleep four to a room in the three-story, organ-equipped 16-room hotel.

The Springs had their heyday around the turn of the century, and a post office was installed in 1901. In 1912 a Dodge four-door sedan was making daily trips to Tahoe for visitors, and by 1919 Pierce-Arrows were making the run. In the 1920's health spas began to lose their vogue and the Springs, after struggling on a few years, closed down. The decaying resort was sold to a power company in 1930 and never reopened. The heavy winter of 1953-54 flattened the hotel, and in recent years the flat has served as a campsite for hiking groups and the Jeepers Jamboree.

Today there is a half-fallen log cabin, the remains of the hotel, a dozen new plywood outhouses, old cement slabs, barbecue pits and a new Geological Survey streamflow measuring station with calibrated depth gauges that rise above the still-bubbling soda springs. The once beautiful Rubicon is now a turbid slough, and the depth gauges suggest that springs and river might be buried under some new water impoundment.

The road above the springs swings southeast away from the river (the branch south along the river soon deadends) and winds through a lush, level forest. Indians must once have found good hunting in these woods; I found a large obsidian spearpoint in the trail, unearthed by jeeps. About ½ mile above Rubicon Springs, after passing the wreck of another ancient car, the trail returns to the sluggish river and crosses to the west bank on a steel I-beam, A-frame bridge. Scheduled signs will reveal that we are here passing from Tahoe to Eldorado National Forest. Immediately we begin to climb steeply through the forest on an incline of dusty, oil-streaked boulders. After a long, straight climb the road abruptly makes a deeply rutted hairpin turn. At the southernmost point of the turn, some jeeper in an attempt at humor has nailed to a tree a purloined yellow highway sign which reads *Watch for Rocks*. Beneath this sign, overgrown with brush and otherwise unmarked, is the northern end of the

Old Rockbound Trail (6380 — 1.4). This virtually unused trail, partly inundated by the expansion of Buck Island Reservoir and blocked by the flooding of Onion Flat to form Rubicon Reservoir, is nevertheless still extremely useful (see Sec. 3A). Above the hairpin, the jeep trail climbs out of the trees to the northwest, then heads west through a little saddle from which Buck Island Reservoir first becomes visible. A little way down we come to

Buck Island Hill Trail (6520 — 0.5), which drops away to the southeast to circle around Buck Island Hill (the 6724' knob that separates Buck Island and Rockbound lakes), and connect with the Old Rockbound Trail. Unfortunately, the raising of Buck Island has flooded enough of the Buck Island Hill trail to make all of it useless. The road continues west along the lake past a usually littered camping area used by jeepers, and down behind a big concrete dam which permanently blocks what used to be the outlet stream, and can raise the original surface level, at high water, by some 21 feet. The reservoir is now drained by a man-made channel that flows west into a 13-foot diameter, 1½ mile tunnel blasted out of solid granite which empties into the northeast corner of Loon Lake.

136

In a little flat about ¼ mile northwest of the lake, the road divides for 50 feet to pass around a ducked boulder. At the north side of the road is a new sign for jeepers reading *Rubicon Springs*, east, *Wentworth Springs*, west. There is no sign (though the USFS has promised one) to indicate that this is the northern terminus of the

New Rockbound Trail (6420 — 0.6). A few ducks on the south side of the trail are all that mark this major trailhead. The jeep road now begins to climb to the northwest up vast sheets of monolithic granite. The route might be hard to follow were it not for the trail thoughtfully left by the jeepers: oil drippings, cigarette butts, broken granite, oil and beer cans, rubber tire marks, broken glass and an endless string of aluminum beer-can pull rings.

The topo map shows the trail-road running up through Big Sluice Box, with an alternate or shortcut route looping north for ½ mile. Actually, Big Sluice Box, a steep, narrow, washed-out canyon, has long been abandoned. Both jeeps and hikers use the more northern route, and the lower of the two junctions is unlikely to be recognized. As we leave the slab granite and enter light timber, the road makes a sudden turn to the north and begins to level off. Unmarked and well hidden on the south side of this turn is an ancient and overgrown road which marks the beginning of the

North Tells Peak Trail (6680 — 0.7). A sign scheduled for installation at the turn in the road is to read *Buck Island Reservoir*, east, and *Tells Peak Trail*, south. A sign to be installed 100 yards south at the top of Big Sluice Box is to read *Lake Winifred 1 mile, Tells Peak 5½ miles, Forni Lake 6½ miles*, south.

Sec. 2
North Tells Peak Trail

	Elev.	Miles from pt. above	Total miles
Big Sluice Box (jeep road)	6680	0.0	0.0
Loon Lake—Buck Island Road	6700	0.8	0.8
Lake Winifred Lateral	6860	0.3	1.1
Lake under Peak 8089	7820	2.4	3.5
North Tells Peak Pass	8460	1.8	5.3
Tells Peak Summit (9125)	8872	0.6	5.9
South Tells Peak Pass	8660	0.5	6.4

The North Tells Peak Trail, running north and south, is entirely separate and distinct (except for the common destination) from the Tells Peak Trail, running east and west, which, making use of a section of the old Highland Trail, approaches the peak from an airstrip on the Van Vleck Ranch. Keeping just east of the ridge for the most part, the North Tells Trail makes a long, slow climb up the gently rising ridge to the northernmost summit of the Crystal Range. Along the way there are marvelous views out across the northern half of Rockbound Valley to the northeast.

This is one of the most remote, least-traveled trails in the Wilderness Area, and signs of foot travel are faint. With no groove to follow, it is constantly necessary to search for blazes and ducks which locate the trail. Some hikers find this difficult and tedious; others find it exhilarating. To identify features of the landscape and thus locate the trail, the 7½′ topo map is almost a necessity.

The route is largely brushless and therefore suitable for travel in shorts. Full-fledged lakes and streams are scarce but drinking water can usually be found. Wood and potential campsites abound. Game is more plentiful in this wild region than people.

Big Sluice Box (6680 — 0.0). When the Wentworth Springs-Rubicon Springs jeep trail northwest of Buck Island Reservoir makes a steep downhill turn out of the timber (see Sec. 1), we leave it and continue south on an overgrown, barely recognizable road through the trees to a little flat where an old hammock-style bedspring and a cast-iron stove mark an ancient camp. A sign scheduled for the road should read *Buck Island Reservoir*, east, and *Tells Peak Trail*, south. Just beyond, the trail turns downhill into the narrow, boulder-strewn canyon of Big Sluice Box. At the head of the canyon there is a pile of rocks supporting a stick which points slightly uphill to the south between two blazed trees. This is the official beginning of the North Tells Peak Trail, which actually starts at the jeep road. A USFS sign is to read *Lake Winifred 1 mile, Tells Peak 5½ miles, Forni Lake 6½ miles*, south.

We pass between the trees and through a patch of brush, coming out on an open slab slope where the trail is conspicuously ducked. A corridor of thick forest that bands the slope on the 6700-foot contour lies just above us. The route shown on the topo map climbs through this corridor and ploughs through brush to the southwest to cross the Loon-Buck Island Road at the high point of the ridge. Then it turns south to Lake Winifred and east-southeast to a little flat where an ancient sign (now gone) read *Lake Winifred ¼ mile*. Unfortunately, the topo map is mistaken. That particular stretch of trail, about a mile in length, simply does not exist, although bewildered travelers over the years have contributed a few ducks in an effort to mark it. The first printing of the first edition of this book describes this section as so vague as to be virtually non-existent.

The actual route of the trail is superior in all regards. It conserves elevation, follows easy ground on a more direct route and is well-marked with ducks and old blazes. A USFS map from the 1950s shows the route clearly and accurately, though all subsequent USFS maps faithfully repeat the topo's error. Instead of crossing the abovementioned thick corridor of forest, the line of ducks contours across the open slope just below it, arcing to the southeast and climbing along the east side of a tiny knob into a little hollow through which passes the crushed rock roadbed of the

Loon-Buck Island Road (6700 — 0.8) built to bring trucks, men and materials into the Desolation Wilderness Area to build the dams, dig the channels and blast the tunnels. This great ribbon of pulverized rock, undifferentiated on USFS maps from wilderness trail, runs 1.0 mile down to the west shore of Buck Island Reservoir, a fast but disappointing trip for the wilderness-seeking backpacker.

From the ducked road crossing, the trail climbs south-southwest up a draw bordered by forest on one side and bare rock on the other. After a 200' climb we emerge onto rolling granite. Here we are rejoined by the imaginary route shown on the topo map. A few yards farther in a shallow saddle, nails in a solitary lodgepole are all that remain to mark the

Lake Winifred Lateral (6860 — 0.3), part of a vaguely ducked, long forgotten trail from Buck Island Reservoir to Lake Winifred.

Beyond the lateral, ducks and blazes lead into a wooded draw beside a stream on the east side of the ridge and we climb along the side hill to the south, crossing and recrossing the stream (usually dry by midsummer), until the trail climbs steeply above the forest, past a 1961 land survey marker (50 feet below the trail) just under summit 7460. Once again we are on top of the ridge, and the trail leads nearly level across open, rolling granite before climbing some 400' in about ½ mile (during which Loon Lake becomes visible to the northwest) to the little, unnamed

Lake under Peak 8089 (7820 — 2.7). The trail now begins to climb more steeply, and above 8000' the hollows and shady, north-facing slopes often lie beneath snowdrifts. The trail levels off and follows the ridgetop south, then slides onto the eastern slope and climbs. After passing a little knob we ascend a draw, come over a shoulder and lose about 100' as we pass under the steep slope leading to summit 8385. After climbing 250' in the space of ¼ mile, we come out on the level ridgetop into a flat which dips slightly to

North Tells Peak Pass (8460 — 1.8). Walking to the eastern edge of the flat we look down an easy backpackers' route to the end of the Rockbound Valley lateral trail at Highland Lake. This route, far superior to the trail through South Tells Pass shown on USFS maps, involves scrambling down a rocky bluff for 100′ or so to a long ramp of monolithic granite leading south-east directly down to the fringe of forest on the lake's north shore.

To continue south up the peak, we follow the trail across the flat to the foot of the summit cliffs, where three big ducks seem to lead us down toward Highland. But at the edge of the cliff, a route of smaller ducks traverses around the side of the mountain, then turns directly upward and we scramble 400-500′ up slab and avalanche chutes (much of the trail beneath snow in early season) to the surprisingly wooded summit of

Tells Peak (8872 — 0.6). A sign reads *Eldorado National Forest, Tells Peak, elevation 9125,* which is 253 feet higher than the elevation given on the topo maps. There is a tin can in a cairn containing notes and names of climbers. Unfortunately the summit is disfigured by names painted prominently in orange on the rock. The trail drops southeast down the ridge, loops north-west around difficult ground, and swings south to a junction about 100 feet west of and below the south saddle. A ducked route heads west toward Forni Lake (visible below) and ducks lead steeply up to the narrow ridge at

South Tells Peak Pass (8550 — 0.5). The USFS maps show 0.8 mile of nonexistent trail linking the pass to the end of the topo-map trail at Highland Lake, almost 750′ below. This is a serious misrepresentation inasmuch as the slope in places is virtually cliff and consequently dangerous to laden, inexperienced hikers. Recognizing the danger, the USFS has agreed to strike this section of alleged trail from its future signs and maps.

Rockbound (Pacific Crest) Trail
(Buck Island Lake to Mosquito Pass)

	Elev.	Miles from pt. above	Total miles
Rockbound Trail (jeep trail jctn.)	6410	0.0	0.0
Loon Lake Road	6500	0.6	0.6
Rubicon Dam Road	6500	0.2	0.8
Tunnel Trail: west end	6550	1.5	2.3
Tunnel Trail: east end	6600	0.2	2.5
Rubicon Reservoir (road's end)	6545	0.2	2.7
Jctn. Old-New Rockbound Trails	6600	1.0	3.7
Lower Rubicon Ford	6700	0.7	4.4
Upper Rubicon Ford	7060	1.8	6.2
Camper Flat (north Jctn.)	7180	0.7	6.9
Camper Flat (North Schmidell Trail)	7180	0.2	7.1
Camper Flat (Velma Trail)	7180	0.0	7.1
South Schmidell Trail	7400	1.3	8.4
Willow Flat) Rockbound Pass) Trail	7460	1.1	9.5
China Flat	7500	0.3	9.8
Jacks Meadows Trail	8050	2.3	12.1
Clyde Lake Trail	8200	0.2	12.3
Mosquito Pass	8420	0.3	12.6

The Rockbound Trail, from Buck Island to Mosquito Pass, climbs 2000 vertical feet in 12.6 miles of trail, most of it close to the Rubicon River, as it gently ascends Rockbound Valley. Travelers should be reminded that the road, channel, dam and tunnel construction necessary to develop water storage in the lower reaches of the valley have so altered the country that the topo map (which fails to show 146-acre Rubicon Reservoir) is less useful than usual and the latest USFS trail map should be carried.

Travelers likewise should be warned that the two trail crossings of the wild Rubicon between Rubicon Reservoir and Camper Flat are dangerous or impossible before the fourth of July after a light winter, and the first of August after a heavy winter. And cross-country travel down the west bank between the two fords may be thwarted by the booming cascade coming over the cliff from Horseshoe, McConnell and Leland lakes.

Rockbound Trailhead: Jeep Trail at Buck Island (6410 — 0.0). The trail begins ¼ mile northwest of Buck Island Lake at a point where the jeep trail splits around a boulder topped by a duck (see Sec. 1). On the north side of the road is a sign for jeepers reading *Wentworth Springs,* west and *Rubicon Springs,* east. There is no sign on the south side to mark this major trailhead (and way station on the Pacific Crest Trail) but the USFS has promised to install one. The three summer cabins shown by the topo map on the east island were removed in 1961. Ducks lead south along a high-standard track which for no apparent reason (except perhaps to avoid a view of the giant scar at the mouth of the Loon Lake tunnel) climbs more than 100' above the lake before descending nearly to the water at a point halfway down the west shore, where we cross the

Loon Lake Road (6500 — 0.6). This 15' swath of crushed rock winds west up the slope and, 1.0 mile above this junction, intersects the North Tells Peak Trail (see Sec. 2) in a broad saddle in the ridge. A sign beside a barricade in the road reads *Rockbound Lake, Rubicon Reservoir, Rockbound Valley,* southeast. No distances are given. A scheduled sign is to read *Buck Island Reservoir,* east, *Loon Lake Trailhead 6½ miles,* west, and *Rockbound Lake 1 mile, Rubicon Reservoir 2 miles, China Flat 9 miles,* southeast. After crossing the road, the trail winds through deep woods and crosses a creek (dry after midseason) before emerging onto the

Rubicon Dam Road (6500 — 0.2). Signs read *Entering Desolation Valley Primitive Area,* and ironically *No vehicles beyond this sign.* A few yards up the road this theme is elaborated in signs explaining that motor vehicles are prohibited *to preserve the primitive environment.* The Rubicon Dam Road, of course, is an extension of the Loon Lake Road, which from Buck Island Reservoir turns southeast toward Rockbound Lake and Rubicon Dam. Between this junction and Buck Island Reservoir, a mammoth barricade has been erected to prevent jeeps from entering the Wilderness Area. (Motorcycles and the like can enter all too easily, as the USFS admits, thanks to a policy which at present allows them, in this one area, to drive right up to the Wilderness boundary. Cyclists caught entering the Wilderness are fined a minimum of $100, but in no other region are they allowed to come so unnecessarily close.)

For the next 1½ miles the graded, banked highway of crushed granite roller-coasters smoothly to the southeast, its path determined by the requirements of heavy vehicles rather than such hiker considerations as economy of elevation change, view, or ac-

142

cess to Rockbound Lake. Since it shows not a trace of erosion or wear after half a dozen Sierra winters, it can probably be expected to last forever. A streamflow maintenance dam on Rockbound Lake raised the surface about five feet in 1955. After fording a creek at the south end of Rockbound (early-season hikers can, with some difficulty, jump across on boulders 50 yards upstream), the road curves around the bottom of the lake and a line of ducks blocking it funnels us south onto the

Tunnel Trail: west end (6550 — 1.5). About 100 yards beyond this point the road plunges into a bulldozed watercourse (roughly equivalent to the flow of the Rubicon, which it replaces) which cannot usually be crossed before midseason. To bypass the channel a trail has been built leading south up the west bank, past a locked cable car, a gauging station, and the mouth of the tunnel draining Rubicon Reservoir. We move up a small wooded draw, climbing above and behind the tunnel mouth, then swing back to the north and out of the trees to emerge again onto the Rubicon Dam road at

Tunnel Trail: east end (6600 — 0.2). There is no sign, but another line of ducks across the road guides northbound travelers into the trail before the road drops into the watercourse. It should be noted, however, that close to the water's edge a vaguely ducked and little-traveled route leads northward $\frac{1}{4}$ mile across level, mostly open ground, to intersect the Old Rockbound Trail (see Sec. 3A). Travelers passing between Camper Flat and Rubicon Springs are urged to use this cutoff and the old trail: it saves nearly 2 miles and avoids all but a fifth of a mile of travel on the construction roads.

Moving southeast on the road from the trail junction, we climb over a low ridge and serpentine down to where the road plunges into the water near a gauging station at a tunnel blasted through the rock at the northwest corner of

Rubicon Reservoir (6545 — 0.2). A highly developed trail leaves the road near the gauging station and goes down the western shore of the reservoir through an open stand of big yellow pine, above and well back from the water. We move east around the bottom of the reservoir to where the high-standard, still raw trail meets the

Old Rockbound Trail (6600 — 1.0). The last of the improvements are now behind. There are no more roads, dams, tunnels or gauging stations; the trail is modest and the river above this point is wild. We turn gradually south across open, rolling slab granite through occasional patches of forest interspersed with sandy fields of wildflowers. After perhaps $\frac{1}{4}$ mile the trail leads down to the beautiful young river splashing down a water-smoothed course of gleaming granite. For nearly ½ mile we walk south near the sculptured riverbank to the

Lower Rubicon Ford (6700 — 0.7). Large ducks at the water's edge inadequately mark the crossing on either side. Unfortunately there are no signs, and many hikers, having failed to pay close attention to either the trail or the map, continue south on a ducked route along the riverbank for as much as ¼ mile before discovering their error.

In addition to signs, cables or cable bridges at both fords are needed to open the country to early-season travel. Because the elevations are low, this region is usually suitable for camping by early June, but runoff from higher in the watershed keeps the Rubicon too high to ford for an additional month, thus blocking the principal trail through the area unnecessarily for fully a third of the season. Considering the unsightly miles of crushed-granite highway a little to the north, a pair of cable bridges could hardly be said to spoil the quality of the wilderness. The USFS has promised to mark the fords better, and agrees to the probable need for a pair of cable bridges.

The trail climbs the nose of a slab ridge, then contours in an arc to the southeast, keeping about 50′ above the water. As it climbs to the east it moves away from a slow, tree-fringed stretch of water. The river moves close below a point at which the trail enters a belt of forest and turns south to ford Phipps Creek. Marked occasionally by faded red paint blazes, the trail climbs south up the west side of a wooded draw, contours around the bare slopes of summit 7310, then drops down into

Upper Rubicon Ford (7060 — 1.8). Like the lower ford this crossing is poorly marked, especially on the west bank, and would benefit greatly from signs and a cable bridge. In early season the water is deep and swift, and fording, if even possible, is dangerous. The northbound hiker will discover it is extremely easy for the unwary visitor to miss the poorly marked ford and continue downstream on a well-ducked trail. Consequently — and because early-season travelers may easily be prevented from crossing the river — it seems appropriate at this point to describe the cross-country route down the west bank between the two fords.

For better than ½ mile, a ducked route leads north on rolling slabs of water-smoothed granite beside an extremely handsome stretch of cascading river. Then the ducks give out and the riverbank steepens, and we find ourselves moving with greater difficulty through a shallow canyon. After ¼ mile the canyon widens, and the ridge hemming us in on the west descends rapidly and

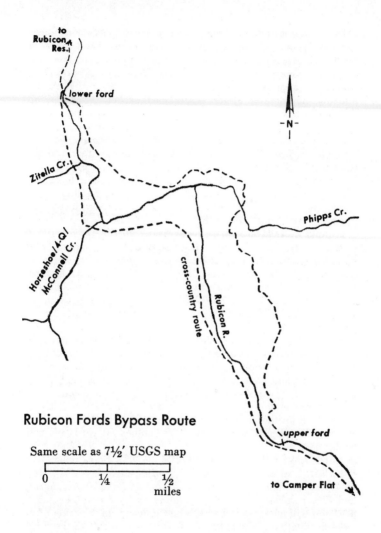

Rubicon Fords Bypass Route

Same scale as 7½′ USGS map

```
0        ¼        ½
                 miles
```

flattens. The river swings sharply to the west around the nose of this ridge, where Phipps Creek enters, but we leave the water ¼ mile south of Phipps Creek and climb perhaps 100′ west over the ridge in order to descend due west on smooth slab slopes to the thickly wooded bend where the river swings back to the north (see map).

145

This brings us to the difficult section of our route. We must force our way up through the brushy forest around the bend and ford the formidable (in early season) cascade that comes booming down the cliffs from Horseshoe, McConnell, 4-Q and Leland Lakes. About 100' above the river there is a short, level run that can be waded at high water by the careful backpacker. After making the crossing, we proceed north, keeping just above the forest, and with little difficulty jump the outlet stream from Lake Zitella. Almost immediately ducks begin to appear and we make our way through low brush back to the river. In the space of ¼ mile we reach the trail at the lower ford.

Returning now to the upper ford, we head south upstream along a trail well marked with ducks and red paint blazes over rolling, open granite beside the lively young river, and into the trees to the trail junction at the northern end of

Camper Flat (7180 — 0.7). Signs read *Trail 16E06* (actually it is 16E04) *4-Q Lakes 1 mile, Horseshoe Lake 3½ miles, Lake Zitella 4 miles, Highland Lake 5 miles, impassable to horses 1 mile beyond 4-Q Lakes,* west, *16E05* (actually 16E07 and 8) *Wrights Lake 8 miles, Desolation Valley 6 miles, Velma Lakes 2 miles,* south, and *Rockbound Lake, Rubicon Springs,* north. A scheduled sign is to read *Pacific Crest Trail,* south, and *4-Q Lakes, Highland Lake,* west.

The trail goes southeast through level forest for perhaps 75 yards before crossing the outlet stream from Lake Schmidell on a log. A little beyond we come to a north-facing sign reading *Camper Flat* and after moving through 50 yards of rather gloomy campground, we pass an identical sign facing south. Another 100 yards brings us to a sign reading *Mineral Springs,* west. (About 30 yards down the path a trickle of cool, pleasantly mineralized water wells up into a little basin.) Another 50 yards of trail brings us to the

North Lake Schmidell Trail (7200 — 0.2). Signs read *Lake Schmidell 2 miles, Leland Lakes 3¼ miles, Lake Lois 2¾ miles,* west, *Rubicon Springs 8¾ miles, Rockbound Lake 7 miles,* north, and *Velma Lakes 2¼ miles, Desolation Valley 6 miles,* south. A new sign will offer somewhat different mileages to the same principal destinations. About 100 yards farther we come to the third and southernmost Camper Flat junction at the

Velma Lakes Trail (7200 — 0.0). Signs read *Rubicon Springs 8¾ miles, Onion Flat 5 miles, Lake Schmidell 2⅛ miles,* north, *16E05, Velma Lakes 2 miles, Emerald Bay 7 miles, Stony Ridge Lake 8 miles, Dicks Pass 6 miles,* east, and *China Flat 3 miles, Desolation Valley 6 miles,* south. New signs will offer basically the same information.

The trail comes out of the woods and moves south near the riverbank for ¼ mile, then abruptly climbs about 100′ up a bluff and levels off in shaded forest out of sight of the river. Two signs, one old, one new, both reading *Lake Schmidell*, mark the junction of an old, unmapped trail that leads west through a little draw to the Schmidell outlet stream and merges with the South Schmidell Trail. Moving south again up the Rockbound Trail, just before crossing the stream from Lake Lois we come to a junction with the

South Schmidell Trail (7400 — 1.3). A sign reads *Camper Flat*, north, *Mosquito Pass*, south, and *Lake Schmidell 1¾ miles*, northwest. The new sign should provide distances of 2 and 5 miles respectively, plus *China Flat 2 miles*, south. Even in early season the stream is easily jumped, and we proceed to the south through alternating stretches of meadow and lodgepole woodland, climbing imperceptibly. We pass a downed barbed-wire fence near the foot of a meadow that sweeps down from Lake Doris and jump the outlet stream from Doris.

At this point the trail in early season is partly flooded, both by Doris Creek and by overflow of the Rubicon, and we splash along multiple tracks at the foot of the meadow, skirting barbed wire and walking on logs for 100 yards before regaining high ground and passing back into the woods at a junction with the eastern end of the

Willow Flat (Rockbound Pass) Trail (7460 — 1.1). Signs read *Willow Flat Trail, Rockbound Pass, Wrights Lake*, west, *Rockbound Trail, Lake Schmidell, Rubicon Springs*, north, and *China Flat, Desolation Valley, 16E05*, south. The new sign should read *Pacific Crest Trail*, north and south, *China Flat ½ mile, Mosquito Pass 4 miles*, south, *Doris Lake 2 miles, Wrights Lake 7 miles*, west, and *Lake Schmidell 3 miles*, north. A little beyond the junction, we come out of the forest into what looks like a Christmas tree lot of several acres. Shoulder-high lodgepole seedlings grow so densely that the ground is entirely hidden. Through the middle of this miniature forest the river runs unusually broad and shallow.

In the heavy winter of 1946-47 a huge avalanche of mud came down off Dicks Peak and spread across the valley floor, damming the river. During the spring runoff, the water rose until it cut a new channel through the barrier. Either the mud slide carried a bumper crop of pine nuts or germination conditions were ideal, for immediately there sprung up millions of seedling lodgepoles. Growth in this classic example of "locked stand" has been unusually slow owing to the stiff competition for sun and soil.

We ford the broad, gravel-bottomed riverbed on stepping stones (a dry crossing except in early season), and move up the east bank through dwarfed forest a few yards before returning to mixed conifer woods of lodgepole and a sprinkling of red and white fir, and western white pine. Almost immediately we come to the old campground (complete with concrete fireplaces) beside the river at

China Flat (7500 — 0.3), a frequent destination of campers although it has no more to offer than unimpressive Camper Flat, downstream. Signs read *China Flat, Rubicon River* and *Please drown your campfire before leaving.* We come out of the woods and cross a meadow (on which cattle brought over the Rockbound Stock Driveway are usually grazing in September) past a sign pointing north into the woods that reads *China Flat Campground,* and return to the river and another ford, this one marked by a sign near the water reading *Trail.* In a normal year this is a wet crossing until after midseason. New signs are scheduled for both entrances to China Flat.

The trail leads more than a mile south along pleasant riverbank through nearly level woodland before fording for the last time (by midseason one can cross dryly a little way downstream, jumping rock to rock). Then the trail swings southeast, away from the water, and begins to climb under Jacks Peak. Following a deep groove marked by occasional red paint blazes, it rises 450' from the ford to a junction with the

Jacks Meadows Trail (8050 — 2.3). A sign reads *Jacks Meadows,* east. This unmapped trail moves down a slight incline on lightly wooded grassland for perhaps ⅛ mile into a lush meadow watered by a rill coming down from beneath Mosquito Pass. The remains of an old cow camp in a fringe of timber suggest this handsome area once knew extensive use. Though damp and buggy to midseason, this seldom-visited meadow offers good late-summer camping.

Back on the Rockbound Trail we climb 150' to the

Clyde Lake Trail (8200 — 0.2). A small but distinct trail, marked by a sign reading *Clyde Lake,* descends southeast down a draw to a talus slope of bright granite, then drops down a gully into a lush strip of meadow beside a pond. The trail swings south around the pond and climbs a few yards to the lakeshore, where it intercepts a fishermen's trail along the north side of the lake. The flow from beneath the gated dam represents the birth of the Rubicon River. The distance from the Pacific Crest Trail to the dam is 0.3 mile.

There is a very reasonable, though virtually unmarked, route for backpackers from Clyde Lake across the crest of the Crystal Range to the trail at Island Lake on the western slope. As we approach Clyde from the east, with a crossing in mind, we see the route clearly: from beneath the low point in the ridge a water-course makes its way 800' down a very steep, grassy slope. The slope, reached from the Clyde Lake dam, can be navigated in either direction in comparative safety by the careful backpacker. The route from Island Lake to the pass (treated in Region 3, Sec. 3), though involving occasional exposure, is roughly comparable in difficulty and safety. The distance from Clyde Lake dam to the trail at the foot of Island Lake is about 1.5 miles.

Back on the Pacific Crest Trail at the Clyde Lake junction a sign reads *China Flat 2½ miles*, north, and *Mosquito Pass ½ mile*, south. The new sign should read *China Flat 2½ miles*, north, *Mosquito Pass ½ mile, Desolation Valley 1 mile*, south, and *Clyde Lake ½ mile*, west. We climb steeply to the south on high-standard trail to a vantage point above Clyde, then swing abruptly east on a long climbing traverse that arcs around a bluff and goes south again into

Mosquito Pass (8420 — 0.4). On the northern edge of the pass, sandwiched between the trail and a dynamited cliff, are the remains of a cabin or shelter with a concrete floor and low cemented masonry walls. In the gully below are the crushed screens that served as windows and the galvanized iron roof. A snarl of rotting, high-pressure rubber hose suggests the onetime presence of a compressor. The position of the cabin, commanding the pass, suggests a toll-taker or sheepherder, but the actual origin of the cliffside hut remains a mystery, at least to me.

A sign at the pass gives the altitude as 8760', an exaggeration of some 340 feet over that shown on the topo map. It should be noted by hikers interested in crossing the Crystal Range between Clyde and Island lakes that an alternative route from the east begins in Mosquito Pass. It is perfectly feasible for a backpacker willing to scramble to climb southwest from the pass to the ridgetop and follow it in a great arc (above the wreck of a small plane on the Lake Aloha slope) above the Clyde Lake cliffs and around to the north into the earlier-mentioned saddle above Island Lake. This route doubles the cross-country distance, but the views are marvelous and the climb is reduced by nearly half.

Old Rockbound Trail

	Elev.	Miles from pt. above	Total miles
Rubicon-Wentworth Springs Jeep Trail	6380	0.0	0.0
Buck Island Lake Trail	6500	0.2	0.2
Fox Lake Jctn.	6550	1.0	1.2
Rubicon Dam Road	6550	0.2	1.4

As mentioned in Sec. 3, the Old Rockbound Trail, though overgrown, unmaintained, sometimes flooded, often vague and mostly unsigned, provides a valuable route for hikers traveling between Rubicon Springs and Rubicon Reservoir. Nearly 2½ miles of hiking can be saved and nearly all of the construction road avoided. Though largely forgotten for nearly a decade, the route is easy enough to follow with the aid of a topo map and this guide. The USFS, acknowledging the trail's value, has promised to resurrect and re-sign it, but lack of funds may cause a delay of several years.

Rubicon-Wentworth Springs Jeep Trail (6380 — 0.0). About 0.6 mile south of the Rubicon River bridge, the jeep trail makes a steep, deeply-rutted hairpin turn to the northwest. At the southernmost point of the turn, beneath a transplanted yellow highway sing reading *Watch for Rocks*, lies the overgrown, almost invisible beginning of the trail. We move southeast through brushy forest a few yards, then come out of the trees and climb on bare granite through a little pass, before passing a fallen barbed-wire fence and dropping to the shore of Rockbound Lake and a junction with the

Buck Island Trail (6500 — 0.2). A sign reads *Rockbound Trail*, with arrows pointing both west and south. A second sign, pointing west, reads *Buck Island Lake ¾ mile, Wentworth Springs 9 miles*. Just to the west the trail, shown on the topo map following the stream to Buck Island, drops into the lake. Since the north end of the trail, as it passes the eastern tip of Buck Island Lake, is also flooded, this trail section, for all practical purposes, can be forgotten.

A fairly distinct groove moves southeast down the shore, generally within 50 feet of the lake, occasionally dipping into the water (or below the high-water mark) for a few yards, to a sandy cove with an old firepit in the middle. At the north edge of the cove a sign reads *Eldorado National Forest, Rockbound Lake*. At the

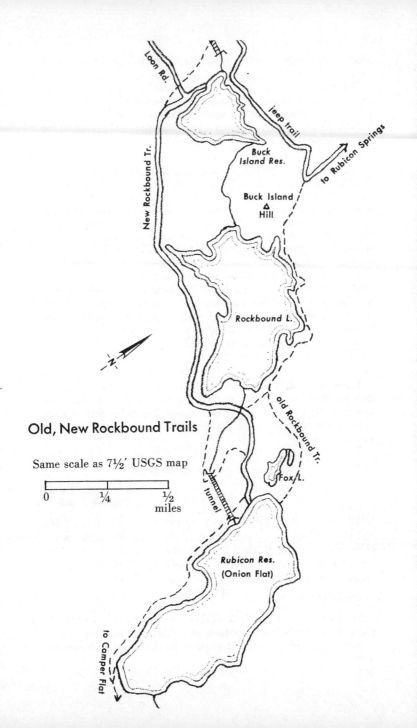

Old, New Rockbound Trails

Same scale as 7½′ USGS map

0   ¼   ½
miles

Loon Rd.

New Rockbound Tr.

jeep trail

to Rubicon Springs

Buck Island Res.

Buck Island
△
Hill

Rockbound L.

old Rockbound Tr.

tunnel

Fox L.

Rubicon Res.
(Onion Flat)

to Camper Flat

south edge a sign on a tree reads *Rockbound Trail, Onion Flat 2 miles*, south.

We continue southeast on a once heavily worn groove now overgrown with brush. Old blazes have grown dim and many ducks have been scattered, but the route for the most part is still plainly visible. At the southeast corner of the lake the trail curves to the east, marking the otherwise undefined

Fox Lake Jctn. (6550 — 1.0). From this point there are a variety of ways to reach the Rubicon Dam Road and the new Rockbound Trail at Rubicon Reservoir. The flattest route leaves the old trail halfway between Rockbound and Fox lakes and follows a vaguely ducked route south to intersect the road where it fords the channel from Rubicon to Rockbound. The hiker then follows the road 1/5 mile over a low ridge, past the eastern entrance to the Rubicon Tunnel Trail, and down the reservoir (see map).

The shortest route follows the old trail past Fox Lake, then strikes off to the southwest below the dam and contours around the northern end of the reservoir to the junction of the road and trail at the gauging station and outlet tunnel. In between these two routes there are several other possibilities. The distance is short and the terrain comparatively easy, but most travelers would benefit by the modest trail the USFS has promised to mark to the

Rubicon Dam Road (6550 — 0.2). For all their vagueness, the old Rockbound Trail and its connecting lateral route are aesthetically superior, easier and nearly 2½ miles shorter than the alternative route (a composite of jeep trail, construction road and new trail).

Sec. 4

Camper Flat to South Tells Pass

	Elev.	Miles from pt. above	Total miles
Camper Flat (north jctn.)	7180	0.0	0.0
4-Q Lakes (ford)	7500	1.0	1.0
Horseshoe Lake (trail jctn.)	7540	2.4	3.4
Lake Zitella	7660	0.5	3.9
Highland Lake	7820	1.7	5.6
South Tells Pass	8660	1.0	6.6

Like the North Tells Peak Trail (Sec. 2) which it supposedly joins, this comparatively remote and little-traveled trail passes through some of the wildest country in the Desolation Wilderness. The link joining the two trails, from Highland Lake to South Tells Pass, cannot honestly be represented as trail. It is included here because the current USFS maps (and signs) show it as trail and, consequently, travelers are liable to depend upon it when planning circuit trips in this region. Admitting that its inclusion is a mistake, the USFS plans to delete it on future maps and signs.

The steep 750' slope is composed of talus, boulders and cliffs, and snow clings to the shaded hollows beyond midseason. There are no ducks to suggest the easiest crossing. A much better connecting route between the two trails, with the possible disadvantage of putting the hiker on the wrong side of Tells Peak, leads northwest from Highland and easily and safely climbs a prominent monolithic slab ridge that runs nearly into North Tells Pass (see Sec. 2).

Camper Flat: North Jctn. (7180 — 0.0). Signs pointing west up the trail read *4-Q Lakes 1 mile, Horseshoe Lake 3½ miles, Lake Zitella 4 miles, Highland Lake 5 miles* and *Impassable to horses 1 mile beyond 4-Q lakes.* (For text of the remaining signs at this junction see Sec. 3.) The trail begins in light forest and climbs gradually in a well-defined, ducked groove through thinning woodland up a series of early-drying stream-beds. We emerge into an open, rocky basin, get a glimpse of a small lake to the north, and make our way out on a peninsula to a ford across the northern arm of the highest and largest of the

4-Q Lakes (7500 — 1.0). The haphazardly located trail through this mysteriously named basin was evidently laid out in the fall, without consideration of early-season conditions, for it repeatedly crosses snowpools, and moves through creek bottoms which in June are normally under water. The ford of the big lake is no exception. Although the crossing is shallow and there are stepping stones and logs, the early-season walker is obliged to wade or make a ¼ mile detour around the northern end of the lake.

Beyond the ford the trail follows the lake shore west, dips disconcertingly into the water, then for no discernible reason climbs north away from the water's edge (where the going is easier on fishermen's trails) only to drop into a snowpool and then pass down a creek bottom to the lower end of the basin. Having barely glimpsed the lower two lakes, we descend steeply through forest for ¼ mile, swinging gradually to the north, roughly paralleling the 4-Q basin outlet stream.

We come down into a pretty, wooded valley opposite the rushing, seldom fished creek from McConnell Lake, then make our way downstream about a mile on well-ducked but little-traveled trail past several campsites to a pleasant wooded flat in slab granite to the outlet creek from Horseshoe Lake.

The topo (and consequently USFS) map shows the trail looping downstream to the north around the flat to cross the combined creeks almost ¼ mile below their junction. Actually, the ducked trail crosses the two creeks individually a few yards above their junction (a dry crossing can be made, even in early season, with a little care), then swings northwest through a belt of trees before climbing steeply up a bare granite slope marked by ducks and faded red paint blazes. Signs of foot travel are nonexistent. Probably this is the stretch the signmakers had in mind when they warned in Camper Flat against bringing horses more than a mile (this is nearly 2 miles) beyond 4-Q Lakes. The route climbs parallel to, but some distance north of, the cascading outlet stream to a profusely signed junction just north of and above

Horseshoe Lake (7540 — 2.4). Signs read *Highland Lake 1½ miles, Tells Peak 2 miles, Van Vleck Ranch 5 miles, 16E04,* northwest, *Camper Flat 3 miles, 4-Q Lakes 2 miles,* east, *Leland Lakes 2 miles, Lake Schmidell 4 miles,* southwest, and *Horseshoe Lake* on one tree and *Hazardous for stock travel* on another. In the brush is an older sign offering all the same information. The most unfortunate inference to be drawn from these signs are that there is a continuous trail from Highland Lake to Tells Peak, which there isn't; that the Van Vleck Ranch is only 5 trail miles away, whereas the distance is closer to 10; and that McConnell and Zitella lakes have been forgotten. New signs happily will omit references beyond Highland and add Lake Zitella; most mileages will be changed.

Horseshoe Lake, in the process of becoming a meadow, is threaded by meandering channels outlined by miniature flowering dikes along its wooded north shore. The scarcity of developed campsites suggests the infrequency of travelers. Our trail from the junction, marked by ducks, switchbacks northwest up an open slope of rock and sand, and we move through a little saddle, veer slightly to the north, then drop to the outlet stream on the northeast shore of

Lake Zitella (7660 — 0.5). There are no signs here and developed campsites are scarce. Distinctive exfoliating cliffs dropping from the northeast ridge of McConnell Peak form the amphitheater that cups this bleakly handsome little lake. The trail crosses the creek on a log jam, continues up the northeast shore past a campsite, then climbs a well-ducked but somewhat circuitously routed trail northwest through the eastern side of the saddle under summit 7865. A more direct but only occasionally

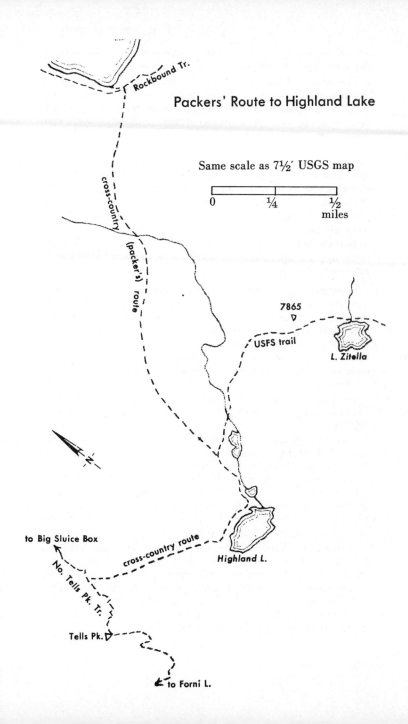

Rockbound Tr.

Packers' Route to Highland Lake

Same scale as 7½′ USGS map

0   ¼   ½
miles

cross-country (packer's) route

7865
▽

USFS trail

L. Zitella

N

to Big Sluice Box

cross-country route

Highland L.

No. Tells Pk. Tr.

Tells Pk. ▽

to Forni L.

ducked route passes a little farther west and climbs directly up the draw and through the lowest point of the saddle.

The section of trail to follow, from the saddle to the crossing of Highland Creek, may well be the most difficult of any in the Wilderness Area. Marked only by occasional ducks, it leads down a steep, wet cliff generally banked with snow until mid-season. Signs of foot travel vanish entirely as we come through the saddle and make our way straight down, duck by duck, often hand over hand. After a quick 300' drop we veer sharply to the west and contour across a steep, slippery slab slope usually streaked with snow and running with snow water.

The route crosses a talus slope, then climbs 150' to the ford of Highland Creek (easily jumped in early season). We move up onto a bare granite bench and circle to the southwest, well away from the lowest lakelet in the chain, before returning to the upper lakelet and switchbacking up a short bluff to a point just above the northern shore of

Highland Lake (7820 — 1.7). Although the single marked trail into the basin is totally impassable to stock, packers serving the area from the north have worked out an easily traveled but unmarked route that inscribes a gentle arc between the bench we have just crossed and the southern end of Rubicon Reservoir. Hikers equipped with compass and map and accustomed to cross-country travel are advised to consider this rugged, 2-mile short-cut (see map).

Deep and handsome Highland Lake fills the bottom of an impressive rocky bowl flanked by the soaring talus slopes of Tells (8872) and McConnell (9099) peaks. A fringe of forest along the north shore offers excellent camping for the few visitors who make their way into this basin. At the west end of the lake, as the topo map shows, the trail ends in sloping meadows which lie at the foot of the snow-streaked jumble of boulders, cliffs and talus that form the head wall of the cirque. A few ducks start up the steepening slope but above the meadow the climber who is really determined to reach the Tells Peak Trail from Forni Lake must scramble up as best he can.

It should be noted that there are two saddles in the head wall between Tells and McConnell peaks, and the trail lies west of the farther north of the two. As indicated in Sec. 2, a safer and much easier route from Highland to the ridgetop, although it puts the hiker north of Tells Peak, leaves the northwest corner of the lake to mount a conspicuous, monolithic, ramplike ridge of granite that leads nearly into North Tells Pass.

Velma Lakes to Horseshoe Lake

(via Lake Schmidell)

	Elev.	Miles from pt. above	Total miles
Middle Velma Lake:			
East Phipps Pass Trail	7950	0.0	0.0
West Phipps Pass Trail	7860	0.5	0.5
Camper Flat: South Jctn.	7180	1.8	2.3
Camper Flat: North Schmidell Trail	7180	0.0	2.3
North-South Schmidell Trail Jctn.	7550	1.1	3.4
Lake Schmidell Lateral	7900	1.0	4.4
Lake Lois Trail	7940	0.1	4.5
Leland Lakes Basin: midpoint	8160	1.5	6.0
McConnell Lake	7820	0.8	6.8
Horseshoe Lake: Zitella Trail	7540	1.4	8.2

In all its 10-mile length, Rockbound Valley is approached from the east by only a single trail: the lateral from Velma Lakes. As a consequence, this trail section often becomes vital to those planning circuit trips in the region. Beautiful Lake Schmidell on the western side of the valley has long been one of the most popular camping spots in the Wilderness Area. Solitude and firewood, however, are generally in short supply. Beyond Schmidell the traffic thins abruptly and it is unusual to encounter travelers at Leland, McConnell or Horseshoe lake.

Middle Velma Lake: East Phipps Pass Trail (7950 — 0.0). Signs read *Tallant Lakes, Meeks Bay, Miller Lakes,* north (see Region 6, Sec. 2) and *Rockbound Valley, Lake Schmidell,* west. Leaving the boulevard of the T-Y Trail we move west through damp, willow-choked woods on a modest track, climb over a little knoll and descend through forest to the

West Phipps Pass Trail (7860 — 0.5). In reality this is only a shortcut lateral to the main T-Y trail — an unmaintained path through swampy woods that can be difficult to find. A sign reads *Velma Lakes, Eagle Falls,* east, *Rockbound Valley,* west, and *Miller Lake 7 miles, Meeks Bay 12 miles,* pointing north into the woods. We continue to the west, moving gently downhill through damp woods on a trail well-marked with ducks, blazed trees and red paint blazes.

After perhaps ¾ mile we come out of the trees to cross an open, rock-strewn slab of granite threaded by a broad, rock-lined corridor that gives the appearance of having just been swept. Beyond this point the country changes. The slope drops more steeply and trees become scarce. We descend rocky gullies and washes onto open, rubble-scattered slabs that tilt down to the fringe of forest that lines the river in the bottom of the valley. The trail fords the Rubicon in a wet crossing (except in late season) on water-smoothed river rock, and we climb a few yards up the west bank past a large campsite to

Camper Flat: South Jctn. (7200 — 1.8). Signs read *Rubicon Springs 8¾ miles, Onion Flat 5 miles, Lake Schmidell 2⅛ miles,* north, *16E05 Velma Lakes 2 miles, Emerald Bay 7 miles, Stony Ridge Lake 8 miles, Dicks Pass 6 miles,* east, and *China Flat 3 miles, Desolation Valley 6 miles,* south. We move north up the trail a few yards to

Camper Flat: North Schmidell Trail Jctn. (7180 — 0.0). Signs read *Lake Schmidell 2 miles, Leland Lakes 3¼ miles,* west, *Rockbound Lake 7 miles,* north, and *Velma Lakes 2¼ miles, Desolation Valley 6 miles,* south. We move west across the level valley floor 0.1 mile, then turn abruptly south through open woodland, easily cross the outlet from Schmidell and climb steadily on a good trail through light forest. We move over a bluff and drop down, guided by freshened blazes, into Schmidell Creek canyon to the junction of the

North-South Schmidell trails (7550 — 1.1). The topo map shows the junction on the south side of the stream, and it may once have been there, but for a long time it has been 100 yards north of the ford. Signs there read *Camper Flat 1 mile, Velma Lakes 3½ miles,* northeast, *Lake Schmidell ¾ mile,* west, and *China Flat 2¼ miles, Desolation Valley 4 miles, Echo Lake 10 miles,* southeast. Signs scheduled for installation are to read, simply, *Camper Flat, China Flat, Lake Schmidell* with appropriate arrows and no distances.

At this point we shall trace the South Schmidell Trail 1.0 mile back to the Rockbound Trail. Heading southeast we almost immediately ford Schmidell Creek, then make our way through level forest on a trail marked by freshened blazes but badly chewed up by stock in the boggier stretches. We pass along the northern fringe of a boggy, buggy meadow where deer often feed, then climb through a sandy pass marked by ducks. The trail turns south and levels off through a parkland of hemlock, red fir and lodgepole before dropping steeply to a junction with the Rockbound Trail just north of the Lois Creek ford. A sign at the junction reads *Camper Flat,* north, *Mosquito Pass,* south, and *Lake Schmidell 1¾ miles,* northwest up the path we have just descended.

Returning to the junction of the North and South Schmidell trails, we move southwest out of the woods and ford the creek, crossing easily on rocks. Multiple tracks move up through steep meadows badly mangled by stock, and onto high ground where the trail is good. We come over a little rise and out into a little meadow with a small lake in the center. Just beyond the lake we come to the

Lake Schmidell Lateral (7900 — 1.0). Signs read *Camper Flat 2 miles, China Flat 3½ miles,* east, *Lake Lois 1 mile, Leland Lakes 1½ miles,* west, and *Lake Schmidell ¼ mile,* pointing north across the meadow to where the outlet stream rises from beneath the gated dam and flows down to the little lake. There are a number of large, well-developed campsites along the eastern half of the lake's shoreline, and some with new concrete fireplaces and grills near a roofless redwood latrine. We move southwest out of the meadow near the lake to a junction with the

Lake Lois Trail (7940 — 0.1). Signs read *Lake Lois 1 mile, Wrights Lake 7 miles,* south, *Lake Schmidell ¼ mile,* north, and *Leland Lakes 1½ miles, Horseshoe Lake 4 miles, Highland Trail 4 miles,* southwest. Scheduled signs omit Highland and Wrights Lake references, and all distances. Immediately the trail begins to climb and we move in an arc up a narrow but adequate groove around the perimeter of the lake, crossing two big all-season creeks, often waist deep in willow and wildflowers. Many smaller rivulets cross the damp trail until late season, and in places it is better to keep to the high ground than to try to stay on the overgrown track.

The important thing is to move continually toward the sandy draw just northeast of Red Peak. The trail eventually emerges from the lush growth and, well marked and ducked, ascends the draw and climbs through a little saddle some 700' above now-hidden Schmidell. Lying north directly below is handsome Leland Lakes basin. The trail down is rough and often dim, but a continuous route, marked by both ducks and pink paint blazes, switchbacks down to the head of the basin, where it becomes quite distinct upon reaching grassland.

The topo map indicates that the trail passes close to upper Leland as it starts northwest down the basin; actually it swings somewhat farther to the north, and the upper lake for the most part remains out of sight as we pass behind a bluff. The USFS trail maps choose a point on the trail halfway between the two lakes in order to designate mileage to and from

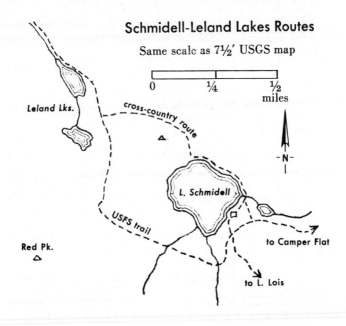

Schmidell-Leland Lakes Routes

Same scale as 7½′ USGS map

0   ¼   ½
miles

- N -

Leland Lks.

cross-country route

△

L. Schmidell

□

USFS trail

to Camper Flat

Red Pk.
△

to L. Lois

Leland Lakes (8160 — 1.5). We use the same point because it happens to mark the beginning of an unmapped knapsacker's route to Lake Schmidell (see map).

Starting between the two Leland lakes, following a line of sight, we move southeast up a gently rising slope through open forest to the more northerly (and higher) of the two saddles between the two basins. Do not be lured to the lower, broader, more easily reached southern saddle, for the descent in brush and talus on the Schmidell side is difficult. Once the northern saddle is reached we find our way down very steep game trails and avalanche chutes to the nearest corner of the lake, where we pick up the fishermen's trail heading southeast toward camp.

Returning to Leland Basin, halfway between the two lakes, we move downhill to the northwest and at last reach the shoreline about halfway down the lower lake, where a sign on a tree (the last sign until the Horseshoe Lake junction) reads *Leland Lakes*. From the foot of the lake, the trail moves down a flower-sprinkled canyon along the north bank of all-year Leland Creek. About ½ mile below the lake we cross the creek to pass through a well-developed campsite, then cross back north. As the canyon flattens we cross the creek again and come out into the meadow that largely surrounds

McConnell Lake (7820 — 0.8). Even in a wet year this rapidly filling lake boasts less than half the area suggested on the maps. And at the end of a dry year it is nothing more than a few channels winding through tall grass. Nevertheless the meadow-lake, lying beneath the impressive McConnell Peak massif, is one of the pleasantest, most peaceful places I know.

The now-faint trail continues northwest across rolling meadowland, well back from the water, then swings north, climbs over a wooded bluff and starts downhill northeast. This is one of the least-traveled sections of the Wilderness and consequently the trails tend to be dim, though this one is fairly well ducked. We descend northwest under the cliffs of McConnell Peak through boulder-studded lodgepole and hemlock woodland underlain with ceanothus and huckleberry oak. The route winds along the base of the cliffs for ¾ mile, then swings to the northeast and, after fording the inlet creek, follows the north streambank down to the trail junction at the lower end of

Horseshoe Lake (7540 — 1.4). A forest of signs, old and new, read *Highland Lake 1½ miles, Tells Peak 2 miles, Van Vleck Ranch 5 miles, trail 16E04*, northeast, *Camper Flat 3 miles, 4-Q lakes 2 miles*, east, and *Leland Lakes 2 miles, Lake Schmidell 4 miles*, southwest. USFS signs scheduled for installation happily omit references beyond Highland Lake.

Sec. 6
Willow Flat Trail to Rockbound Pass; Lake Doris Trail to Lake Schmidell; Rockbound Stock Driveway (East Side)

	Elev.	Miles from pt. above	Total miles
Willow Flat Trail (east end)	7460	0.0	0.0
Lake Lois Trail	8340	1.4	1.4
Rockbound Pass (8650)	8550	0.5	1.9
Lake Lois Trail	8340	—	—
Rockbound Stock Driveway (east end)	8400	1.3	2.7
Lake Schmidell (trail jctn.)	7940	0.6	3.3
Rockbound Stock Driveway (east end)	8400	—	-—
Rockbound Stock Driveway Pass	9180	1.7	4.4

Sec. 6 (really three trails strung together) begins at the Rubicon River, climbs to Rockbound Pass, retreats to the junction below Lake Doris, then heads north to Lake Schmidell, from which it backtracks to the eastern end of the Cattlemen's Stock Driveway and climbs to the pass. It is not designed as a trip itinerary but, since it includes both the genuine pass trails coming into Rockbound Valley from the west, it does suggest a circuit trip from Wrights or Dark Lake through wild, high, beautiful country.

Rockbound Pass is the choice of probably 90% of the travelers crossing the Crystal Range from the west, and for good reason: it is served by a well-signed and well-maintained trail that connects directly to the roadhead at Wrights Lake and the Rockbound Trail on the Rubicon River. By comparison the Rockbound Stock Driveway leads from nowhere to nowhere over a rarely maintained and unsigned route. It runs 600' higher and several miles longer than the Rockbound Pass (Willow Flat) Trail, but it offers a marvelous walk through delightful country for those with the time and inclination to try it. The

Willow Flat Trail: East End (7460 — 0.0) is probably better known, unofficially, as the Rockbound Pass Trail. Its junction with the Rockbound Valley Trail is on high ground just south of a large, spongy meadow, a few yards west of the Rubicon River. Signs at the junction read *16E08, Willow Flat Trail, Rockbound Pass, Wrights Lake*, west, *Rockbound Trail, Lake Schmidell, Rubicon Springs*, north, and *16E05, China Flat, Desolation Valley*, south. (For scheduled signs see Sec. 3.)

The modest but continuous and well-ducked trail climbs gently west through open forest, just above the southern margin of the meadow. The slope steepens as we swing a little north above the meadow, then the trail turns abruptly south in a ¼ mile climbing traverse. We move back to the northwest to switchback up a steep, wooded slope, coming out of the trees onto an open, easier slope that leads up to a junction with the

Lake Lois Trail (8340 — 1.4). Signs read *16E07 Lake Lois 1 mile, Lake Schmidell 2 miles, Leland Lakes 4 miles*, north, *China Flat 2 miles*, east, and *Rockbound Pass ½ mile, Wrights Lake 7 miles*, west. New signs will offer virtually the same information. Heading west toward the pass we move up a tundralike meadow into windy Doris Lake basin, swinging to the south of the small clump of trees that vainly attempt to shelter the uninviting campsites by the lake.

The trail climbs along the southern margin of the basin, moving up on grass beneath talus slopes to the south. Snow often covers the highest sections of the trail beyond midseason. We pass just south of a pond that provides drinking water in all seasons and come out into

Rockbound Pass (8550 — 0.5). An old sign reads *Rockbound Pass, elevation 8650*, which is a hundred feet higher than the topo map indicates. Farther through the pass, west-facing signs read *Entering Desolation Valley Wilderness Area* and *No Motorized Vehicles Permitted.* (For the western half of the Willow Flat Trail see Region 3, Sec. 6.) Returning to the

Lake Lois Trail (8340 — 0.0) below Doris Lake, we head north on a traverse across tilting meadow, with occasional fine views out over Rockbound Valley, and into a handsome lodgepole and hemlock parkland. The trail contours north around the slope and comes out of the trees onto a lovely sloping meadow with a shallow lake.

We move northwest across the meadow past a pair of ponds and drop gently downslope to the western arm of Lake Lois. The trail passes several of the more sheltered campsites before we move out on the windy eastern shore to climb over a little knoll and, turning west, cross the outlet stream on the small, gated rock dam. After passing several camps on the northern shore, the trail begins to climb, and we swing away to the north. The trail levels off on the flat nose of a lightly-wooded ridge, halfway across which we come to the

Rockbound Stock Driveway: East End (8400 — 1.3), also known as the Red Peak Stock Trail. A collection of five signs read *16E09, Rockbound Stock Driveway, Barrett Lake Red Peak Trail*, southwest, *Rockbound Pass, Lake Lois*, south, and *Lake Schmidell*, north. New signs are to offer most of this same information, with no distances. We continue north along the ridge a few hundred yards, then abruptly drop almost 600′ down a steep, dusty, switchbacking track northwest into the handsome granite bowl that holds deep, blue Lake Schmidell. Above the southeast corner of the lake we come to the

Lake Schmidell: Trail Jctn. (7940 — 0.6). Signs read *Lake Schmidell ¼ mile*, north, *Leland Lakes 1½ miles, Horseshoe Lake 4 miles, Highland Trail 4 miles*, southwest, and *Lake Lois 1 mile, Wrights Lake 7 miles*, southeast. The lakeshore lies only 100 yards north. Returning to the

Rockbound Stock Driveway: East End (8400 — 0.0), we begin a gentle climb up a broad grassy slope on a vague and intermittent track marked by big cairns. Almost immediately we come to the remains of a log shelter at what once must have been a cow camp. For travelers concerned with the likelihood of encountering a herd of cattle, it should be noted that the grazing permit allows for no more than 150 head of cattle to visit the Wilderness Area between August 1 and September 20, and as a matter of practice none are brought over the pass before Labor Day. And for those curious about the footing, so long as one travels before the cattle come in the fall, there is less dung to contend with than on the trails favored by packers, such as Willow Flat.

We move up through a succession of lush little valleys on a track broad enough for a truck, marked by large heaps of rock spaced some distance apart. This big trail, built by and for cattlemen, at their expense, makes an interesting contrast with the smoother, more tailored trails built by the Forest Service. As we leave the lovely, tree-flanked meadows for steeper slopes of rock, the trail becomes a huge, rocky trench that climbs via long, well-built switchbacks, and we move out into the open, high above Lake Lois, with marvelous views out over forested Rockbound Valley to Dicks and Jacks peaks.

After a long climbing traverse south, during which we pass vast banks of wildflowers fed by rivulets falling from shaded snowbanks above, we zigzag upward through talus on a rough track that leads into shallow, unmarked

Rockbound Stock Driveway Pass (9180 — 1.7). This slight dip in the barren ridge that runs south from Red Peak is the second highest pass (after 9380′ Dicks Pass) in the Wilderness. There are no signs to welcome the traveler or tell him how high he has climbed, but a little to the west there is an exceptional view over Rockbound Pass to Mt. Price and Pyramid Peak. (For descriptions of the western approach to the pass, see Region 3, Sec. 6.)

Phipps Peak

Sec. 1 UPPER GENERAL CREEK TRAIL: MILLER LAKE JEEP ROAD
TO TAHOE-YOSEMITE TRAIL, INCLUDING THE LAKE GENE-
VIEVE LATERAL TO THE TAHOE-YOSEMITE TRAIL

Sec. 2 TAHOE-YOSEMITE TRAIL: MEEKS BAY TO MIDDLE VELMA
LAKE, INCLUDING THE GROUSE LAKE LATERALS

Sec. 3 LOWER GENERAL CREEK TRAIL: SUGAR PINE POINT TRAIL-
HEAD TO UPPER GENERAL CREEK TRAIL

The Phipps Peak Region, embracing the northeastern corner
of the Wilderness Area, is bounded by the Miller Lake Jeep Road
in the north, Middle and Lost Corner mountains in the west, Middle Velma Lake in the south and Meeks Bay in the east. The trail
beside General Creek divides neatly into two sections, which for
clarity are labeled "Upper" and "Lower." The two join officially
at a signed junction with the General Creek Lateral to the Miller
Lake Jeep Road, near where the north-flowing creek abruptly
swings east toward Lake Tahoe.

Almost the entire region is heavily forested, in contrast to most
of the Wilderness Area. There is contrast, too, between the three
trails. The T-Y Trail is a heavily used, highly developed, high-
speed stock trail, completely rebuilt in 1967-68. The Upper General Creek Trail, on the other hand, is a little-traveled, modest,
well-aged track, reworked in 1968. The Lower General Creek
Trail is a recent restoration of an old, abandoned route, which
seems destined for considerable use. Pack trips into the region
may be arranged by writing: Patricia E. Hudson, Meeks Bay
Stables, P. O. Box 234, Meeks Bay, Calif. 95723.

Upper General Creek Trail

	Elev.	Miles from pt. above	Total miles
Richardson Lake Road	7150	0.0	0.0
Trailhead	7150	0.5	0.5
Trail-Logging Road Jctn.	7340	0.7	1.2
Upper-Lower General Creek Trail Jctn.	7160	0.3	1.5
Lake Genevieve Lateral	7480	2.0	3.5
Under Summit 8235	8180	1.6	5.1
Phipps Creek Ford	7620	2.0	7.1
Tahoe-Yosemite Trail	8100	1.6	8.7

The Miller Lake Jeep Road leaves Highway 89 beside Lake Tahoe just south of Chambers Lodge. At the north corner of the junction a street sign reads *Rubicon Rd.* while a large sign on the south corner advertises *McKinney Estates*, and beneath it a smaller sign reads *Miller Lake Jeep Rd.* For a full description of the road see Region 5.

After leaving the pavement behind McKinney Estates, the dirt jeep road, passable to most passenger cars carefully and slowly driven, climbs past McKinney, Lily and Miller lakes to an unmarked junction with the southbound Richardson Lake Road. Below the junction the Richardson Road immediately passes a cow camp, and after several hundred yards it is blocked by several deep mudholes. Just beyond these lies the difficult, rocky ford of the Miller Lake outlet stream. Since these obstacles prevent crossing by passenger cars, our trail begins at the

Richardson Lake Road Jctn. (7150 — 0.0). Beyond the creek the road leads into a little flat and then forks. About 100 yards up the eastern branch is a usually unlocked gate signed *Private Road, No Trespassing.* The rough logging road (headed for Lost Lake) passes a cabin beyond the gate and climbs south to rejoin the trail at the top of the hill. The Richardson Lake Road swings southwest from the fork through a little flat, and just before fording the stream from Richardson Lake we come to the unmarked

Trailhead: North Lateral to the General Creek Trails (7150 — 0.5). (See map.) The trail at first is faint, partly because the few travelers who enter here use the logging road, and partly because the USFS neglected this lateral when it reworked the Gen-

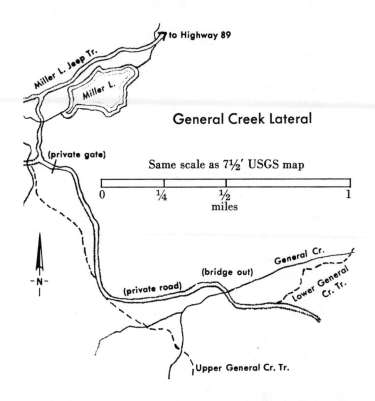

to Highway 89

Miller L. Jeep Tr.

Miller L.

General Creek Lateral

(private gate)

Same scale as 7½′ USGS map

0   ¼   ½   1
miles

General Cr.

(bridge out)

Lower General Cr. Tr.

-N-

(private road)

Upper General Cr. Tr.

eral Creek Trail in 1968. A little way into the woods the trail leaves the stream and, becoming better defined, follows the gently climbing route of a barely recognizable old road up a flat ridge through mixed conifer forest. After crossing a barbed-wire fence in flat meadowland, we return to the logging road and walk several hundred yards up it to the brow of the hill and a signed

Road-Trail Jctn. (7340 — 0.7). A weathered sign by the roadside reads *General Creek, Velma Lakes*, pointing southeast down into a wooded draw. An arrow carved in a nearby tree points in the same direction. The logging road descends to the east down a steep, sandy slope for ½ mile to a ruined bridge at a ford of the Lower General Creek Trail shown on the topo map (see Sec. 3).

From the junction at the top of the hill, which has for all practical purposes become the junction of the Upper and Lower trails, we move southeast down a ducked, blazed faint groove through lodgepole pine and then aspen to a tributary of General Creek. Signs on the south bank mark the official

Upper-Lower General Creek Trail Jctn. (7160 — 0.3). The signs read *Miller Lake 3 miles, Rubicon Springs 9 miles,* northwest, *General Creek Trail, Lake Tahoe 5 miles,* east, and *Velma Lakes 6½ miles,* southeast. A modest groove marked by both freshened and old blazes and a few ducks drops down the tributary a few yards, then circles to the south as it climbs up around a little knob and through a gap above General Creek. We climb southeast under a little knob where the forest thickens, then settle into a gentle ascent through a boggy meadow. After moving south through damp wooded meadow for ¾ mile, we come to the

Lake Genevieve Lateral (7480 — 2.0). A repetitious, contradictory trio of signs read (in summary) *Tallant Lakes* (now named *Genevieve, Crag, Hidden, Shadow, Stony Ridge and Rubicon) 3 miles, Velmas via Tallant Lakes 8 miles, Meeks Bay 7½ miles,* east, *Rubicon Springs Road 4½ miles,* north, and *Velma Lakes 2¼ miles,* south. We turn east on the 2.0 mile trail to Lake Genevieve, climbing gently through light timber past a Land Survey marker. After ascending about 100', the trail levels off across rolling, wooded country for nearly a mile. The route is dim and winding but blazes and gentle country make it easy enough to follow.

A great many deadfalls blocking the trail were bucked in 1969. We descend very slightly past a lily pond, then climb again over a hillock before winding down to the north end of Lake Genevieve. After crossing one branch of the outlet stream on a log jam, we make our way through brushy forest along the shore to cross a second stream on a log and come out into a bare, open camping area. Just to the east is the T-Y Trail and a sign reading *Crag Lake ¼ mile, Stony Ridge Lake 2 miles,* south, and *Meeks Bay 5 miles,* north. No mention is made of the 2.0 mile trail just traversed from General Creek.

Returning to the copiously signed junction by General Creek, we move south into another boggy meadow which apparently once was logged, cross the creek, and climb steeply up switchbacks some 200' under summit 7975 onto a level, flat-topped ridge running southeast. After nearly a mile along the western side of the ridge, we climb steeply another 200' to a little promontory

Under Summit 8235 (8180 — 1.6). This, the highest point on the trail, offers an excellent view west over Rockbound Valley and its reservoirs to the northern peaks of the Crystal Range. There now begins a long, gentle descent southeast through continuously wooded country on modest but generally excellent trail.

We move through a shallow valley, climb over the top of a little ridge, and drop into the drainage of an all-summer creek. At the creek-crossing the trail, which had swung to the east, hooks back to the south and gently descends onto a wooded flat to

Phipps Creek Ford (7620 — 2.0), which in early season we cross on a log just upstream. The trail climbs gradually through pleasant, shady forest for a mile before steepening slightly to mount a low ridge. We drop a few feet southeast into a hollow to a signed junction with the

Tahoe-Yosemite Trail (8100 — 1.6). Old signs read *Phipps Pass, Tallant Lakes, Meeks Bay,* northeast, *Velma Lakes, Rockbound Valley,* south, and *Miller Lakes,* northwest. No distances are given.

SEC. 2

Tahoe-Yosemite Trail

(Meeks Bay to Middle Velma)

	Elev.	Miles from pt. above	Total miles
Meeks Bay Trailhead	6250	0.0	0.0
Lake Genevieve: General Creek Lateral	7420	3.1	3.1
Crag Lake Campground	7500	0.4	3.5
Hidden Lake Trail	7550	0.4	3.9
Stony Ridge Lake	7820	0.8	4.7
Lower Grouse Lake Trail: Rubicon Lake	8380	1.7	6.4
Upper Grouse Lake Trail	8800	0.8	7.2
Phipps Pass	8825	0.1	7.3
West Ridge: Phipps Peak	8740	1.2	8.5
Upper General Creek Trail	8100	1.3	9.8
Velma Trail: Middle Velma Lake	7950	1.0	10.8

The Desolation Wilderness portion of the T-Y Trail was relocated and rebuilt in 1967-68 into a high-speed, minimum-grade wilderness boulevard for backpackers and stock. Much of track remains raw after several winters and some stretches are so highly developed as to be inconsistent with wilderness. In some places the builders have gone to ridiculous lengths to maintain high standards, so that speed and ease of travel cost considerable extra miles.

From the trailhead to the pass the traveler is never far from a lake or stream. The string of lakes from Genevieve to Rubicon, once known as Tallant Lakes, offers many good campsites, but use is considerable and the shady, well-watered country harbors a thick population of mosquitoes that remain past midseason. The view from the southern approach to Phipps Pass may be the finest the Wilderness Area offers. Missing from this predominantly forested country, however, are the vast slopes of bare granite common in Desolation Valley.

The dirt road that winds 1½ miles to the southwest up Meeks Creek valley to the trailhead begins opposite the Meeks Bay Theater on Highway 89 at Lake Tahoe. A USFS sign at the entrance to the road uninvitingly reads *14N00, Meeks Creek Government Trail.* Although rough (and muddy in early season) the road is passable to carefully driven passenger cars. A sign at the spacious parking area at the trailhead reads *Private property behind this sign* (referring to Girl Scout Camp Waisu) *park here.* Other signs beside garbage cans request the traveler to *pack out unburnable refuse and deposit in cans* and remind him to obtain a campfire permit.

Tahoe-Yosemite Trailhead (6260 — 0.0). A sign just west of the road reads *Tahoe-Yosemite Trail, 17E01, Desolation Wilderness Area ½ mile, Lake Genevieve 3 miles.* The big dusty track climbs steadily to the southwest, passing an old road dropping to the Girl Scout camp and an old rock-lined spring. Largely obscured by trees below the trail is an enormous water tank belonging to the camp. The pitch eases as we turn south to contour along the slope, then steepens again as we climb over a little rise to the north fork of Meeks Creek.

For the next mile the trail runs virtually level southwest along the north side of the creek through sandy flats and handsome groves of fern- and snow-plant-floored, mixed-conifer forest. After a 100′ climb, we wind through level forest to a faint branch leading west (a section of the pre-1967 T-Y Trail). A sign at the junction reads *Trail abandoned, not maintained,* and some wag has added "You said it!" A little beyond, the main trail wetly fords Meeks Creek, but 50 feet short of the water a path turns upstream through ferns to a willow and alder thicket, passes several campsites and old tracks, then mounts a long fallen tree which emerges from the thicket to cross the creek.

Beyond the log we have a choice of climbing directly up the steep slope to rejoin the new trail, or following a more gradually climbing old trail to rejoin 100 yards farther south. The topo map shows the trail fording the two forks of the stream separately, but the relocated new trail fords 50 yards below the confluence, and the log crossing is just below it. After swinging south along

170

the creek we turn east and climb ½ mile in a semicircle around a little canyon; the purpose of this ½ mile detour is apparently to maintain a gentle grade. The trail returns to the creek and we complete the climb to

Lake Genevieve (7420 — 3.1). A sign reads *Crag Lake ¼ mile, Stony Ridge Lake 2 miles,* south, and *Meeks Bay 5 miles,* north. There is no mention of the 2.0 mile trail west from this junction to the Upper General Creek Trail (see Sec. 1). Beyond Lake Genevieve we move southeast up a gentle slope, pass the gated rock dam at the foot of Crag Lake and, midway up the shore, come to

Crag Lake Campground (7500 — 0.4) consisting of two large, two-seater, galvanized iron outhouses and a score of concrete fireplaces — all scheduled for either destruction or removal under the new USFS policy of decentralizing camping and minimizing man-made improvements in the Wilderness Area. At the south end of the lake the trail forks. The lower branch quickly peters out as it reaches the stream in the meadow; the upper branch continues southeast, climbing to ford the Shadow Lake outlet, then veering back south a few yards to the

Hidden Lake Trail (7550 — 0.4). A sign reads *Hidden Lake ¼ mile,* southwest, *Stony Ridge Lake 1 mile, Velma Lakes 6 miles,* southeast, and *Lake Genevieve 1 mile,* north. A new trail leads down to Hidden Lake (elevation 7510), where excessive pasturing of stock has somewhat marred the small lake's principal campsite. From the junction we climb east up a rocky open bluff and cross a low ridge to come out above rather marshy Shadow Lake. To the east rises peak 9183. Rubicon Peak was named by the Wheeler Survey Party of 1877 in jesting analogy to Caesar's crossing of the Rubicon. The trail again leads southeast and makes a long, well-graded ascent up a relocated track to

Stony Ridge Lake (7820 — 0.8), where we pass large campsites on the long, wooded western shore. At the upper end of the lake the trail splits: the lower, southeastern branch quickly mires in boggy meadow, while the new, upper track climbs over a little rise, then moves south on high ground in the trees above the meadow. Just below, the old trail can be seen crossing the boggy meadow on a rotting, half-floating ancient boardwalk.

A sign on the ground at the edge of the meadow reads *Trail 17E01, Velma Lakes 5 miles,* south, and *Meeks Bay 9 miles,* north. From the edge of Stony Ridge Meadow the trail makes a stiff, switchbacking climb up a 500′ rocky wall staircased with waterbars. We come through a little draw flanked by snowbanks until midseason and drop to the shore of Rubicon Lake (8340). Big campsites lie along the western shore and the trail passes among them as it turns south and climbs 100 yards past the lake to a junction with the

North Grouse Lake Lateral (8380 — 1.7). Signs read *Velma Lakes 4 miles*, southwest, *Grouse Lake ¼ mile*, southeast, and *Stony Ridge Lake 2 miles, Lake Genevieve 3 miles*, north. The Phipps Pass (T-Y) Trail makes a long traverse northwest above Rubicon Lake, then climbs on a constant grade through a little gap and onto the steep upper slopes of the north ridge of Phipps Peak. As we move southwest on a staircased, climbing traverse of the slope, Upper Grouse Lake becomes visible below, and in the distance we see a part of Cascade Lake through a notch. From a little farther up the trail, Lower Grouse also becomes visible.

Much of the highly engineered trail to the pass was relocated in 1968. Six-by-six timber waterbars, pegged into the granite with steel reinforcing rods, form a series of waterfalls in early season and present knee-wrenching obstacles for the backpacker. It is ironic that these manicured and staircased sections of the trail, thanks to erosion, now offer more difficult footing for both man and beast than the conventionally constructed stretches of the old trail. And despite all the development, snow lies in deep drifts across the trail in several sheltered notches until midseason.

The new trail makes several unfortunate dips to pick up stretches of the old trail (distinguished by faded red paint blazes and ducks). We come around a bend about 50′ above and north of the saddle which forms Phipps Pass to a ducked but unsigned junction with the

South Grouse Lake Lateral (8800 — 0.8). The topo map no longer shows this junction accurately because the new T-Y Trail no longer descends into the saddle (see map). The section of old T-Y Trail, marked by faded red paint blazes and ducks, leading down into the saddle, has become the highest section of the South Grouse Lake Lateral. From this point onward the new T-Y Trail has been relocated far to the north of the old route, which is the one shown on the topo map.

In order to trace the loop of trail visiting Grouse Lakes, we now return to the junction just above Rubicon Lake with the

North Grouse Lake Lateral (8380 — 0.0). Leaving the T-Y Trail we head southeast downhill through a deeply cut trough into a marshy meadow, then circle back to the north and come down the west side of the meadow to Upper Grouse Lake (8180). After passing this shallow, rather uninviting lakelet, the trail grows vague and then forks at a sign reading *Lower Grouse Lake ½ mile*, southeast. The southeastern branch leads over a little rise and down toward now visible and more interesting Lower Grouse (8020).

The southern branch leaves the fork and, turning southwest, leads steeply up a continuous groove marked by culverts and a few ducks and crossed by occasional deadfalls. Following a small creek flowing from the saddle ahead, the no-longer-maintained or signed trail climbs nearly 600' on switchbacks to the saddle, then turns abruptly north up the old T-Y Trail to the earlier-mentioned junction with the

New Tahoe-Yosemite Trail (8800 — 1.2). We now resume our journey southwest on the new trail, but instead of dropping into the saddle and starting down toward Velma Lakes as shown on the topo map, we continue to climb toward Phipps Peak, gaining an additional 50' before reaching the sign that marks

Phipps Pass (8825 — 0.1). Behind the sign on the north side of the trail, a ducked route leads only 50' higher to a pass in the ridge and then drops northeast some 300' to the shore of attractive, well-wooded Phipps Lake, about ½ mile from the T-Y Trail.

From the Phipps Pass sign the backpacker is amazed to discover that the trail continues to climb (passing two more ducked routes leading across the ridge to Phipps Lake). After ascending perhaps 50' more (while the old trail heads south downhill) our boulevard settles into a groove on the 8800' contour line and, with only minor dips and climbs, proceeds to circle for better than a mile around Phipps Peak to the northwest. The peak was named for a General William Phipps.

As we proceed, there unfolds one of the finest panoramic views in the Wilderness. Starting in the southeast with Mt. Tallac and following around in a giant arc to the northwest, we look out upon the three Velma lakes, Dicks and Fontanillis lakes, Dicks and Jacks peaks, Pyramid Peak, Mt. Price, Rockbound Pass, Doris and Lois lakes and finally Red, Silver, McConnell and Tells peaks.

At last forsaking the 8800' contour, the trail drops slightly northwest to a shallow saddle in the

West Ridge of Phipps Peak (8750 — 1.2). A few yards' walk north through the saddle rewards us with a view down into the seldom-visited, officially unnamed lake (known as Lower Phipps) and adjacent meadow that lie a mile downstream from Phipps Lake. The trail leads west along the south side of the ridge toward Middle Mountain (8333) and makes a hairpin turn to the southeast around a rock wall built (unsuccessfully) to prevent short-cutting. We move down a ½ mile traverse to the southeast, but before reaching the old trail we make another hairpin turn

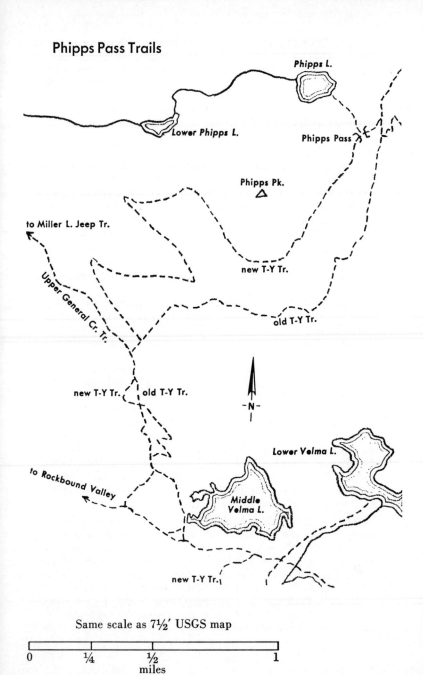

Phipps Pass Trails

Phipps L.

Lower Phipps L.

Phipps Pass

Phipps Pk.
△

to Miller L. Jeep Tr.

Upper General Cr. Tr.

new T-Y Tr.

old T-Y Tr.

new T-Y Tr.   old T-Y Tr.

–N–

Lower Velma L.

to Rockbound Valley

Middle
Velma L.

new T-Y Tr.

Same scale as 7½′ USGS map

| 0 | ¼ | ½ | 1 |

miles

around another wall and traverse nearly ½ mile to the west.

We make two more long, exasperating traverses before finally coming to the old T-Y Trail 100 yards above the Upper General Creek Trail junction. It is impossible to defend the ridiculous length of this trail on the basis of maintenance of grade because the route circles more than a mile from the pass before beginning to descend. We move down the trail 100 yards to a signed junction with the

Upper General Creek Trail (8100 — 1.3). Signs read *Phipps Pass, Tallant Lakes, Meeks Bay*, pointing up toward the pass, *Velma Lakes, Rockbound Valley*, south, and *Miller Lakes*, north. No distances are given. We move south through pleasant parkland several hundred yards on the old trail before the relocated route splits off to the west, drops down a rocky hillside near a small creek, then swings back across the old trail to the east and descends in elaborate sharp switchbacks to the bottom of the slope, where it once more merges with the old trail at an unmarked junction (see map).

Northbound travelers are apt to find the junction confusing because the old trail, though a few sticks have been thrown across the mouth, looks more inviting and substantial and appears to lead in the proper direction; the raw, dusty relocation seems headed around the north shore of Middle Velma. The only possible excuse for this absurd and expensive relocation is a reduction in grade for the benefit of pack animals. The old route, despite lack of maintenance, remains in good condition and is easily followed; I find it clearly superior to the new route.

The merged trails leave the bottom of the slope to enter a wooded meadow west of the lake, and westbound travelers must be extremely vigilant to find the unmarked junction of the inferior shortcut to Camper Flat shown on the topo map. This is an old, obscure, wet trail, little used principally because its northern end is difficult to find. A little way into the woods on the T-Y Trail, we pass a sandy ditch which marks the junction. By heading southwest from the ditch we will come upon a dim groove (often filled with water) and a line of old blazes.

This dim groove weaves through the damp woods and willow thickets, jumps the outlet stream from Middle Velma and finally reaches high ground, where all at once it is well marked with ducks. In less than 100 yards we emerge from the woods at a signed junction with the Velma Trail to Camper Flat (see Region 5, Sec. 5).

Returning to the junction at the sandy ditch, we move south on the T-Y Trail, ford the outlet stream and wind uphill southeast (with minor trail relocations) to the serrated western shore of

Middle Velma. After passing a 100-yard shortcut to the Velma Trail, we come to a signed junction with the

Velma Trail (7950 — 1.0). Signs read *Tallant Lakes, Meeks Bay, Miller Lakes*, north, and *Rockbound Valley, Lake Schmidell*, pointing west toward Camper Flat. No distances are given. For the trail to Camper Flat, see Region 5, Sec. 5. For the trails in Velma Lakes Basin see Region 7.

Sec. 3

Lower General Creek Trail

	Elev.	Miles from pt. above	Total miles
Sugar Pine Point Trailhead	6340	0.0	0.0
General Creek Ford No. 1	6340	0.6	0.6
Burn Pile	6460	0.5	1.1
General Creek Ford No. 2	6420	0.6	1.7
General Creek Ford No. 3	6820	2.0	3.7
Lost Lake Road	7160	0.4	4.1
General Creek Ford No. 4	7100	0.2	4.3
Miller Lake Lateral	7340	0.5	4.8

Neglected for many years, the Lower General Creek Trail became virtually abandoned when the USFS closed the 2½ mile dirt road from Highway 89 to the trailhead. Then, in 1969, as the state began building an enormous (200 unit) campground complex just across the creek, the USFS resurrected (and in a few places relocated) the trail, planning access to come from the new (Sugar Pine Point) campground. So once again a modest but well-marked path leads gently upward through pleasant country beside General Creek.

Although the access afforded to Upper General Creek, Lost and Duck lakes is inferior to that provided by the Miller Lake Lateral from the jeep road of the same name, the new Lower General Creek Trail is a worthwhile end in itself and, being comparatively low in elevation, offers pleasant walking as early as May and as late as November. By early 1970 the precise location of the trailhead (the point on the road beyond which cars will be prohibited) had not yet been determined, but it clearly will be at the western edge of Sugar Pine Point Campground, just south of the settlement of Tahoma.

Driving north along Lake Tahoe on Highway 89 we encounter the first signs mentioning Sugar Pine Point just north of Meeks Bay. The highway dips to cross General Creek at the USFS Guard

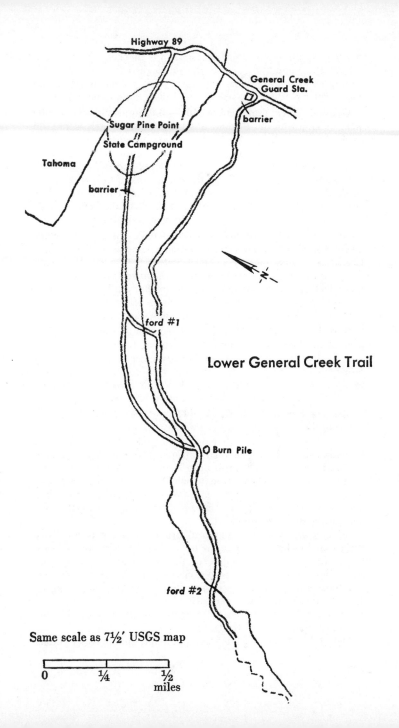

Highway 89

General Creek
Guard Sta.

barrier

Sugar Pine Point
State Campground

Tahoma

barrier

N

ford #1

Lower General Creek Trail

O Burn Pile

ford #2

Same scale as 7½' USGS map

0   ¼   ½
                    miles

Station (where the original access road is blocked), then climbs a bluff a few hundred yards to the well-signed road west into the campground. Future signs and state park personnel will guide the traveler to a parking area behind the campground at the

General Creek Trailhead (6240 — 0.0) approximately a mile west of Highway 89. Beyond a (future) barrier across the old road we begin walking up a broad, shallow, wooded valley perhaps ¼ mile north of General Creek. Moving southwest through level country, the old road comes out of the trees and forks: a branch continues southwest ¼ mile up the north bank of the creek before fording and intersecting the General Creek Road at the Burn Pile. We choose the slightly more direct branch to the south, which passes a yellow section marker and immediately dips to

General Creek Ford No. 1 (6340 — 0.6). The crossing is dry (except in early season) and we climb a few feet to the General Creek Road from the USFS Guard Station (see map). Following the road to the southwest along the streambank, we climb a few more feet into a big, sandy, logged-over flat studded with occasional large ponderosa pine. On the margin of the flat sits a partly charred, house-high pile of logs and debris known as the

Burn Pile (6460 — 0.5). The construction of a 200-unit campground produces a considerable volume of forest debris, which is hauled to this point and periodically burned. For perhaps ½ mile we move across the flat, which in spring is a sandy, flowered meadow, before entering thick pine and fir forest, and winding some 200 yards to a long-ago-washed-out bridge at

General Creek Ford No. 2 (6420 — 0.6). Beyond this dry crossing the overgrown road passes through pleasant mixed-conifer forest interspersed with patches of quaking aspen. After ¼ mile the road ends and the trail continues through young red-and-white fir forest up what must have been a logging road nearly a century ago. The winding track comes out of the forest and turns nearly due west through level, meadowed woodland for more than a mile before the valley begins to narrow and the north slope becomes a steep canyon wall.

Occasionally the relocated trail branches to the north above the partly-blocked old route for better footing. New ducks begin to appear regularly to supplement old blazes and blue plastic ribbons (left over from the trail construction) beside the modest but continuous groove. We pass a "Forest Survey" metal tag on an old barbed-wire fence and switchback steeply 100′ above the creek to circumvent an unusually steep slope, then descend 50′ on the other side to the old trail.

The old trail through this stretch, though dim, is mostly intact and close to the water, and may be preferred by hikers allergic to unnecessary climbing. We make our way through fields of huckleberry oak and buckthorn up the steep-walled, narrow canyon to where the trail forks around a ducked boulder. The west branch continues 50 feet upstream to a small campsite and ends. The south branch drops through brush to

General Creek Ford No. 3 (6820 — 2.0). Beyond the dry crossing on rocks, the trail climbs a few log steps past several handsome pools and abruptly turns south on a looping, switch-backing trail (with several confusing relocations) to mount a bare granite bluff. Just across the canyon a jagged blue cliff rises above us. At the top of the bluff the trail turns back to the west and closely spaced ducks lead us a few yards to the

Lost Lake Road (7160 — 0.4). A pair of large ducks embracing a tree branch mark a junction which hopefully will be signed. We follow the old logging road downhill to the west to the washed-out remains of a huge bridge. A detour moves upstream to the west 50 yards through the trees to make a crossing at

General Creek Ford No. 4 (7100 — 0.2) and return to the bed of the logging road. The trail shown on the topo map from this point to the junction of the Upper General Creek and Miller Lake Lateral trails has virtually ceased to exist, the logging road having taken its place. We consequently are obliged to climb west up the straight dusty road which has been cut into the steep slope, passing the bucked deadfall that blocked it until late 1969, to the top of the hill and a junction with the

Miller Lake Lateral (7340 — 0.5), marked a little obscurely by an arrow cut into a large lodgepole and an old sign reading *General Creek, Velma Lakes,* southwest. For descriptions of the 1.2 mile trail to the Miller Lake Jeep Road in the north and the Upper General Creek Trail in the south see Sec. 1.

Velma Lakes Basin

Velma Lakes Basin, lying west of Lake Tahoe's Emerald Bay, offers, along the scalloped shores of its three handsome lakes, some of the finest campsites in the Desolation Wilderness. In terms of forest cover, the Velma country falls halfway between the brilliant bare granite of Desolation Valley and the dense lodgepole forests of the Phipps Peak region. The basin lacks the configuration of the familiar alpine cirque, and Middle and Lower Velma lakes, though separated by only a very low ridge, drain in opposite directions.

Dicks and Fontanillis lakes occupy a higher, wilder, more barren basin to the south and offer correspondingly more limited camping. Cascade basin, for lack of a mapped trail, sees the fewest visitors of the three, though it offers lower elevation and easier access. In visitor use Velma basin ranks second to Desolation Valley. Though the trail distances to the two are roughly equivalent, the climb to the Velmas is nearly twice as great.

The entry points are both on Highway 89 at Emerald Bay. A foot trail rises from Eagle Falls Campground at the western corner of the bay, and a horse trail climbs from Bay View Guard Station at the southernmost point of the bay. At both trailheads there are rest rooms, picnic areas, campgrounds and parking lots. At Bayview there is also a general store, gas station and telephone.

Except for the highly unofficial route into Cascade basin, the trails are excellent, highly developed and well signed, especially

181

the new portion of the T-Y Trail which passes north-south through the basin. Campsites are plentiful, water is abundant and wood supply is adequate. Brush is minimal, except in lower Cascade basin. Use tends to be heavy at Middle and Upper Velma, and mosquitos are active well into midseason. Cascade Stables (H. R. Ebright, Box 7034, South Lake Tahoe, Calif. 95716, tel. KL 1-2055) offers services ranging from pony rides to pack trips.

SEC. 1
Eagle Falls Trail to Middle Velma Lake

	Elev.	Miles from pt. above	Total miles
Eagle Falls Campground (trailhead)	6600	0.0	0.0
Eagle Lake Trail Jctn.	7000	1.0	1.0
Eagle Falls-Bay View Trail Jctn.	8180	1.6	2.6
Dicks Pass-Velma Lakes Trail Jctn.	8180	0.7	3.3
Old Tahoe-Yosemite Trail Jctn.	7960	0.8	4.1
New Tahoe-Yosemite Trail Jctn.	7980	0.1	4.2
Middle Velma Lake (west end)	7950	0.3	4.5

The Eagle Falls trail comes close to being a backpacker's ideal. Horses are not permitted, location is sensible and grade is controlled intelligently. Deadfalls, waterbars, staircases, unnecessary climbs and poor footing are at a minimum. In these respects it contrasts vividly with the Bay View horse trail, which should be avoided by the backpacker—or at least never ascended.

At the western corner of Emerald Bay on Highway 89 a large sign at the mouth of Eagle Creek Canyon reads *Eldorado National Forest Campground, Eagle Falls*. Behind it lies a paved parking lot flanked by restrooms and a picnic area to the south and a campground to the north. At the western end of the parking lot (which on weekends may be full) is the

Eagle Falls Trailhead (6600 — 0.0). A sign reads *17E03, Emerald Bay Trail, Desolation Wilderness ¼ mile, Eagle Lake 1 mile*. Just beyond, a second sign warns, *Horse travel unsafe beyond this point*. A third sign, at a branch to the campground, reads *Trail* and points south toward a small waterfall. After ascending a steep, rocky staircase in the bottom of the canyon, the trail splits into two tracks (the lower, southern branch is better) which rejoin after a few yards and climb around a point of rock to cross a wooden bridge just above the waterfall.

Under soaring cliffs on the south side of Eagle Creek we climb steeply over boulders onto a broad trail of springy duff that winds upward through deep-shaded pine forest. The trail splits from time to time, and the branchings are all unmarked, but as we move up the canyon all tracks eventually return and we climb up out of the woods on open granite under high cliffs to a junction with the

Eagle Lake Trail (7000 — 1.0). A sign reads *Eagle Lake,* southwest, *Velma Lake Camp 3½ miles, Dicks Lake 4 miles*, south, and *Eagle Falls Camp*, north. Impressive Eagle Lake immediately becomes visible in its barren, handsome amphitheater through an open stand of giant red fir as we climb steeply to the south on a long traverse that gains 700′ in ½ mile.

We dip a few feet through a hollow to cross an all-summer creek, then switchback steeply up a wooded ravine near the rattling cascade, occasionally following recent relocations of the trail, and finally coming out into a wet, flowered meadow and passing through a sandy saddle. The trail drops 50′ to the west, then swings south to contour on a gentle incline across a steep, sandy slope for ½ mile. We then switchback steeply but briefly, climbing now to the southwest, and move up a sandy draw through patches of timber into a saddle to the

Eagle Falls-Bay View Trail Jctn. (8180 — 1.6). A variety of old and new signs read *Bay View 2½ miles, Azure Lake ¾ mile, Granite Lake 1 mile*, pointing to a staircase rising to the southeast, and *Velma Lake 2 miles, Rockbound Valley, Dicks Lake 4 miles*, pointing west. To this point, the Eagle Falls Trail has climbed 1600′ in 2.6 interesting miles. By comparison, the Bay View Trail has risen 1650′ in 3.2 miles of dull, dusty horse trail.

Now on the combined (Emerald Bay) trail, we move west-southwest across rolling, rocky, open lodgepole woodland, dipping through a shallow basin at the bottom of which, at an unmarked junction, a trail leads southeast down a gentle incline to Azure Lake. Because the trail down becomes difficult and dim, the USFS plans to eliminate it on future maps. We climb gradually west through a little saddle to the

Dicks Pass-Velma Lakes Trail Jctn. (8180 — 0.7), which, though unsigned, is well marked by an "X" carved in a tree and a pile of rocks (which once supported a signpost) at the edge of a shallow snowpool. (The USFS promises to re-sign this junction.) The trail northwest through a saddle drops through open, rolling woodland past several lakelets and snowpools, skirts an unnamed lake between Upper and Lower Velma and fords the pleasant creek which joins them. (By midseason it can easily be jumped about 50 yards downstream.) We pass several campsites and 50 yards west of the stream come to a junction with the

Old Tahoe-Yosemite Trail (7960 — 0.8). An old sign reads *Emerald Bay 4½ miles, Bay View 4½ miles,* pointing back east. (The USFS plans a more informative sign to include the Camper Flat and Old T-Y trails.) This junction marks the most popular point of departure for Lower Velma Lake, via an unmapped path that runs northeast down a gentle, wooded slope beside the stream. Continuing west, we move uphill into thick forest for several hundred yards to a junction with the

New Tahoe-Yosemite Trail (7980 — 0.2) built in 1968. New signs read *Dicks Lake 1¼ miles, Dicks Pass 2½ miles, Glen Alpine Springs 7 miles,* south, and *Middle Velma Lake ¼ mile, Rockbound Valley 2 miles,* west. A few yards north, the trail comes out of the trees and we look out across the roughly triangular surface of island-studded Middle Velma to the forested slopes of 9234′ Phipps Peak. We turn west to parallel the south shore and at the west end of the lake in a thicket of lodgepole we come to a junction with the

Middle Velma Lake (west end) (7950 — 0.3). Signs read *Tallant Lakes, Meeks Bay, Miller Lakes,* north, and *Rockbound Valley, Lake Schmidell,* west, with no distances. For trails to the north see Region 6, Sec. 2. For trails to the west see Region 5, Sec. 5.

Sec. 2
Bay View Trail to Old Tahoe-Yosemite Trail

	Elev.	Miles from pt. above	Total miles
Bay View (Cascade Stables Corral)	6850	0.0	0.0
Granite Lake Roadend	7350	0.7	0.7
Granite Lake Jctn.	7700	0.5	1.2
Bay View-Eagle Falls Trail Jctn.	8180	2.0	3.2
Dicks Pass-Velma Lakes Jctn.	8180	0.7	3.9
Dicks Pass-Old T-Y Trail (north jctn.)	8270	0.7	4.6

The Eagle Falls trailhead warns against horse travel; the Bay View trailhead should offer a warning to backpackers. Besides being exceptionally steep in spots, the dusty, dung-splattered trail is unusually dull. The logical route from Bay View to Velma Basin would ascend Cascade Creek (see Sec. 5) but because that route is blocked by a parcel of private land the USFS has been obliged to run the Bay View trail nearly to the top of 8700′ Maggies

Peaks. So, despite a trailhead 250′ higher than Eagle Falls, the climb up this trail is greater by about 50′.

A sign at the southernmost point of Highway 89 in Emerald Bay reads *17E04, Bay View Trail, Granite Lake 1 mile, Desolation Wilderness 1¼ miles.* The sign marks the entrance to a dirt road which skirts the southern edge of Bay View Campground for 0.2 mile before arriving at a corral sign, *Cascade Stables, fishing, hunting, pack trips, KL 1-2055.*

Cascade Stables Corral (6850 — 0.0). At the corral the road forks: the south branch, passable to passenger cars, leads over private property to a saddle above Cascade Lake; the west branch leads to within ½ mile of Granite Lake, but loose rock and extreme grade make it passable only to jeeps, so we park among the trees at the corral.

Just west of the corral a USFS sign reads *Granite Lake Trail,* pointing up the west branch of the road. After 100 yards' walk we come to the trailhead and a sign reading *Granite Lake 1¼ miles, Azure Lake 3 miles, Velma Lakes 4½ miles, Rockbound Valley 6½ miles.* The trail moves away from the road to the south in a series of long, carefully graded switchbacks that climb up a gloomy, dust-filled trench through dense forest.

After ½ mile we return to the steeply climbing road as it makes a sharp turn. (There is no sign at the road-trail junction but if the downward-bound hiker misses the trail he will discover the road offers a steeper but more direct and less confined route to the trailhead.) We climb steeply to the northwest into a parking area on a little point at the

Granite Lake Roadend (7350 — 0.7). The trail leaves the parking area toward the southwest, climbing a steep, lightly wooded slope through large trees on a dusty, occasionally switchbacking groove to

Granite Lake Jctn. (7700 — 0.5). We pass above the oval, shaded lake (which lies at 7670′) and the large campsite beside it, and begin climbing very steeply up dusty switchbacks that ascend directly up a wooded cliff to the west. The trail makes one long traverse to the south, then switchbacks to the southwest up a slope threaded by a variety of old trails and shortcut chutes.

Nearly 800′ above Granite Lake we emerge suddenly from the trees to find a marvelous, almost aerial view of Emerald Bay, Cascade Lake and Tahoe. Having reached nearly 8500′ the trail passes between Maggies Peaks and levels off to cross the flat western slope of the higher, more southerly peak. We then move gently down through open parkland offering occasional views to the north of the cliffs rising above Eagle Lake toward Phipps

Peak. After ½ mile we drop steeply by staircase into a gap where a sign reads *Granite Lake ¾ mile, Bay View 2 miles,* northeast, and *Velma Lakes 1¾ miles,* southwest.

From this sign we move out along the narrowing ridgetop that extends southwest from Maggies Peaks, gradually dropping almost 300′ before abruptly turning north around the nose of the ridge and descending a flight of stairs to the

Bay View-Eagle Falls Trail Jctn. (8180 — 2.0). A variety of signs offer a variety of distances (see Sec. 1) and we move off to the west on the combined (Emerald Bay) trail across rolling, rocky, open woodland, dropping slightly into a shallow basin, at the bottom of which, at an unmarked junction, a trail leads southwest toward Azure Lake. We climb gradually west through a little saddle to the

Dicks Pass-Velma Lakes Trail Jctn. (8180 — 0.7). The junction, though unsigned, is marked by an "X" carved into a tree in front of a pile of rocks beside a small snowmelt pond. The trail to the northwest (see Sec. 1) drops into Velma Basin. We take the trail to the southwest which makes its way across rough and rocky but nearly level ground, climbs over a rounded granite knoll and drops into a shallow ravine, crossing an all-summer creek just below a lakelet. Though the blazes were freshened in 1968 the track at times is dim. We climb directly toward dome 8619 for several hundred yards to an unsigned junction with the

Old Tahoe-Yosemite Trail (8270 — 0.7). The junction, in bare rock, is hard to recognize. A 4′ log, sawn on both ends, has been placed at the mouth of the trail down to Upper Velma (which has been officially abandoned), evidently to block it. Except for overgrown blazes there is nothing more to mark the junction. The USFS has promised to maintain and re-sign the old trail from the Dicks Pass-Velma Lakes junction to Dicks Lake.

Sec. 3
New Tahoe-Yosemite Trail
(Middle Velma Lake to Dicks Pass)

	Elev.	Miles from pt. above	Total miles
Middle Velma Lake (south end)	7980	0.0	0.0
Fontanillis Lake (outlet)	8300	0.9	0.9
Dicks Lake Trail Jctn.	8440	0.7	1.6
Old Velma Trail	8460	0.1	1.7
Dicks Pass Trail	8600	0.3	2.0
Dicks Pass	9380	1.4	3.4

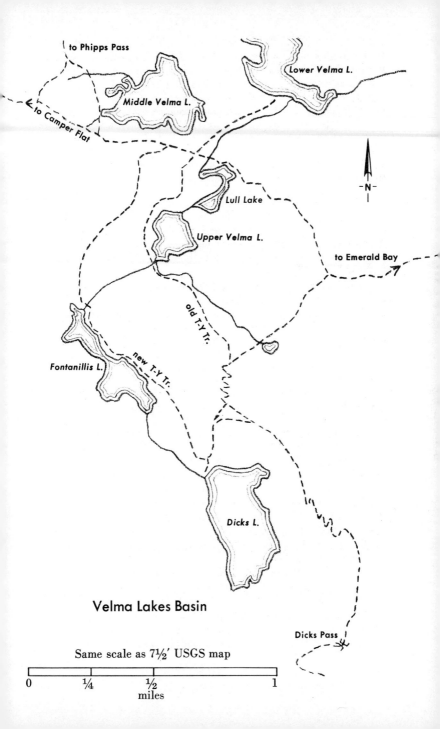

to Phipps Pass

to Camper Flat

Middle Velma L.

Lower Velma L.

-N-

Lull Lake

Upper Velma L.

to Emerald Bay

old T-Y Tr.

Fontanillis L.

new T-Y Tr.

Dicks L.

Velma Lakes Basin

Dicks Pass

Same scale as 7½′ USGS map

0   ¼   ½   1
miles

The southernmost section of the old T-Y Trail through Velma Basin makes a stiff 540' climb on slippery slabs up a shaded north slope that generally is buried under a snowdrift until midseason and streaming with water thereafter. This route has long plagued packers, hikers and USFS trail-maintenance crews, so in 1968 a completely new trail, ½ mile west of the old one, was opened to connect the Velma-Camper Flat Trail in the north with the Dicks Pass Trail in the south.

The 3.4-mile new route, which efficiently spreads the short steep climb into a long pleasant grade, is shown only on the newest USFS map, and then somewhat inaccurately. With the opening of the new trail the 1-mile stretch of the old trail (shown on all maps) between Upper Velma and the next junction to the south has been officially abandoned and all signs referring to it have disappeared. Since it nevertheless is still both useful and passable, accounts are supplied here for both T-Y trails, the old and the new (see map).

Middle Velma Lake: south end (7980 — 0.0). New signs read *Dicks Lake 1¼ miles, Dicks Pass 2½ miles, Glen Alpine Springs 7 miles*, south, and *Middle Velma Lake ¼ mile, Rockbound Valley 2 miles*, west. The trail passes through deep forest up the nose of a small ridge for several hundred yards, then, climbing at a controlled grade on a duff-floored track, swings to the south, dips slightly and drops to cross a small creek usually running to mid-summer.

Marked by a continuous new groove and fresh blazes but no ducks, the trail climbs out of the woods on the south side of the creek and turns southwest to ascend a strip of tilted meadowland before re-entering the forest and climbing a low, flat-topped ridge. We drop 50' to the ford at

Fontanillis Lake (8300 — 0.9), crossing the outlet stream on rocks. The trail clings tightly to the northeastern shore for ½ mile, then moves uphill to the southeast above a barren-looking lakelet. We climb an excellent groove up a steepening, open slope and move into a patch of timber to the

Dicks Lake Trail (8440 — 0.7). A sign beside a large log reads *Dicks Lake ¼ mile*. This sign was made for the old junction, and we discover it to be only 50 yards to a sign at the shore near the outlet reading *Dicks Lake, elevation 8420*. The trail turns abruptly north up a gentle slope, coming out of the trees to an unmarked, easily missed junction with the

Old Tahoe-Yosemite Trail (8460 — 0.1). The two trails diverge only slightly as they move northward: the old T-Y Trail continues faintly northward into a saddle, while the new T-Y

Trail gradually curves to the east and is heading southeast by the time we reach the

Dicks Pass Trail (8600 — 0.3), which has come directly southeast from the above-mentioned saddle. The shortest route from Emerald Bay, as the map shows, goes southwest from the Emerald Bay Trail to the old T-Y Trail, climbs to the saddle, then turns southeast on the old Dicks Pass Trail and intersects the new trail at this junction in a little flat above the northeast corner of the lake.

With the last junction behind us we climb south on a broad, high-standard track that was completely rebuilt in 1968. It leads continuously upward at a controlled grade through dusty switchbacks across a tree-studded sandy slope above the eastern shore of Dicks Lake. An overabundance of waterbars and an excess of switchbacks make travel arduous for the backpacker. Under the southernmost point of a switchback halfway to the pass, an icy spring issues from the ground. This is the last dependable source of water until Gilmore Lake, some 3 miles southeast over the pass. After switchbacking to better than 9000', the trail takes off on a long, climbing traverse to the south (often buried beneath snowdrifts until midseason) that ends in a barren, broad, cobblestoned flat at

Dicks Pass (9380 — 1.6) halfway between a little knoll to the west and summit 9579 to the east. A sign reads *Dicks Pass, elevation 9500*, the 120' exaggeration evidently meant to flatter the perspiring hiker.

Sec. 4

Old Tahoe-Yosemite Trail

(Middle Velma to Dicks Pass Trail)

	Elev.	Miles from pt. above	Total miles
Middle Velma (southeast end)	7960	0.0	0.0
Upper Velma Lake (south end)	7940	0.5	0.5
Emerald Bay Trail Jctn.	8270	1.0	1.5
Old Dicks Lake-Dicks Pass Trail Jctn.	8500	0.5	2.0
New Tahoe-Yosemite Trail (Dicks Lake)	8460	0.2	2.2
Dicks Pass Trail	8600	0.3	2.3

Since the new T-Y Trail was opened in 1968, the old one has been neglected. All signs referring to it have disappeared and there has been no maintenance, despite the USFS promise that all but the abandoned 1.0 mile south of Upper Velma will be maintained in its transportation system. The heavily used northern section remains in good condition but the remainder, though passable, has somewhat deteriorated.

Middle Velma, southeast end (7960 — 0.0). This junction, out of sight of Middle Velma though only a few hundred yards distant, lies 100 yards west of the ford of the Upper-Lower Velma Creek. It is marked by a sign, *Emerald Bay 4½ miles, Bay View 4½ miles.*

Moving south on the old trail we almost immediately cross a small creek and pass along the margin of a number of large campsites in an open grove of lodgepole before coming to a sign on the meadowed shore reading *Upper Velma Lake, elevation 7960.* The trail climbs away from the water over a low peninsula, then returns to pass beween the lake and a pond close beside it to the inlet stream at

Upper Velma Lake, south end (7940 — 0.5), which cascades down a bare granite slope from Fontanillis Lake. The trail continues to climb southeast up bare slab which gives way to a creekbed coming down the slope from the east. We cross and recross the creek — at times the trail is indistinguishable from the creek — splashing upward on a rocky, open slope to the dim junction with

Emerald Bay Trail (8270 — 1.0). Except for a few overgrown blazes, the junction is marked only by a 4′ log, sawn on both ends, that blocks the entrance to the abandoned section we have just ascended. We continue upward to the south through steepening gullies that are often streaming with snowmelt water, crossing slippery slabs into which footsteps have been chiseled to help stock keep their feet. A snowdrift on the highest slope under the saddle forces us, before midseason, to detour to the west close beneath summit 8619, then angle back into the saddle above the snow, where we find the junction of the

Old Dicks Lake-Dicks Pass Trail (8500 — 0.5). From this junction in the saddle we have a choice of trails. The old Dicks Lake Trail takes us southwest to the new T-Y Trail and to Dicks and Fontanillis lakes, while the old Dicks Pass Trail takes us southeast to an unmarked junction with the new Dicks Pass Trail. The old Dicks Lake Trail follows a series of ducks through the saddle and gently descends southwest across a sandy, almost treeless plain under summit 8619 until it merges, at a junction marked only by a faint groove and an old blaze, with the

New Tahoe-Yosemite Trail: above Dicks Lake (8460 — 0.2).

Cascade Basin
(Emerald Bay to Snow and Azure lakes)

	Elev.	Miles from pt. above	Total miles
Emerald Bay (Cascade Corral)	6850	0.0	0.0
Cascade Rim trailhead	6900	0.2	0.2
Cascade Falls	6900	0.7	0.9
Azure-Snow Lake Trail Jctn.	7300	1.6	2.5
Snow Lake	7380	0.5	3.2
Azure Lake	7700	0.7	3.7

Anyone who has driven south from Emerald Bay has looked down on Cascade Lake and the waterfall at the mouth of the small basin above it. Flanked by Maggies Peaks on the north and Mt. Tallac on the south, this deep and impressive little basin contains an all-year stream and four lakes of varying size and accessibility. Because Cascade and the lands surrounding it are privately owned and posted against trespassers, the Forest Service has been unable to build a public trail into the region, and has been forced to build its Bay View Trail almost to the top of Maggies Peaks.

But a trail of sorts does exist. Often hard to find and difficult to follow, it passes from Bay View on Emerald Bay across a currently unposted corner of private land, and up into the lake basin above the falls onto land which is a part of the Wilderness Area. A road from Cascade Stables Corral (under the same ownership as Cascade Lake) climbs to Cascade Rim. Since several brushfields must be crossed, hikers are advised to wear full-length trousers.

Cascade Stables Corral (6850 — 0.0) is reached by 0.2 mile of dirt road from a Forest Service sign at Bay View Guard Station at the southernmost point of Highway 89 on Emerald Bay. The road forks at the corral and the branch to the south, passable to passenger cars, heads up a little draw and ends on the flat top of

Cascade Rim (6900 — 0.2), where there is adequate room to park. The beginning of the trail, though unsigned and unmarked, is not difficult to find. From the roadhead it drops 20-30′ due south down a dusty gully in the brush toward Cascade Lake, visible below, then swings southwest toward the falls, leveling off near the 6800′ contour. There follows an exasperating, hot ½

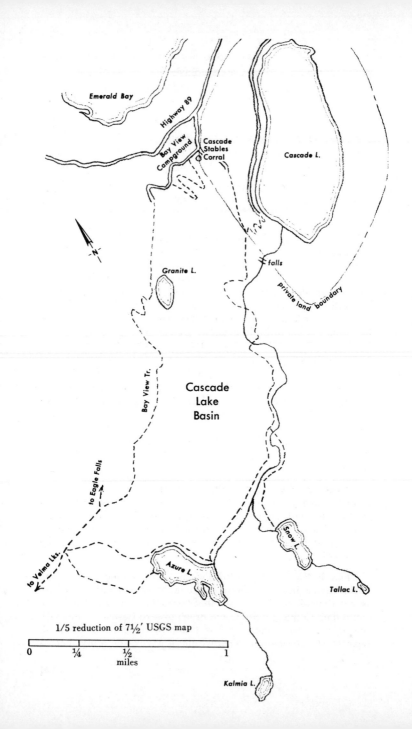

Emerald Bay

Highway 89

Bay View Campground

Cascade Stables Corral

Cascade L.

N

Granite L.

falls

private land boundary

Cascade Lake Basin

Bay View Tr.

to Eagle Falls

to Velma Lks.

Snow

Azure L.

Tallac L.

Kalmia L.

1/5 reduction of 7½′ USGS map

0   ¼   ½   1
miles

mile during which the trail roller-coasters across a steep, largely shadeless slope through dense brushfields of waist-high manzanita, whitethorn and huckleberry oak.

At times the path grows so faint as barely to qualify as game trail; other stretches offer a well-traveled track and even a few ducks. In places there are multiple paths where travelers have been unable to agree on the best course. Near the west end of the lake, we intersect a well-defined trail switchbacking up from the end of the private road beside the lakeshore. From that point on the route is much improved.

The brushfield ends at the granite barrier over which Cascade Falls drops from the basin above. With considerable relief we exchange brush for rock and make our way upward on conveniently located ledges that lead into the mouth of the upper basin, several hundred yards north of and 100′ above

Cascade Falls (6800 — 0.7). The trail continues southwest, almost unmarked, across rolling, open granite until it reaches the handsome tree-shaded stream near a campsite. Almost immediately the way is blocked by a swampy alder thicket, and we are forced to veer north on granite along its eastern margin, to where a highly visible track moves across in grass through a patch of wild onion; a second route crosses the thicket on a log. Beyond the alders the trail turns back to the south to cross the stream on stepping stones to a smooth granite slab above a waterfall.

Moving southwest once more, we climb up a sparsely ducked, dry ravine on sloping slab and cross the creek at the foot of a massive, monolithic sugarloaf of granite. The ducked route edges to the north around the low end of the barrier, then climbs south up the ridge above a lily pond and over the top into the flat, wooded valley through which Cascade Creek flows.

The trail is clear and easily followed in this more easily marked woodland; there are ducks on granite slabs and new blazes on some of the trees. About ½ mile above the sugarloaf barrier the trail comes close to the creek and divides at the

Azure-Snow Lake Trail Jctn. (7300 — 1.6). Though the junction is not signed, a fancy duck, lying within a circle of small stones, contains a pair of sticks which indicate the general directions in which the two trails lead. Just west of this exotic duck, close to the creek, are a boulder topped with dead branches and a giant deadfall through which travelers have worn a notch. From the otherwise unmarked junction the Azure trail continues southwest along the north side of the stream in a noticeably fainter but continuous groove.

193

The Snow Lake Trail, which we first shall trace, makes a somewhat precarious crossing of the creek on a small, partly submerged log and heads south up a well-worn track. We pass through a duff-bottomed snowmelt pool (dry before the summer season) and turn southwest to climb parallel to the stream.

In heavy forest the trail turns west and passes between the stream and a lily pond, then arcs gently south away from the water and passes a land-survey marker dated 1929. We return to the stream and a much-littered campsite, and climb out of the trees up over a rocky bluff and down to the shore of

Snow Lake (7380 — 0.7). This unusually attractive lake, hemmed in by cliffs to the west and south, offers a variety of fine campsites despite an appalling volume of debris. Just west of the lake, partly hidden by forest, rises a spectacular mound of granite, so smooth and so white that at first glance through the trees it looks more like a snowdrift or sand dune than rock. Hard-to-reach Tallac Lake lies in a little bowl some 500′ up the cliffs, south-southwest of Snow Lake. Returning to the

Azure-Snow Lake Trail Jctn. (7300 — 0.0) we skirt a jumble of boulders and downed trees and move southwest along the edge of the woods on the northern margin of the valley. The trail grows progressively fainter as we proceed, but almost ½ mile above the junction a line of ducks materializes to lead us west up a brushy ravine which opens into a small box canyon.

At first there seems no feasible route up a steep cleft in the granite wall but, looking up carefully, we see a 20′ length of hemp rope hanging across the steepest pitch. With the help of the rope we move up the cleft and out onto a steep granite slope. Ducks lead a little to the north, away from the falls coming down from Azure, and we ascend a series of draws and gullies that eventually swings back to the outlet stream through several large camps and passes through a little notch to the eastern shore of

Azure Lake (7700 — 0.7). Except for those just mentioned, the only good camps on this majestic, cliff-ringed lake are on the north end, from which a trail climbs steeply northwest out of the basin to intersect (at an unmarked junction) the Velma Basin Trail from Emerald Bay (see Sec. 1). Kalmia Lake, possibly the most remote named lake in the Wilderness Area, can be reached by an exceptionally steep 900′ climb up the west side of the inlet stream at the south end of Azure Lake. There are several good places to camp.

Chapter 13—Region 8

Fallen Leaf Lake

The watershed draining east from Desolation Valley to Fallen Leaf Lake is bounded on the north by the high, barren ridge running from Jacks and Dicks peaks to Mt. Tallac, and on the south by an almost equally impressive wall running from Keith's Dome to Echo Peak. The western apex of this roughly triangular region is the junction of the T-Y and Pacific Crest trails at the northeast corner of Lake Aloha.

Contained within this valley are a dozen attractive lakes, a large, all-year stream, excellent accessible campsites, a soda spring, several roadhead resorts and a fine network of trails in addition to high, remote ridges and paths among the peaks. In terms of visitor use, the region ranks third behind Echo and Emerald Bay. In terms of access to Desolation Valley, the trail is half again as long as from Echo, and the climb is more than 1000′ greater. Although Angora Lakes and Tallac Creek do not drain toward Fallen Leaf, the trails at each fall most logically into this region.

There are three main roadheads, all of which are reached from Highway 89 at the south end of Lake Tahoe. Just west of Camp

195

Richardson, at a sign reading *Fallen Leaf Lake 5 miles,* a narrow paved road turns south into the timber, passes a large USFS campground and 2 miles above the highway comes to a junction signed *Fallen Leaf 4 miles, Glen Alpine Springs 6 miles,* pointing south on the paved road, and *Angora Lookout 4 miles, Angora Lakes 6 miles,* pointing east up a dirt road (see Sec. 9). The paved road winds among the trees to the south end of Fallen Leaf, to a marina, store, lodge and rental cabins, gas station, coffee shop and telephone. Fallen Leaf apparently was named for Delaware Indian Chief Falling Leaf, who guided a Tahoe-Sierra exploring party in the late 1840's. The nearest pack station is Camp Richardson Corrals (write Allen Rose, P. O. Box 126, Camp Richardson, Calif. 95716) although Echo Corrals (see Region 1) also packs in this area.

A few hundred yards beyond the lodge, the road forks again at what is locally called "the crossroads." A paved road branches north and immediately crosses Glen Alpine Creek. It threads its way 0.6 mile north through Stanford University Alumni summer camp to end by the lakeshore trailhead of the Cathedral Trail (see Sec. 8). The south branch from the crossroads is the Clark trail, which switchbacks 850' up Angora Peak to the parking lot by the locked gate below Angora Lakes. From the fork in the road at the bridge, we continue west up the Glen Alpine Spring Road and immediately pass signs reading *Private Campground, Private Property.* Despite the exclusive tone, the public is welcome. We pass through the campground and follow a winding paved road which climbs 0.2 mile to a sign on the south side of the road reading *Triangle Lake 3 miles, Haypress Meadows 4 miles.* This is the northern end of the Tamarack Trail.

The road crosses the creek on a wooden bridge as the pavement ends, and we make our way on gravel along the north shore of uninspiring Lily Lake, passing over a cable which blocks the road in the winter, and crossing a stream-bed (which flows in early spring) on cobblestones. A little beyond Lily the rough and rutted road begins to climb and, just 1.0 mile above the fork at Fallen Leaf, we come to a forest of signs reading, in part, *Private Road, Park below this point. No fires, littering, hunting, shooting. Desolation Wilderness Trails ¾ miles,* pointing west up the road, and *No unauthorized vehicles beyond this point.*

As might be apparent, the road above this point runs on private land and the owners are quite serious about keeping vehicles out (hikers and horsemen are welcome). Beyond this point there are additional signs and a cable across the road, which locks to a tree and is labeled *Private Road, absolutely no vehicles.* Even if the road over private land were open to the public it could not

196

be considered passable to passenger cars, so for all practical purposes the trail may be considered to begin at the public-private land boundary at the bottom of the hill, which we will call the "Lily Lake Parking Lot" (see Sec. 1).

To reach the remaining roadhead (to the Floating Island trail up Tallac) we continue northwest on Highway 89 1½ miles beyond the Fallen Leaf Lake road and turn south at a large sign reading *Spring Creek Summer Home Tract.* Avoiding the numerous roads turning west, we drive due south up a paved road beside Tallac Creek for 0.8 mile to a bend in the road close to the water, where several signs mark the trailhead.

SEC. 1

Glen Alpine Trail

(Fallen Leaf to Lake Aloha)

	Elev.	Miles from pt. above	Total miles
Lily Lake Parking Lot	6540	0.0	0.0
Glen Alpine Springs	6800	1.0	1.0
Grass Lake Trail	7000	0.5	1.5
Susie Shortcut (east end)	7800	1.4	2.9
Dicks Pass Trail	7940	1.4	3.3
Susie Shortcut (west end)	7700	0.4	3.7
Susie Lake (outlet)	7780	0.6	4.3
Heather Lake (outlet)	7900	1.0	5.3
Pacific Crest Trail: Lake Aloha	8100	1.0	6.3

As described above a mile west of Fallen Leaf Lake Lodge, just west of Lily Lake, we come to the end of public land at a collection of signs (none of them USFS) which warn us to drive no farther. This is the

Lily Lake Parking Lot (6540 — 0.0). Since the road beyond this point is private and posted against vehicles, we are obliged to park (space is limited) and begin hiking. The rutted road climbs steeply in loose gravel, passes a side road and a cluster of cabins, then levels off at a cable across the road (sometimes locked) just below a new A-frame named "WigWam Ranch." The road passes through a patch of lodgepole forest and comes out into the tree-shaded, parklike meadow at

Glen Alpine Spring (6800 — 1.0). We pass a large barn and the ruins of several old buildings before reaching a handsome glass-and-stone chalet beside the wishing-well-like shelter that houses the bubbling spring. Of all the mineral springs in this guide, this one unquestionably is the best-tasting. A sign on the chalet boasts of the charged carbonic acid spring: . . . *its action is diuretic, laxative and stimulative to the entire digestive tract; beneficial in dyspepsia, torpid liver, kidney and bladder irritations; is also a tonic* . . . Nathan Gilmore's wife named the springs from Sir Walter Scott's *Lady of the Lake.*

At the opposite end of the chalet, housed in a blue box, is a pay telephone (541-9711). At the upper end of the meadow are picnic tables, concrete stoves, garbage cans and the official trailhead. A USFS sign reads *17E06, Glen Alpine Trail, Desolation Wilderness* ½ *mile, Susie Lake* 2½ *miles,* and a second sign warns that all motor vehicles are prohibited beyond this point.

A virtually new trail, reconstructed in 1968 to the highest USFS standards, leads south out of the lush, shady meadow and winds upward at a controlled grade through jumbled terrain of alternating boulders and brush. After 0.4 mile we leave the brush and come into the trees quite close to the creek, to pass the old Grass Lake Trail, now blocked with a line of stones. The old trail is both more modest and more direct. I find it adequately marked and preferable to the new trail. We pass a waterfall and an inviting pool and 100 yards farther up the Glen Alpine Trail come to the junction of the new

Grass Lake Trail (7000 — 0.5). A sign reads *Grass Lake 1 mile, Trail Ends 1 mile,* southwest. Almost immediately we begin to climb a steep, rocky slope along the east bank of Gilmore Creek on a newly located track. Long, sharply turning switchbacks studded with waterbars saw their way monotonously up the slope. Sections of the old, steeper, less elaborate trail frequently come into view.

About ¾ mile upstream the rocky brush gives way to light lodgepole forest and the slope eases slightly. Angling to the northwest we cross some 75 yards of boardwalk overlaid with granite sand. After only two years it was already partly washed out and growing hazardous. As a trail-building technique in country of this sort boardwalks, covered or otherwise, are absurd. With creaking knees we ascend another long flight of waterbar steps as the trail, closely following the creek, gradually arcs to the west into a patch of lodgepole to the

Susie Shortcut: east end (7800 — 1.4). Signs read *Gilmore Lake 1 mile, Half Moon Lake 2 miles, Dicks Pass 3 miles,* northwest, *Glen Alpine Springs 3 miles,* east, and *Susie Lake* ½ *mile,* southwest. The Susie and Glen Alpine distances are unusually inaccurate. Travelers bound for Susie Lake and points beyond should avoid the 0.8 mile main trail, which climbs 340′ then promptly loses 240', in favor of the 0.6 mile Susie shortcut which travels on the level through a snowpool-studded, wooded draw, then drops 100' before hooking to the north to rejoin the main trail.

From the shortcut's east end the main trail crosses a wooded flat, then climbs a steep woodland slope on a switchbacking staircase to an unfortunate and somewhat confusing double junction with the Half Moon Trail and

Dicks Pass Trail (7940 — 0.4). At the southern (lower) junction on a little knoll above a snowpond, our trail intersects the T-Y Trail going from Dicks Pass to Susie Lake. There is no longer any sign and the junction is confused by several shortcut paths and sections of old trail. Some 50 yards up the Dicks Pass Trail to the north (out of sight) is the clearly marked and signed northern (upper) junction at which the Half Moon Lateral (see Sec. 5) intersects the T-Y Trail. Signs read *Gilmore Lake 1 mile*, *Velma Lakes 6 miles*, north, *Half Moon Lake 1½ miles*, northwest, *Glen Alpine Springs 2 miles*, southeast, and *Susie Lake 1 mile*, southwest. (According to the trail signs, Glen Alpine has come closer while Susie is now farther, while just the opposite is true.)

From the unsigned lower junction on the knoll, we move down a broad, switchbacking, elaborately built staircase on a fill of crushed granite. The track descends a steep, lightly wooded open slope through denser forest to a patch of meadow and a reunion with the

Susie Shortcut: west end (7700 — 0.4). Signs read *Gilmore Lake 1¼ miles*, *Velma Lake 6¼ miles*, north, *Fallen Leaf Lake*, *Glen Alpine Springs*, east, and *Susie Lake ½ mile*, *Desolation Valley 2 miles*, south. We cross a stream, move up onto a little bench, then turn south and follow the lakeshore through several campsites to the outlet stream of

Susie Lake (7780 — 0.6). We make our way around the south shore, where the trail is freshly relocated, over fields of small, sharp, red-brown rock whose color intensifies the deep green of the predominantly hemlock forest that encircles the lake. To the north the reddish talus slope seems to sweep directly from Susie to the slight dip in the ridge that marks Dicks Pass, effectively hiding the sizable basin containing Half Moon and Alta Morris lakes. We pass a tree-studded peninsula of shattered rock on which there are several inferior campsites, and move steadily west up barren rock through a broad draw to the narrow eastern bay of

Heather Lake outlet (7900 — 1.0). We move up the north shore on a handsome trail carved out of the red rock, ranging

199

50-100′ above the water on a steep, bare slope. Near the western shore the old trail, shown on the topo map, curls to the south onto flat meadow interspersed with clumps of graceful hemlock, past the USFS campground shown on the topo map. But in 1969 the trail was relocated so that it hugs the bottom of the cliffs to the north, and the campground improvements, in keeping with a new USFS policy to decentralize camping, have been removed. Camping is still good by the lake and up the little canyon to the northwest. The new trail continues due west, well above the lake, crossing one creek from the north on a fancy bridge but requiring the hiker to jump a second stream of equal size.

Elegant switchbacks, complete with waterbar staircases and fill-covered boardwalks, cling to the bottom of the shady north wall, where the hiker is obliged to contend with sizable snowdrifts to midseason, while below to the south portions of the old trail may be seen wandering down the flowered meadow. After climbing out of Heather Lake basin we turn south a few yards to the junction of the T-Y and Pacific Crest trails at the northeast corner of

Lake Aloha (8100 — 1.0). Signs read *Mosquito Pass 1 mile, Rockbound Valley 1 mile,* west, *South end Desolation Valley 2 miles, Echo Lake 5 miles,* south, and *Heather Lake ½ mile, Susie Lake 1½ miles, Glen Alpine Springs 4 miles,* east.

SEC. 2

Tamarack Trail

(Lily Lake to Triangle Junction)

	Elev.	Miles from pt. above
Glen Alpine Road: Trailhead	6540	0.0
Triangle Jctn.	8180	2.5

Offering the easiest route from Fallen Leaf to Echo, this old, largely abandoned trail was officially reopened in 1968 when deadfalls and brush were cut and minor repairs made. The 1700′ climb was not designed for and is inaccessible to horses, and since the trail clings to a steep, shaded north slope and often follows the bottoms of washes, it should be considered impassable to hikers because of snowdrifts in early season and likely to be damp until midseason. The USFS has promised to maintain the trail for foot travel and to replace the long-missing signs at either end.

Though comparatively unused for lack of signs, especially at the Echo end, the trail traverses wild, handsome country and affords excellent views of Indian Rock, Mt. Tallac, Dicks and Jacks peaks and Glen Alpine Canyon. Together with the trail around Keiths Dome and the Lake Lucille lateral to Grass Lake, it provides an outstanding (if long) one-day circuit trip from Fallen Leaf. A sign on the south side of the Glen Alpine Spring road 0.2 mile above the fork in the road at the south end of Fallen Leaf reads *Triangle Lake 3 miles, Haypress Meadows 4 miles.*

Glen Alpine Road: trailhead (6540 — 0.0). A modest, blazed groove leads southwest from the road through rocky, brushy forest, climbing a gentle slope just east of but never in sight of Lily Lake. In the first ¼ mile several unmarked paths intersect the trail from the cabins to the south of Lily. We climb, often in stream-beds, through junglelike thickets of willow and alder, and come out into a sandy, parklike flat of brushless forest before switchbacking steeply up a treeless slope of huckleberry oak.

For several hundred difficult yards the trail climbs a deep, narrow, rocky watercourse (dry by midseason but a torrent in early June) under overhanging brush, then climbs on bare rock west over a little bluff, from which the soaring cliffs of Indian Rock are easily viewed, and crosses both forks of all-year Lily Lake inlet stream, the second at a mossy waterfall. We switchback steeply for 200' up the west bank of the stream, then cross to climb less steeply on switchbacks up the east bank.

Crossing the creek for the last time, the trail climbs steeply for 100 yards along the west bank, then abruptly leaves the stream to climb southwest up a flattening, grassy slope. We move through open forest, with fine views across Glen Alpine Canyon, over a gently sloping western spur of Echo Peak to the highest point on the trail at 8240'. The trail then descends gently southwest through thickening forest and, barely 100 yards from Triangle Junction, we pass a rock cairn (on the south side of the trail) that marks the faint but continuous Echo Peak Trail (see Region 1, Sec. 4). Nearby on trees are triangular orange signs reading *Echo Rim Ski Trail* and *Echo Rim Trail.* The trail at this junction levels off and turns west, and we walk the last few yards to

Triangle Jctn. (8180 — 2.5). A sign reads *Triangle Lake ½ mile, Lost Lake 1 mile,* north, and *Desolation Valley,* pointing west up the Keiths Dome Trail to Haypress Meadows. The signs indicating the trail south to Echo and the Tamarack Trail just ascended have long since disappeared. The USFS has agreed to re-sign this important four-trail junction.

Lake Lucille Lateral from the Glen Alpine Trail

	Elev.	Miles from pt. above	Total miles
Glen Alpine-Grass Lake Trail Jctn.	7000	0.0	0.0
Old-New Grass Lake Trails (east jctn.)	7100	0.4	0.4
Grass Lake (west jctn. of old-new trails)	7220	0.4	0.8
Lake Lucille Trail	7220	0.2	1.0
Lake Lucille (northeast outlet)	8180	1.0	2.0

For many years the old trail down the cliff from Lucille to Grass Lake was left off the maps, signed *Abandoned Trail* and generally forgotten. But in 1968 the USFS decided to restore it for foot travel and a maintenance crew cut deadfalls and brush, unplugged culverts and added a few blazes. Unfortunately, the old Grass Lake lateral to the Glen Alpine Trail, which it intersects, has in the meantime been replaced by a new trail which lies farther north. As a consequence, it presently is necssary to transfer from the new Grass Lake Trail to the old one in order to reach the Lake Lucille Trail (see map).

Though steep and narrow the Lucille Trail, unlike the Tamarack Trail from Lily Lake, might be navigated by experienced horsemen, though not by pack animals. The 1180' vertical climb compares favorably with the 1700' rise of the Tamarack Trail. USFS plans call for minimum maintenance, signs at both ends, and a more reasonable connection between the Lucille and Grass Lake trails. The route appears, though somewhat inaccurately, on the newest USFS trail maps. As on the Tamarack Trail, snow on the steep, shaded north slope makes early-season travel inadvisable.

Glen Alpine-Grass Lake trail jctn. (7000 — 0.0). Signs at this new junction read *Grass Lake 1 mile, Trail ends 1 mile*, southwest. The old trail to Grass Lake, now blocked by a conspicuous line of stones, lies about 100 yards east down the Glen Alpine Trail. This old junction is relevant for hikers to Lucille because the Lucille Trail junction may be approached more directly from this point than from any other. From the new junction a broad, high-standard trail, more intent on maintaining proper grade than on direct access, swings west around a shallow, rocky basin before moving on a staircase up a little bluff to merge for a few yards with the

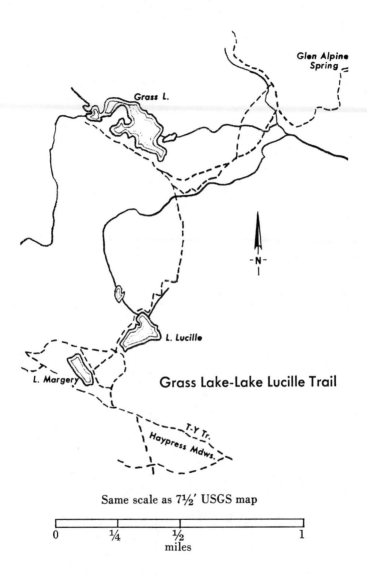

Grass Lake-Lake Lucille Trail

Same scale as 7½' USGS map

0   ¼   ½   1

miles

Old Grass Lake Trail: east jctn. (7100 — 0.4). No sign, of course, marks the junction, but the alert hiker, using the accompanying map, should be able to find the old trail branching northeast down the meadow off the bluff, and a few yards up the new trail, branching southwest (left) up into the brush. Travelers interested in the most direct route to Lucille from this point (at the expense of visiting Grass) should take the old trail ¼ mile to the signed Lucille junction. Travelers to Grass should stick to the new trail which climbs directly west across rocky country and ascends a little draw on waterbars to the southeastern tip of

Grass Lake: west jctn. of old-new trails (7220 — 0.4). The new high-standard boulevard continues through lodgepole forest, past several adequate campsites, to the western end of the lake, where it abruptly ends. The junction of the old and new trails near the southeast end of the lake can be extremely hard to find. The best procedure is to start at the lake and move slowly down the trail, scrutinizing the southern margin of the trail, about 50 yards from the water, for a faint track heading southeast toward the cliffs. Once the junction is found a modest but continuous groove leads out of the trees and into the brush to a signpost marking the junction of the

Lake Lucille Trail (7220 — 0.2). The sign reads *Grass Lake ¼ mile*, pointing northwest up the old trail we have just traveled. From the clearly marked junction the Lucille Trail turns south past the last trees, crosses the northwestern outlet creek from Lake Lucille (usually dry by midseason) and switchbacks steeply up a shadeless slope of talus and waist-high ceanothus and huckleberry oak. Despite numerous corrugated iron culverts the rough trail is often no better than a rocky watercourse.

After ¼ mile we climb steeply up a rocky gorge onto a wooded ledge with a shady campsite, and a small stream that flows to midseason. After traversing the ledge to the west the trail climbs steeply south onto a second, larger, wooded ledge on which there also is water in early season. Moving again to the west across the ledge, we climb a switchbacking trail that crosses and recrosses the northeastern outlet stream from Lucille (usually flowing to midseason) as it mounts a clifflike slope just east of a long, steep talus slope. The pitch lessens slightly as the trail ascends up a series of hollows and dells to the northeastern outlet at

Lake Lucille (8180 — 1.0). No sign marks the indistinct junction with a good fishermen's trail which leads down the northwest shore, crosses the northwest outlet (down which there are a number of good campsites and a lakelet) and passes behind a little peninsula, through several more excellent campsites, on the way to a trail junction a little above the lake's west end on the inlet stream from Lake Margery. For the adjoining trails see Region 2, Sec. 3.

Tahoe-Yosemite Trail
(Glen Alpine Trail to Dicks Pass)

	Elev.	Miles from pt. above	Total miles
Glen Alpine-Dicks Pass Trail Jctn.	7920	0.0	0.0
Mt. Tallac Trail: Gilmore Lake	8300	0.6	0.6
Dicks Pass	9380	2.0	2.6

In 1968-69 the Dicks Pass Trail was rebuilt to the highest USFS standards, which means soil-filled, wood-framed staircases, waterbars and a wide track suited to laden pack trains. Dicks is the highest pass in the Wilderness Area, and running water on the south slope is not to be found above Gilmore Lake after mid-season. Deep snow, especially on the north slope, obscures much of the trail in early season. The best views to the south and west are somewhat below the pass. As indicated in Sec. 1, the trails from Susie Lake and Glen Alpine Spring meet at an unsigned lower junction, while 50 yards north, at the upper junction, we come to the Half Moon Lake Trail at the

Glen Alpine-Dicks Pass Trail Jctn. (7920 — 0.0). Signs read *Gilmore Lake 1 mile, Velma Lakes 6 miles,* north, *Half Moon Lake 1½ miles,* northwest, *Glen Alpine Springs 2 miles,* southeast, and *Susie Lake 1 mile,* southwest. We move north up a long, climbing traverse on a knee-breaking staircase constructed of creosoted 4 x 4's filled with gravel. Maintaining maximum grade, the trail turns sharply east to mount a little bluff. Below the trail on the bluff at 8000-8200 feet, the pits and trenches of the Josie gold claim may be found which, though abandoned in 1938, produced samples assaying as rich as $50 a ton. We switchback to the north briefly, then climb parallel to but west of the strip of forest that shelters Gilmore Creek. This stretch of trail has been relocated about 50 yards west of the route shown on the topo map leading to the

Mt. Tallac Trail: Gilmore Lake (8300 — 0.6). Signs read *Gilmore Lake ¼ mile, Mt. Tallac 1½ miles,* north, *Dicks Pass 2 miles, Velma Lakes 5 miles,* northwest, and *Glen Alpine Springs 3 miles,* south. The big trail climbs on a controlled grade up a bare, rocky slope only occasionally shaded by trees, and after ¼ mile we for the first and last time look out over large, circular Gilmore Lake, bordered by bare talus on the north and grass-floored open forest on the south and east.

Leaving the last of the forest behind, we move steadily up-

205

ward on rock and talus, past clumps of trees, through grassy flats sprinkled with wildflowers. The view improves immensely (see cover) when Half Moon and Alta Morris lakes become visible directly below to the west in their beautiful little basin under Dicks and Jacks peaks. Dicks was named for Captain Dick Barter, hermit of Emerald Bay, and Jacks honors Carson Valley pioneer Hardin Green Jacks. Susie, Grass, Aloha, Lucille and Triangle lakes are revealed as we move higher. The trail passes into a saddle that marks the low point of the high ridge between Dicks Peak and Mt. Tallac, but instead of dropping through and starting down, we swing sharply east and start up the ridge. The slope north of the saddle is both too snowy and too steep for a trail of reasonable usability, so the weary traveler is obliged to climb an additional 200 vertical feet into a bare, cobblestoned flat where the highly developed trail shrinks to a line of ducks sticking up through snowbanks in early season. We move up the last few yards into a very shallow, windy saddle to

Dicks Pass (9380 — 2.0), where a sign reads, erroneously, *Dicks Pass, elevation 9500 feet,* an exaggeration of approximately 125 feet. For a description of the northern approach to Dicks Pass from Velma Basin see Region 7, Sec. 3.

Sec. 5
Half Moon Lake Trail

	Elev.	Miles from pt. above	Total miles
Dicks Pass-Half Moon Lake Trail Jctn.	7940	0.0	0.0
Half Moon Lake (east end)	8140	1.4	1.4
Half Moon-Alta Morris Lake Jctn.	8140	0.5	1.9

Beginning at the Dicks Pass-Glen Alpine Trail junction described in Sec. 4, the Half Moon trail climbs into one of the loveliest lake basins in the Wilderness Area. Visitors, campsites and firewood are scarce.

Dicks Pass-Half Moon Lake Trail Jctn. (7940 — 0.0). A sign reading *Half Moon Lake 1½ miles* points northwest. A modest but continuous and easily followed track leads northwest up a wooded ravine, winding among trees, occasionally crossing creeklets and dodging deadfalls. After about a mile, during which the grade is constant but not excessive, we come out of the woods at the base of high talus slopes into the mouth of a basin paved with pink sedimentary rock. Ducks replace tree blazes as we move across rolling, open rock, passing several flower-rimmed ponds and lakelets. The trail crosses a small, wooded promontory on which there is an improved campsite and drops to

Half Moon Lake: east end (8140 — 1.4). We move in an arc around the northern lakeshore in a lush strip of flowered meadow that lies beneath the tall, gray talus slopes descending from the Dicks Pass ridge. Tongues of grassland and low brush reach far up the rocky slope, making it easier for backpackers to drop cross-country into the basin from Dicks Pass and for unburdened hikers to ascend the same route. At the west end of the lake we move around the base of a little bowl, cross a creek that falls from between Dicks and Jacks peaks, coming to the small, wooded peninsula that separates

Half Moon and Alta Morris lakes (8140 — 0.5). The topo map shows a trail crossing between the lakes and leading to the eastern end of Alta Morris; this is a portion of the fishermen's trail that encircles both lakes.

Sec. 6
Mt. Tallac Lateral from Gilmore Lake

	Elev.	Miles from pt. above	Total miles
Mt. Tallac Trail: Gilmore Lake Jctn.	8300	0.0	0.0
Cathedral Trail Jctn.	9340	1.5	1.5
Mt. Tallac Summit	9735	0.3	1.8

The fifth-highest peak in the Wilderness Area, Tallac is easily the most often climbed. Trails from Fallen Leaf and Tahoe merge into the Cathedral Trail, which joins the lateral from Gilmore Lake at a poorly marked junction not far beneath the summit. The modest trail is continuous and well defined and the views and the wildflowers are often spectacular. The highest dependable water comes from a small spring above the path about ¾ mile up the trail. From

Mt. Tallac-Dicks Pass Trail jctn. (8300 — 0.0), the Tallac trail leads up Gilmore Creek and forks, one branch (the horse crossing) immediately fording the creek and swinging north to the lake, the other branch continuing upstream to the lake, then crossing the creek on the gated streamflow maintenance dam. In a parklike meadow under big trees on the southeast shore the trails rejoin. We leave this sizable area of excellent campsites and begin to climb northeast, directly toward the summit, on a long, comparatively gentle slope.

Passing the last timber we move up a ravine into a marshy

hollow beside a talus slope where the trail makes an abrupt turn that can be momentarily confusing. We then move steadily up a good groove across a treeless, rocky slope largely covered by grass, wildflowers and low-growing sagebrush. After passing a trickle of water from a spring above the trail (the last dependable source), we arc gently to the north toward but not into a low pass, then turn east to climb parallel to the ridge. From this open slope the view across Gilmore, Susie and Aloha to the Crystal Range is excellent. The trail makes a shallow loop to the south to join the

Cathedral Trail (9340 — 1.5) at an unsigned junction. To mark the junction a short section of low rock wall has been built, and the faint track from Cathedral Lake enters at its lower end, between two rock cairns. A modest sign would greatly improve chances of recognizing the junction. The combined trails climb northeast up the still-gentle slope toward the upthrust heap of brown rock that marks the summit. We turn east once more for several hundred yards to a small clump of weathered trees and an equally weathered sign inaccurately reading *Mt. Tallac, elevation 9785 feet, Summit 200 yards*. The trail abruptly turns north and we scramble up the rough, brown rock, to

Mt. Tallac Summit (9735 — 0.3). Like Flagpole Peak, Tallac flies, on a flagpole made from a guy-wired branch, whatever flags climbers happen to have brought with them. On an August day in 1969, for instance, there floated on the stiff breeze a canvas laundry bag (from Lake Tahoe City Linen) inscribed with the peace symbol, and one blue and one red bandana. The white-veined black summit rock bristles with pitons, and birds and butterflies flutter in the surprising crop of wildflowers that grow from crevices and on arid-looking patches of sand. Visible from the summit are Take Tahoe in its entirety, Azure, Kalmia, Gilmore, Susie, Aloha, Heather, Grass, Middle Velma, Lucille, Triangle and Fallen Leaf lakes.

Sec. 7
Floating Island Trail

	Elev.	Miles from pt. above	Total miles
Floating Island Trailhead	6460	0.0	0.0
Floating Island Lake (outlet)	7220	2.0	2.0
Lateral to Cathedral Trail	7260	0.2	2.2
Cathedral Trail	7540	0.4	2.6
Cathedral Peak Ridgetop	8600	1.2	3.8
Gilmore Trail	9340	1.1	4.9

The Floating Island Trail from Spring Creek follows an ancient road that served long-departed Tallac Creek Fish Hatchery. Happily the road has deteriorated to the status of a wide and pleasant trail. To the surprise of most travelers there really is a floating island in the lake of the same name, though it certainly is not the one that inspired the lake's name in the 1890's, when fishermen were said to have poled the island to the lake's center to catch the giant trout that lived there.

The Floating Island Trail was virtually abandoned until 1968 when it was resurrected and partly re-signed. In 1969 work was completed and the adjoining Cathedral Trail up Mt. Tallac was put in shape, although some critical signs are still missing. Because the trailhead is off the beaten track and well removed from public facilities, the Floating Island Trail is comparatively little used. It is reached by driving 1.3 miles west of the Fallen Leaf Lake Road on Highway 89, then turning south (left) at Spring Creek Summer Home Tract and driving 0.9 mile, keeping to the left as the road repeatedly forks.

Floating Island Trailhead (6460 — 0.0). At a bend in the road, close to the creek (directly across the road from a cabin signed *The Hams, lot 126*), a USFS sign reads *Floating Island Trail, Floating Island Lake 2 miles, Mt. Tallac 4 miles.* A more modest, privately posted sign nearby reads *Trail to Floating Island Lake, Cathedral Lake and Mt. Tallac.* From the signs the trail leads down to the edge of the creek, where it splits, one fork continuing up the west bank to peter out, while our trail crosses the creek on a log. Some 50 yards into a dense thicket of lodgepole saplings, a local path joins our trail from the north.

We push through the thick forest on a newly relocated stretch of trail that gives evidence of flooding in early season. About ¼ mile from the trailhead we emerge from the trees onto a broad avenue recognizable as an ancient road, passing through more open forest beneath occasional giant ponderosa pine. The road climbs through pleasant, mixed-conifer forest, never far from Spring Creek, and after ½ mile we pass an iron gate post sunk in concrete. About 100 yards farther we pass a second post, and shortly thereafter make our first ford (on stepping stones except in early season) of the creek.

Still on the road we pass a third gate post and make a second crossing of the creek. About ¼ mile beyond the trail leaves the road and somewhat vaguely, despite occasional ducks, moves through a rockpile, splitting harmlessly for 50 yards, and for the first time climbs steeply. At the top of the pitch we recross the creek and climb a few yards to

Floating Island Lake: outlet (7220 — 2.0). The shallow, oval, tree-encircled lake offers several campsites, one with an iron stove and battered picnic tables, but mosquitos tend to persist beyond midseason. The island, at least in 1969, consisted of a badly trampled rectangle of turf about 8' wide, 20' long and 2' thick, which drifts with the wind until it runs aground. It appears to have been hewn out of the small meadow at the lake's north end, probably by unnatural forces.

By an old signpost at the south end of the lake the trail splits, an old path leading south (right) into the trees, while the new track climbs up a staircase to the southeast (left), then hooks to the west before heading south. In a jumble of gray rock a ducked route leads east toward Cathedral Creek and Cathedral Trail, soon petering out. About 50 yards farther up the new trail we come to a more reliable version of the

Lateral to the Cathedral Trail (7260 — 0.2). A sign nailed to a tree 10 yards above the trail reads, *Floating Island Lake* ¼ *mile*, north, *Fallen Leaf Lake 3 miles*, east, and *Cathedral Lake* ¾ *mile, Mt. Tallac 3 miles*, south. A very dim, little-used, unmaintained path drops into the wooded canyon and crosses the creek. In the creek bottom a confused snarl of old blazed paths finally sorts itself into a trail that climbs the far side of the canyon through grass and brush to join the Cathedral Trail at a ducked but otherwise unmarked junction at the top of the cliffs.

Returning to the Floating Island Trail at the junction with the lateral, we follow up the Floating Island inlet stream, cross over a little knob and climb along a little rill in the next drainage south, the trail studded with waterbars. We cross the rill, move south through grass-floored forest on the level, then cross Cathedral Creek to a bare signpost at the junction with the

Cathedral Trail (7540 — 0.4). For the rest of the trail up Mt. Tallac, see Sec. 8.

SEC. 8
Cathedral Trail

	Elev.	Miles from pt. above	Total miles
Cathedral Trailhead	6380	0.0	0.0
Fallen Leaf Trail Jctn.	6480	0.4	0.4
Lateral to Floating Island Trail	7260	1.1	1.5
Floating Island Trail	7540	0.3	1.8
Cathedral Peak Ridgetop	8600	1.2	3.0
Gilmore Trail	9340	1.1	4.1
Mt. Tallac	9735	0.3	4.4

The shortest and most popular trail up Tallac, the Cathedral Trail is probably the steepest track in the Wilderness Area, climbing 3355' in 4.4 miles. Nevertheless, since it begins on a road near a center of summer population, it gets a good deal of use, especially from visitors to the Stanford Alumni Camp. The trail was touched up in 1968 and '69 although the long-missing sign at the trailhead has yet to be replaced. As indicated earlier the trailhead is reached by turning north at the fork in the road at the south end of Fallen Leaf, crossing the bridge and driving 0.6 mile north through the Stanford camp.

Cathedral Trailhead (6380 — 0.0). The trail begins at a signless white post in a jog in the road about 200 yards short of road's end. A well-defined groove runs north, parallel to the road and 50 yards to the west, through rocky brush, past the last cabins and close to the shore at the bottom of a steep brush slope. We roller-coaster near the water until cliffs force us to climb 50' up a draw, after which we contour across the slope about 75' above the water to a junction with the

Fallen Leaf Trail (6480 — 0.4). There is no sign but a rock cairn marks the intersection of two clearly defined grooves. The Fallen Leaf Trail leads north-northeast along the lake shore past summer cabins to a dirt road coming around the lake from the north. The Cathedral Trail turns due north and climbs steeply through shadeless brush for $\frac{1}{2}$ mile, to a stand of lodgepole which survived a fire in the early 1930's, before turning west and switchbacking directly up the south ridge of the canyon containing Cathedral Creek. At the top of the cliff, at a junction marked only by sentinel ducks, we come to the

Lateral to Floating Island Trail (7260 — 1.1), which drops down a grassy slope to cross the canyon on the way to Floating Island Lake (see Sec. 7). The slope eases considerably beyond the lateral junction and we move in open woodland across a little flat, past an all-summer pond, to climb steeply up through a parklike stand of large red fir to a junction, marked by a signless post, with the

Floating Island Trail (7540 — 0.3). Turning south our trail moves several hundred yards through forest on a slight incline to the northeast shore of shallow, somewhat disappointing Cathedral Lake. Signs read *Cathedral Lake, elevation 7640, Floating Island Lake 1 mile, Gilmore Lake 3 miles,* west, and painted in white on a rock, *Three miles to the Holy rock.* The trail climbs steeply out of the pocket of forest sheltering the lake to switchback through waist-high brush for $\frac{1}{4}$ mile before crossing all-season Cathedral Creek (highest dependable source of water) for the last time.

At the creek the trail forks, one branch ascending the stream, the other crossing. A yellow-painted arrow recommends the crossing but the two forks rejoin a few yards higher. Throughout this stretch of trail there are occasional relocations, and sections of old trail may be seen nearby from time to time. The ducked groove climbs out of the brush and we enter a bowl of shattered rock bounded by cliffs and steep talus slopes. The trail moves directly west across the barren rock floor and switchbacks up the exceptionally steep headwall of talus. Unfortunately another corniced snowfield usually covers the upper reaches of the trail until after midseason, and we are forced to detour around on rock to the

Cathedral Peak Ridgetop (8600 — 1.2). A weathered sign at the top reads *Gilmore Lake 1¼ miles, Mt. Tallac 1¼ miles,* north, and *Floating Island Lake 2½ miles, Fallen Leaf Lake 3 miles,* east. Cathedral Peak, which lies southeast down the slightly tilting sage plain, is actually the nose of Tallac's southeast ridge, although from Fallen Leaf it appears to be a formidable mountain. It might be noted that the trail, in the process of climbing out of the bowl, dips unfortunately to the south, so if the upward-bound hiker detours north around snowfields, he can shave almost ¼ mile off the climb. The cross-country climbing up the talus slope is no more difficult than the trail.

From the sign on the ridgetop, ducks lead northwest on a gentle incline across a windy sage plain paved with slate-colored cobblestones, running roughly parallel to the eastern cliffs. As we climb higher the trail becomes better defined, through patches of meadow, fields of flowers and occasional clumps of pine. The country is very similar to the southern summit slope of Echo Peak. A little below the Gilmore junction the trail grows somewhat faint in rolling grassland, but by searching out ducks we make our way to an unsigned junction with the somewhat deeper groove of the

Gilmore Trail (9340 — 1.1). We enter between cairns at the bottom of a low rock wall and turn northeast. After heading directly toward the upthrust mass of brownish rock that marks the summit, we veer to the east to a clump of trees where a weathered sign reads, *Mt. Tallac, elevation 9785 feet, Summit 200 yards.* This elevation, it might be noted, is exactly 50' higher than that given correctly on the topo map. The trail turns north and we scramble on rough rock, not far from the northeastern cliffs, to

Mt. Tallac Summit (9735 — 0.3). For the description of the view see Sec. 6.

Sec. 9
Angora Lakes to Echo Peak

	Elev.	Miles from pt. above	Total miles
Locked Gate: Angora Road	7200	0.0	0.0
Angora Lakes Resort: upper lake	7460	0.9	0.9
Echo Peak	8895	1.2	2.1

Two miles up the Fallen Leaf Road from Highway 89 a dirt road signed *Angora Lookout 4 miles, Angora Lakes 6 miles*, climbs to the southeast, and after less than a mile, at an unsigned junction, a fork drops southeast through a little pass on the way to U.S. 50. The Angora road at this junction turns southwest and mounts the ridge that separates Fallen Leaf from Lake Valley. We pass Angora Lookout on a patch of pavement, moving directly toward the dark cliffs of Echo and Angora peaks. The peak was named for the Angora sheep that pioneer Nathan Gilmore pastured at its base. The road turns south and then west, and we come into a little flat with ample parking space at the

Locked Gate: Angora Road (7200 — 0.0). Only the owners of summer cabins and the resort are permitted to drive beyond this point but the public is welcome to walk. There are boats for rent in the upper lake and the resort sells sandwiches, drinks, ice cream and candy to visiting hikers. From the northeast corner of the parking area the little-used Clark Trail switchbacks 850' northwest down Angora Peak, to the fork in the road by the Glen Alpine Creek bridge. A dusty road switchbacks up through light forest, but there are well-constructed sections of trail short-cutting between the loops. At the foot of the lower lake the road levels off, leads down the western shore and climbs through the trees to

Angora Lakes Resort: Upper Lake (7460 — 0.9). The 10 housekeeping cabins rent for $125-185 weekly, and shopping service and taxi service from the gate are provided. Winter address: 739 Arden Ave., Glendale, Calif. 91202. Phone: (213) 244-3582. From the resort the unofficial, unmapped trail leads southeast down the lake in front of cabins, crosses the outlet stream on a bridge and circles behind a storage shed to a boulder by a tree bearing a weathered sign reading *Echo Peak*. (See map.)

Climbing left around the boulder, we follow a sparsely ducked route up a boulder-and-talus slope onto a rocky spur. The route turns south and, where the spur joins the steep slope, the path becomes more distinct. We move south parallel to the shore 100' above the water, climbing gradually until we reach the southern

213

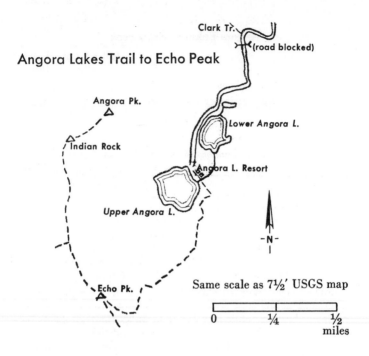

Angora Lakes Trail to Echo Peak

Clark Tr.

✗(road blocked)

Angora Pk.
△

Indian Rock
△

Lower Angora L.

Angora L. Resort

Upper Angora L.

– N –

Echo Pk.
△

Same scale as 7½′ USGS map

0   ¼   ½
                  miles

end of the lake. Then the trail starts up steeply on a sandy, lightly wooded slope, dividing into faint multiple tracks made by descending hikers. Rather than spend a lot of time trying to find the single best track, the hiker is advised to rely primarily on ducks and move southeast toward the peak on a steep, climbing traverse.

Toward the top of the slope the trail becomes more distinct, and we move up into a level sandy flat, cross its corner on ducks and move directly up the steep wooded slope of the peak. As we rise higher the slope steepens and the trail begins to switchback. We pass a diamond-shaped highway sign posted by some wag which reads *Caution: maximum speed 25 mph.* The trail climbs onto a little ridge, passes a little dell and, following ducks, moves up steeply through an area often choked with snow until midseason.

We turn west with the ridge, climbing directly toward the black summit cliffs for a few yards; then the ridge swings south and we climb over often corniced snowfield and up a sandy chute onto the mountain's main east ridge, marked by a cairn of rocks on a

214

boulder. For the most direct route to the summit we turn northwest at a point 25 yards short of the cairn and move directly up the back of the ridge, close to the northern cliffs. It is only a few yards farther to climb past the cairn onto the south-side sage plain, and then turn northwest and ascend the easy slope to

Echo Peak (8895 — 1.2). For routes to the summit from the west and south see Region 1, Secs. 4 and 7.

Chapter 14

Desolation Angling

Within Desolation Wilderness and the surrounding country there are nearly 100 trout-bearing lakes, a river and a dozen large creeks. Averaging less than ½ mile in diameter, these small lakes range in elevation from 7000 to 9000′, occupying glacially scooped-out hollows in the granite. Since granite basins rarely provide fertile water, food tends to be relatively scarce, and since most lakes are frozen over for about half of each year it is not surprising that trout were almost non-existent in the region before the arrival of the white man.

Owing to the scant feed and short growing season, Desolation trout tend to be slower-growing and smaller than trout found in lower, larger, lusher surroundings. Environmental conditions also affect reproduction. The California State Department of Fish and Game (DFG) which administers the fishery estimates that there is limited natural reproduction in no more than half the area's lakes, and only 5-10% show sufficient reproduction to be considered self-sustaining and in no need of further planting.

Lest this sound overly pessimistic, it should be stated at once that despite considerable angler pressure in some areas and less than ideal trout-growing conditions, Desolation each year affords fine sport and good eating to fishermen with at least some basic knowledge of angling. Inexperienced or impatient visitors who want substantial catches are advised either to patronize commercial trout ponds or to fish in the popular roadside waters where catchable trout are regularly planted.

While the majority of waters were originally barren, there may in very early times have been rainbow trout, descended from the sea-run steelhead, that climbed the Rubicon River (which reaches the sea through the Sacramento River) to populate the waters of Rockbound Valley. And the cutthroat trout which eons ago evolved from ocean species and were stranded in the inland waters after the oceans receded certainly made their way up the Tahoe tributaries into Fallen Leaf, Cascade and Echo lakes.

The first recorded planting of game fish came in 1887 when Nathan Gilmore planted 20 black bass in what is now Gilmore Lake. There were sporadic plantings of small numbers of trout

217

by interested fishermen early in the century but the first significant, systematic stocking (by the DFG) began in the early 1930's.

No account of the region's angling activity would be complete without mention of the pioneering activities of the Mt. Ralston Fish Planting Club (MRFPC), formed in 1925, mainly by Echo Lake cabin-owners, as "A non-profit organization planting trout fry in the Echo Lake-Desolation Valley Region." In the 10-year period ending in 1935, the MRFPC planted more than a million trout fry (fingerlings supplied principally by the DFG) of half a dozen species in nearly 100 back-country locations, many of them previously barren.

Besides being barren, many Desolation tarns were then still unnamed, so the MRFPC whimsically devised Indian-like names from the names of such early club presidents as George Foss (Gefo), Walter Campbell (Waca), Ross Pierce (Ropi) and Frank Talbot (Frata). In 1935 the MRFPC (now with more than 1000 members) maintained a pack train, consisting of two wranglers and 10 pack horses, which each year spent three months planting not only trout fry but also fresh-water shrimp and salmon-fly larvae for them to feed upon, as well as such aquatic plants as wild water lily and water hyacinth.

At the same time, the club's determined opposition in the Legislature effectively killed a drastic trespass bill aimed at keeping the sporting public off of wild private lands. One of the MRFPC's principal and most lasting achievements was the construction of streamflow maintenance dams throughout the wilderness area. The additional water stored behind each dam is released gradually through the dry months of late summer and early fall in order to maintain sufficient downstream flow to protect trout in the creek below. By 1953 some 23 of these dams had been built.

But also by 1953 air planting had passed the pioneering stage and only a handful of lakes required the services of the MRFPC pack train. What had taken the pack train two long months on the trail now took the DFG airplane two or three days. By 1958 the club's efforts were being channeled into catchable-trout planting, streamflow maintenance dams and legislation affecting sportsmen. One of the largest and most recent accomplishments of the MRFPC was the completion in 1960 of a dam on Ralston Lake storing 150 acre-feet of water to be used to keep Ralston Creek flowing into Echo (and Echo Creek flowing into the Upper Truckee River) during dry months.

As recently as the middle 1960's the Desolation region was basically an eastern brook trout fishery, with an occasional lake planted to rainbow. Lakes containing other species could be counted on one hand. But in the last five years, in an effort to increase variety and better match trout to the appropriate waters, the DFG has provided the angler considerable diversity. The 1969 tally, reflecting the presence of more than one species in many lakes, showed: brook 78 lakes, rainbow 50 lakes, golden 19 lakes, brown trout 16 lakes, cutthroat 4 lakes, kokanee salmon 3 lakes, mackinaw (lake) trout 1 lake, and Arctic grayling 1 lake.

Most angling guides rate the quality of the fishing (good, fair, poor, etc.) and list the size fish that may be expected in a given water. In the largely artificial fishery of the Desolation country, with its utter dependence on planting, there simply is no way that such ratings can accurately be provided. The presence or absence of fish, as well as the species, may be determined by the supply at the hatchery at the time planting is scheduled.

The excellence of the fishing varies with the recent fishing pressure, feeding activity, phase of the moon, available food, skill of the angler, time of day, weather, season and of course that great imponderable — luck. But the biggest factor is the fish-planting program of the DFG. Consider, for example, a short history of Triangle Lake, which I have fished regularly for some years. DFG management calls for biennial planting of fingerling brookies in odd-numbered years. The effect on this small, shallow, 8000′ lake, with unusually good feed, is considerable.

In 1965, with the fishing good for 9″ brookies, the DFG made a small plant late in the season. Fishing stopped as the 9-inchers ignored anglers to go after the fingerlings. In 1966 there was good fishing for 10-12″ fish. In early 1967 the fishing was fair for 7-inchers with an occasional 12-13″ fish; then in midseason a fresh planting of fingerlings ruined the fishing for the rest of the season.

Angling was fair in early 1968 for 5″ and 9″ brookies, but then, for some unknown reason, there came down from the sky in the off year a shower of rainbow trout fingerlings! The fishing suffered for the rest of the year, as was to be expected, and it failed to improve in 1969 when the fishing was fair to poor for 7-8″ and 9-11″ brookies.

Another important variable is streamflow fluctuation. Consider very shallow, 8000′ Desolation Lake. The DFG planted brookies annually until 1965 but the fish did so poorly that a shift was made to annual plantings of rainbow, beginning in 1966. Desolation is the lowest in the Chain of Lakes below Aloha Dam, and as such is completely dependent on the flow from beneath the gated PG & E dam. When the flow is cut off or greatly reduced for significant periods, the surface of Desolation will drop as much as 18 inches, which in a shallow lake is highly destructive to the fishing.

The flow released from above by PG & E is affected by down-stream commitments, season of the year, heaviness of the pre-ceding winter, etc. — enough factors to keep streamflow unpre-dictable. In years when the lake was full in early season I have made good catches of both rainbow and brook running to 14". In other years at the same season when conditions seemed just as good, except that the lake surface was very low, I have more than once been skunked.

These two examples hopefully will illustrate why accurate rep-resentations as to the quality of the fishing or the size of the fish simply cannot be made.

Insofar as angling methods are concerned, still-fishing with bait, spin-fishing with lures or bait, fly-casting and trolling all are effective when conditions are right and the angler exercises the requisite skill and persistence. Fly fishermen are particularly fond of the region because trout rise readily in the small lakes, and the bare granite offers unusual casting room. Such natural baits as helgramites, grubs, grasshoppers and worms are generally more effective than salmon eggs.

While brook, rainbow and golden all readily take flies, brook trout tend to shift their feeding to deeper water when the surface becomes warm in August. Brown trout, except in streams, are inclined to be deep feeders, and the kokanee salmon in Echo and Fallen Leaf, rarely rising for insects, are most easily taken troll-ing. In streams, rainbow favor the fastest water, while the other trout lie in more sheltered spots, waiting for the current to bring them food.

It is popularly believed that trout fishing is successful only at dawn or dusk. The principal bases in fact for this contention are that poor light conceals the fisherman and the artificiality of his offerings, and trout are apt to venture farther from shelter to feed when protected by shadow. Consequently, trout tend to feed on the surface, especially in lakes, more at dawn and dusk than during the brighter part of the day. However, the very early fishing does not justify very early rising. Trout tend to have several spurts of feeding each day; if the angler happens to hit one, the fishing will be unusually good.

Many fishermen likewise believe that as soon as they reach wild, remote, untraveled country, the fishing will be simply fan-tastic. By the same token they scorn easily accessible waters as offering no chance of good sport. But distance from civilization is no substitute for skill. The clever fisherman will repeatedly make good catches from good water, even though it is heavily fished, while the novice may very well be skunked at a rarely fished, well-stocked, back-country lake. A somewhat more reliable generalization suggests that the higher and smaller the lake, the smaller the fish; and the lower and larger the lake, the larger the trout produced — whether or not the lakes in question are heavily fished.

Although there is always considerable variation in size within any given generation of trout, as well as variation in the food supply and competition in the water in question, certain generalities can be made as to the size of the average eastern brook and rainbow trout of a given age in the waters of Desolation Wilderness. At the time of planting in July the fingerling trout measure 2-3″, a year later they have reached 6-8″, two years later 8-10″, and three years later 10-12″. The expected life span of Desolation trout is only about four years and the maximum size for brook and rainbow, except in the largest, lowest lakes, is about 15-16″.

Golden trout, planted only in the highest, most remote lakes, commonly take two years to reach 7-8″. The more difficult to catch brown trout grow considerably larger, and fish of from two to six pounds have been taken. Some of the mackinaw (lake) trout in Stony Ridge Lake probably exceed five pounds. Kokanee salmon occasionally reach lengths of 14-16″, but the average fish caught is half that size.

Most anglers prefer the rainbow trout to the brook trout because he attacks all manner of foods and lures with abandon and fights energetically. Unfortunately, Desolation is a fishery built around small lakes, and rainbows rarely spawn in lakes, requiring strongly flowing streams with beds of gravel on which to lay their eggs. Brook trout, on the other hand, often spawn in spring-fed lakes that have no visible stream. And generally they can be expected to spawn under broader and poorer conditions than the rainbow.

Spawning ability was the prime reason for the wholesale planting of brookies in the previously sterile tarns of Desolation. Golden trout, like rainbow, need a gravel-bottomed stream for spawning and spawn in the spring. Brook trout spawn in the fall, usually in November.

In the last few years DFG experiments have revealed that brookies do better in the higher lakes and rainbows do better at lower elevations. The dividing line has arbitrarily been set at 7500′, and henceforth — with many exceptions — it will be DFG policy to plant brookies above 7500′ and rainbows below. Some of the experimental evidence came from 8000′ Lake of the Woods, which for years has produced a few large rainbow but not much fishing.

Beginning in 1966, yearly plants were made at a ratio of two rainbows for each brook. Samplings taken in the fall of 1968 showed brookies outnumbering rainbows by a spectacular 10 to 1! Other experiments have disclosed that rainbows are less severely affected by fluctuations in streamflow; as a consequence they will in the future be stocked in the Chain of Lakes below Aloha Dam as well as in other lakes and streams which are at the mercy of an upstream dam.

It is DFG policy to plant the exotic golden trout in the highest, most remote waters, both to maintain its status as a rare prize and because it neither competes well with other species nor withstands heavy angler pressure. Because goldens occur naturally at extremely high elevations in the southern Sierra, it is popularly believed that they cannot live at lower levels. But they have been flourishing for years in marshy McConnell Lake at an elevation of only 7800′.

Diversity, in the last few years, has become one of the prime aims of DFG management, and in keeping with their effort to provide a variety of species they have proposed the planting of Arctic grayling (allied to the trout but having a higher, longer dorsal fin). The grayling, it is hoped, would provide sport in at least a dozen shallow, accessible lakes that presently are barren because they freeze nearly to the bottom. "Winter kill" of trout occurs when the oxygen content of the water beneath the ice becomes exhausted, causing the fish to suffocate.

Grayling commonly survive in the arctic in water with no measurable oxygen content. In the Desolation Wilderness they will not only add spice to the fishing, but will open waters to angling that are now devoid of fishlife.

In the index to lakes at the end of the chapter, there are better than a dozen barren lakes in which grayling should flourish. For a start, the DFG in 1969 planted 500 grayling fingerlings (at 10 to the ounce) in shallow Fawn Lake, ½ mile north of Buck Island Lake.

In keeping with its aim toward diversity and increased trout production, the DFG has been increasing the number of lakes in which it is planting a second species of trout or salmon. A second species may more fully utilize the environment. During midsummer in the deeper lakes, brookies occupy the deeper water while rainbow feed in the shallows and on the surface. And since food is nearly always scarce in Desolation waters, the fact that not all food is shared by the two species (there are morsels a rainbow might pass by that would be eaten by a brook, and vice versa) means that, despite competition, there should be at least slightly greater fish production with two species than with one.

These considerations were responsible for the addition of kokanee salmon, beginning in 1962, to the basically rainbow populations of accessible, heavily fished Echo and Fallen Leaf lakes.

Because of the long winter dormant season and the small amount of food in the geologically young, rockbound lakes, the DFG estimates an average fish production in the Desolation region of only 10-20 pounds per acre each year.

For some years now, ever since the DFG inaugurated its catchable-trout program (planting 5-to-the-pound trout measuring 8-10″) there has been pressure from sportsmen to plant them everywhere in greater quantity. Because catchables have a far higher survival rate than fingerlings the DFG conducted experiments (notably in Crag and Gilmore lakes) to determine the feasibility of extending its catchable program to air planting beyond the roads.

The tentative conclusion, however, is that it is generally better management (trout production per dollar) to plant fingerlings if the planting cannot be managed by truck. For, while catchable planting triples the survival rate, the cost per fish is five times that for fingerlings, and growth after planting is negligible. The time may come, however, when fishing pressure on such close-to-the-road lakes as Eagle (above Emerald Bay) and Tamarack (above Echo) may require catchables to keep up with demand.

The earlier in the season that fingerlings are planted, the greater their chances for survival, so the DFG operation — in the interest of economy — customarily begins soon after the highest lake has thawed, sometime in July. The trout are trucked from the hatchery to the South Lake Tahoe airport, ready to plant in 7-10 gallon steel cans containing about 1000 fish each. The DFG plane, equipped with a hopper for dumping, carries a pilot and bombardier and 20 cans of fingerlings for each half-hour flight.

Early risers in the back country may see a stubby twin-engined plane swoop to within 100′ of the water and drop what looks like a bucket full of water (if they're close to the drop site) before pulling up just high enough to clear the next ridge. Brook, rainbow and brown trout are planted in July. Golden trout reach the hatchery as eggs soon after their spring spawning high in the Cottonwood Lake Basin of the southern Sierra, but by the time the eggs hatch and the fingerling trout are robust enough to survive transplanting and an air drop, it is fall. So golden, along with spring-spawning cutthroat and Kamloops rainbow, are generally planted in September or October.

Fishery biologists work their way through the country as often as possible. A party of three or four men may pack into a lake basin, set lightweight, nearly invisible monofilament nets (ideally overnight) in the most critical waters, then set off to fish and inspect additional waters and talk to packers and fishermen. Information thus gathered is added to file cards kept on each lake, which are evaluated to determine appropriate management policy.

All trout anglers over the age of 15 are required to purchase and carry a valid State of California fishing license. The cost is $5 for Californians, $12 for nonresidents. The season in the Desolation country customarily runs from the Saturday closest to May first until November 15th. See the published DFG regulations for restrictions and closures (principally on Lake Tahoe tributaries). The daily limit is 10 fish; there is no minimum size, but sportsmen keep nothing healthy under 7″ and nothing at all that will not be eaten, carefully releasing their fish underwater — or at least with wet hands.

Unlike some game fish, trout should be killed promptly, cleaned as soon as possible and kept as dry and cool as possible. Trout cared for in this manner can be kept fresh for days without refrigeration or snowbank. The considerate angler will take care to bury entrails well away from both water and campsites.

Legend: In the alphabetical listing of lakes that follows, *EB* represents eastern brook trout, *RT* rainbow, *RT Kamloops* kamloops trout, *GT* golden trout, *BN* brown and loch leven trout, *CT* cutthroat trout, *G* grayling and *K* kokanee salmon. Approximate lake elevations are shown in parentheses. The word "annual" means the lake is scheduled for yearly air plantings of fingerlings by the DFG. "Biennial even" means plantings are scheduled every two years in the even years (e.g., 1970, 1972, etc.). It may be assumed, unless otherwise indicated, that there is little or no known natural reproduction. The information that follows was gathered from DFG biologists and their files, and augmented by my own experience.

Index to Lakes

Aloha Lake (8100)—Traditionally RT but recent EB plants doing better. Annual RT, EB. Some large fish. Lake is half-drained every fall.

Alta Morris Lake (8150)—Annual GT beginning in 1968. Fish not abundant but survival good.

American Lake (8100)—Annual EB. Highest in Chain of Lakes.

Angora Lakes, Upper and Lower (7400)—Annual CT in both lakes. Presence of golden shiner population makes Angoras candidates for chemical treatment.

Avalanche Lake (7300)—EB every three years. This lake is actually a wide spot in Pyramid Creek, just above Horsetail Falls.

Azure Lake (7700)—EB and RT in alternate years. Both doing well. Some big fish. Fair natural reproduction.

Barrett Lake (7600)—EB planted before 1966 are reproducing sufficiently well. Annual RT begun 1967.

Beauty Lake (7000)—Too shallow for RT or EB. A prime candidate for grayling.

Bloodsucker Lake (7400)—Sterile, popular lake well suited to grayling.

Boomerang Lake (8050)—EB present, indicating natural reproduction. Last planted 1951.

Buck Island Reservoir (6450)—EB and RT in alternate years. Natural reproduction of BN. Large fish of all three species.

Cagwin Lake (7750)—EB biennial even, but heavy fishing offsets natural reproduction, so RT tried experimentally in 1968.

Cathedral Lake (7600)—EB last planted in 1964 disappeared; GT planted experimentally in 1967-68.

Chain, also known as Upper Channel Lake (8050)—EB occasionally, stocked primarily by EB from other lakes in the chain.

Channel Lake (8050)—Annual EB through 1966, then annual RT beginning in 1967.

Cliff Lake (8400)—GT planted in 1966-67 failed owing to self-sustaining resident population of EB.

Clyde Lake (8050)—Annual RT until 1962. Annual GT beginning 1966. Stream below dam well stocked with GT.

Crag Lake (7450)—Self-sustaining population of BN.

Cup Lake (8700)—EB through 1964; some natural reproduction continuing. GT 1966-67; biennial odd-year plants thereafter.

Dark Lake (6900)—Annual BN fingerlings augment annual RT catchables.

Desolation Lake (8000)—Annual EB through 1965, then annual RT beginning 1966.

Dicks Lake (8400)—Annual EB until 1963 when self-sustaining reproduction became evident. RT Kamloops tried experimentally 1966-7-8.

Doris Lakes, Upper and Lower (8350)—Despite natural reproduction of EB, fish remain scarce, so better-suited GT were planted 1967-8.

Duck Lake (7600)—Too shallow for RT or EB. A candidate for grayling.

Eagle Lake (7000)—Annual RT.

Echo Lakes, Upper and Lower (7420)—Chemically treated in 1960 to remove rough fish, annual RT thereafter. Massive plantings of kokanee salmon 1962-3-4 have become self-sustaining. RT catchables planted occasionally at dam.

225

Elliott Lake (8350)—This tiny lakelet between Dicks and Fontanillis planted to GT biennially beginning 1966. The larger lakes above Fontanillis last planted to EB 1962.

Fallen Leaf Lake (6377)—Annual RT fingerlings and catchables. Massive plantings of kokanee salmon 1962-3-4 have become self-sustaining.

Fawn Lake (6350)—First plant of grayling fingerlings in the area, in 1969.

Floating Island Lake (7200)—EB annual. Population of lahontan red side minnows suggests need for chemical treatment but access is difficult.

Fontanillis Lake (8350)—EB annual plus a few RT descended from Dicks Lake.

Forni Lake (7950)—This lake beneath Tells Peak was planted to EB with little success until 1965. Annual GT began 1968.

Forni Lake (7600)—This lake beneath Pyramid Peak is too shallow for RT or EB and is a candidate for grayling.

Fox Lake (6550)—Biennial odd EB, with some rough fish.

Frata Lake (8050)—EB last planted 1965, RT in 1967. Planting discontinued due to winter kill. This popular pond seems well suited to grayling.

Gefo Lake (7850)—Biennial EB until winter kill 1966-67. This shallow, now-barren lake is a candidate for grayling.

Gem "Lost" Lake (7800)—Shown on topo as Lost Lake, NW of Barrett Lake. Not planted, probably barren, shallow. Another candidate for grayling.

Genevieve Lake (7400)—Annual BN, some EB, hordes of red side minnows. Halfway to Crag Lake, the "Dipper Pond" contains spawning EB plus annual RT.

Gertrude Lake (8000)—EB until 1965, then biennial GT beginning 1968.

Gilmore Lake (8300)—Scene of experiments: black bass in 1887, catchable RT Kamloops in 1967. Annual RT supplements naturally spawning EB and BN. Contains chubs, suckers, red side minnows. Too deep for chemical treatment.

Granite Lake (7650)—Annual EB.

Grass Lake (7200)—Self-sustaining EB and BN with RT Kamloops experimentally planted 1967-68. Some giant browns.

Grouse Lake (8150)—Annual RT until 1965, when self-sustaining reproduction became evident. This lake located between Wrights and Smith lakes.

Grouse Lakes (8200)—Planted to EB in 1964, RT in 1966; now Upper Lake only planted EB biennial even. These shallow lakes lie between Rubicon Lake and Phipps Pass.

Half Moon (8150)—Annual EB until 1964 showed self-sustaining reproduction. Annual RT Kamloops begun 1968 for diversity.

Heather Lake (7900)—Annual BN beginning 1966. Earlier plants of both RT and EB. Natural reproduction of all three species. Big browns.

Hemlock Lake (8400)—Biennial EB.

Highland Lake (7800)—Remoteness makes biennial RT sufficient.

Hidden Lake (7700)—Annual EB plus trial plant of RT Kamloops in 1967.

Horseshoe Lake (7550)—Biennial EB and RT discontinued because of winter kill. Grayling planned for this shallow lake.

Huth Lake (7550)—Unnamed on most maps, Huth lies between Shadow Lake and Tells Peak. Planted 1962 and 1964 EB, and 1968 CT.

Island Lake (8150)—Biennial EB until 1965. If reproduction does not prove self-sustaining, shift will be to GT.

Jabu Lake (8500)—EB planted in 1962 failed. Annual GT since 1966 survive but growth is slow.

Kalmia Lake (8600)—GT in 1965, then biennial even beginning 1966. Good survival but slow growth.

Lake No. 3 (8200)—GT 1968. Not previously planted.

Lake No. 5 (7950)—Biennial EB.

Lake No. 9 (8200)—Too shallow for RT, EB. A candidate for grayling.

Lake of the Woods (8050)—RT only until 1965; then annual plants of EB and RT (2:1) yielded spectacular 10:1 ratio favoring EB. Now EB annual.

Lawrence Lake (7800)—Annual EB until 1965, RT Kamloops in 1967, then annual RT beginning 1968.

Le Conte Lake (8200)—Annual RT through 1968. Annual EB begun 1969.

Leland Lakes, Upper and Lower (8150)—GT 1967, then biennial even beginning 1968.

Lily Lake (6600)—Self-sustaining population of BN, RT and EB. Not stocked.

Lois Lake (8300)—EB planting discontinued 1964 due to overpopulation. Self-sustaining EB population.

Loon Lake (6400)—Annual RT and EB plus RT catchables.

Lost Lake (7700)—This lake between Meeks and General creeks receives both EB and RT annually.

Lost Lake (8100)—This lake adjacent to Triangle Lake was planted annually until 1964 with EB, then RT in 1966 and GT in 1968. Biennial odd GT began 1969.

Lost Lake (7600)—The Lost Lake NW of Barrett Lake, for simplicity's sake, is listed under its older name "Gem," but is probably barren.

Lucille Lake (8200)—Annual EB.

Lyons Lake (8400)—Annual RT.

Margery Lake (8200)—Annual EB plus RT experimentally in 1968.

Maud Lake (7700)—Annual RT.

Miller Lake (7115)—Annual RT plus apparently reproducing EB and BN. Large fish.

McConnell Lake (7800)—Fast turning to meadow, this no-longer-planted lake supports natural reproduction of GT.

Osma Lake (7650)—Not planted EB since 1938 owing to natural reproduction of EB. RT in 1966.

Phipps Lake (8550)—Last planted 1965. Self-sustaining EB fishery.

Lower Phipps Lake (8200)—Located west of Phipps Lake on Phipps Creek, this never-planted, unnamed lake probably contains self-sustaining EB descended from Phipps.

Pitt Lake (7500)—A wide spot in Pyramid Creek containing EB.

Pyramid Lake (8050)—Biennial EB.

Pyramid Peak Lakes, Upper and Lower (8800)—Upper first planted to GT 1965, then biennial even beginning 1966. Shallow lower lake planned for grayling. These two usually unnamed lakes lie just northwest of the peak.

4-Q Lakes, Lower and Middle (7450)—Planted to EB until 1967, then annual RT beginning 1968. EB reproducing naturally. Remaining lakes too shallow for trout, planned for grayling.

Ralston Lake (7800)—Annual RT until 1966, EB 1966-67, RT 1968, then both species annually beginning 1969. EB expected to improve fishery.

Richardson Lake (7400)—EB.

Rockbound Lake (6550)—Annual plantings of EB, RT until EB reproduction established, then annual plantings of RT (which outnumber EB 2:1). Also some natural reproduction of BN.

Roddie Lake (6900)—Shown on the topo map east of Loon Lake as "Hidden Lake." EB natural reproduction plus CT plants every three years.

Ropi Lake (7600)—EB until 1967, then annual RT beginning 1968.

Rubicon Lake (8300)—Annual EB except RT in 1967.

Rubicon Reservoir (6550)—Annual RT augment the limited natural spawning of EB and BN.

Saucer Lake (8600)—EB until 1965, then biennial GT beginning 1968.

Schmidell Lake (7850)—EB planting discontinued 1962 due to overpopulation. Self-sustaining EB fishery.

Secret Lake (8300)—This barren, shallow lake east of Wrights Lake under Blue Mountain is a candidate for grayling.

Shadow Lake (7650)—This marshy lake under Rubicon Peak up Meeks Creek needs a streamflow maintenance dam. Annual EB with some BN reproduction and red side minnows.

Shadow Lake (7450)—This lake between Loon Lake and Tells Peak contains some RT and gets biennial EB.

Sixteen Shot Lake (7100)—This unnamed lakelet east of Loon Lake forms a triangle with Hidden and Winifred lakes. EB planted occasionally.

Smith Lake (8700)—EB planting discontinued in 1964 due to overpopulation. Self-sustaining EB fishery.

Snow Lake (7400)—Annual EB.

Spider Lake (6700)—EB until 1965, then annual RT beginning 1966.

Stony Ridge Lake (7800)—This fertile lake contains a self-sustaining fishery of EB, BN and a few Mackinaw lake trout left over from an early plant, as well as red side minnows. Last plant 1966.

Susie Lake (7800)—Annual RT Kamloops beginning 1968 augment self-sustaining EB fishery. Also chub, red side minnows, probably BN.

Sylvia Lake (8050)—Biennial EB.

Tallac Lake (7900)—Shallow lake planted 1968 to GT.

Tamarack Lake (7800)—Annual EB except RT in 1966-67 due to EB scarcity.

Toem Lake (7650)—Annual EB through 1967, then annual RT.

Top Lake (8300)—EB until 1964 when natural reproduction seemed well established. GT planted as supplement in 1965-6-8.

Triangle Lake (8000)—Biennial odd EB, except RT in 1968.

Twin Lakes, Upper and Lower (8000)—Annual EB both lakes, except RT Kamloops tried in lower lake 1968.

Tyler Lake (8000)—Annual EB.

Umpa Lake (7900)—No DFG records. Possibly EB.

Lower Velma Lake (7700)—Good natural reproduction of self-sustaining EB and RT with some BN. Some large fish. Last planted 1956.

Middle Velma Lake (7900)—Annual RT in this fertile lake with no natural reproduction. Some large fish.

Upper Velma Lake (7950)—RT annual planting augments self-sustaining EB fishery. Last planted to EB 1965.

Waca Lake (8200)—Annual EB.

Winifred Lake (6850)—Annual EB with RT added in 1969.

Wrights Lake (6941)—Annual RT, RT Kamloops and BN, plus RT catchables.

Zitella Lake (7650)—Annual RT through 1966. Shallow. Grayling planned.

Index to Streams

Barrett Creek—Upper reaches of Bassi Fork of Silver Creek. EB, RT

Bassi Fork of Silver Creek along Red Peak Trail. EB, perhaps BN

Cascade Creek—RT and EB

Eagle Creek—RT

Echo Creek—RT

General Creek—EB plus RT descended from Lost Lake

Glen Alpine Creek—Both RT and EB catchables

Highland Creek—RT

Jones Fork of Silver Creek—EB and RT

Lyons Creek—EB, RT and BN

Meeks Creek—EB and BN

Phipps Creek—EB

Pyramid Creek—EB and RT catchables

Ralston Creek—RT and EB

Rubicon River—GT from Clyde Lake to trail crossing, RT-GT hybrids to China Flat, RT and EB from China Flat to Rubicon Reservoir

Wrights Lake Inlet—RT and EB

Wrights Lake Outlet—RT catchables

Index